BEAT

To the healers of the world, the doctors and the peacemakers: in particular, you, Professor Georges Audry, and the beautiful operation you carried out on 13 October 2011.

BEAT

the true story
of a suicide bomb
and a heart

ROWAN SOMERVILLE

THE LILLIPUT PRESS
DUBLIN

First published 2017 by
THE LILLIPUT PRESS
62–63 Sitric Road, Arbour Hill
Dublin 7, Ireland
www.lilliputpress.ie

ISBN 978 1 84351 705 4

A CIP record for this title is available from
The British Library.

10 9 8 7 6 5 4 3 2 1

Set in 11.5 pt on 15 pt Caslon with
Knockout display by Marsha Swan
Printed by GraphyCems in Spain

CONTENTS

CONTENTS

PART III: TRIBES

Of course two peoples and two languages will never be able to communicate with each other so intimately as two individuals who belong to the same nation and speak the same language. But that is no reason to forgo the effort at communication. Within nations there are also barriers, which stand in the way of complete communication and complete mutual understanding, barriers of culture, education, talent, individuality. It might be asserted that every human being on earth can fundamentally hold a dialogue with every other human being, and it might also be asserted there are no two persons in the world between whom genuine, whole, intimate understanding is possible – the one statement is as true as the other. It is Yin and Yang, day and night; both are right and at times we have to be reminded of both.

Herman Hesse, *The Glass Bead Game* (1943)

Prologue

A small hand pulls at the refrigerator, the seals around the door resist and then give with a familiar sucking sound. Light, so yellow in the early morning, floods the shelves. An eager little face peers up at the treasures. There's orange juice, and milk, wine in a half-corked bottle, a plastic tray with a wilting lettuce and the flash of colour from a forgotten tomato. There's part of a roast chicken, a pat of butter repackaged in its crumpled wrapper and sausages straining against a roll of greaseproof paper. Below are cheeses and a chocolate mousse.

Defrosting on the top shelf is a fist-sized mass of dark tissue, purple-red, mottled with spots of clotted-cream fat. As it collapses, its cling-film covering sloughs off like the skin of an old snake.

The boy hardly gives it a glance. It's a heart, he knows this, like the one in his own chest. Not alive, but no less human.

PART I
Blood

ONE

I June 2001

It's the first night of June 2001. A crowd of people are gathering, mostly young women, the oldest twenty-three. They are queuing outside a nightclub, milling about, breaking ranks to greet, shriek and hug. There is much admiring of outfits, talk of hair, of exams and shoes and the coming holidays. Groups of teenagers flock from one cluster to the next like birds breaking from one tree to another. There are comments on other groups, on looks, recent histories and loves.

The sea is no more than fifty metres away, rising and falling like the chest of a sleeping giant, heaving and subsiding against the concrete of the sea wall. A single-storey building of exposed concrete stands between the crowd and the water, which follows the coast in a gentle S. Two lamp posts cast light over the car park, over the gathering crowd of young people. The lamp posts were painted blue last week, a shade of blue just lighter than evening sky. Peals of laughter explode in the warm night like muted fireworks, mingling with the whining screech of scooters and clacking of an old Mercedes taxi unloading a couple of smartly dressed girls.

There are boys, too; teenagers and a few young men in their early twenties, mooching around, pretending not to look, waiting in the queue, chatting, wanting to blend in, fidgeting to be noticed but affecting disdain, greeting friends with hugs and handshakes. Some are hoping their new jeans look good, or touching the faint dark clouds of recent facial hair, the scars of pimples. They are hoping for a dance, for a kiss or something more.

It's a Friday night, the beginning of a holiday. Girls will be allowed in for free before midnight on this particular Friday, but the doors are still closed. It's after eleven o'clock, and there are more than a hundred and fifty young people outside, but for some reason the doors are closed. They should be flung wide by now, but they are not; they won't be until the security guard cracks open the gate and steps out.

His name is Jan Blum. He's just checked the fire exits and is now heading to the car park to look around. A Ukrainian, Jan was living in Kiev with his wife Irena and their two-year-old daughter only six months ago. Now he has a new life, a new country, and a new language. He'd never dreamed of becoming a doorman in a nightclub, but it's regular money with friendly people and a good atmosphere. He likes it. He goes to work contented and comes home tired.

Jan is twenty-five, a solid young man with thick forearms, short cropped hair on a somewhat rotund head and features that seem concentrated in the middle of his face. His eyes are close together and deep-set, giving an impression of seriousness. This should be a useful trait for a club doorman, but here at the Dolphi there's very little trouble, especially tonight: a disco for teenagers for International Children's Day. Jan's job is more to protect the young people than to police them. They're nice kids, friendly, almost all from Russia and former Soviet states. They, like him, are grateful for their lives here.

This afternoon he picked up his daughter from kindergarten and settled down for a nap with Irena. Tomorrow their first proper holiday will begin, and they would fly back to Kiev to see the rest of their family.

An hour after falling asleep, Jan woke, heavy with the dreams of a hot summer afternoon. From the comfort of a bed shared with his wife and baby daughter he wondered aloud whether to miss his final shift. Should he go, shouldn't he … Then he remembered that his cousin Sergei would be bartending that night, which decided it. He resolved to do his final shift and then enjoy his holiday.

———

The two girls who climb out of the Mercedes taxi are sisters, Lena and Julia. They wait in the queue, one in jodhpurs, the other in tight trousers. Julia has her hair in braids, secured with tiny white rubber bands, and her sister has green polish on her fingernails, a colour that upset her mother but promises to glow thrillingly under the ultraviolet light of the nightclub. The girls are chatting, about their exams, music, their little brother Sasha, the dream Lena had the night before.

Lena, an artistic girl with her sights set on going to university, was woken by a haunting image. She was standing in a white bridal gown. On her finger was an embossed gold ring. But next to her, where a groom should have been, there was nothing.

Julia, two years younger, doesn't care about dreams. Her interests are trance music and her ever-expanding menagerie of fluffy toys. Furthermore, their grandmother – an expert on all superstitious matters, like many Soviet women of her generation – had told them not to worry. A white dress could only be a positive sign.

———

A few hundred metres away Uri approaches. He has no intention of going to the Dolphinarium, but his car is parked in the car park and he's strolling along the seafront after a busy shift at work. Uri is thirty-two and a social worker, or a 'house father' at the community centre. Unmarried, good with children, he is a man with a kind face and thick dark eyebrows that seem to struggle to avoid each other over his nose. Uri is one of those men with a particularly square jaw, like a cartoon hero. It juts out when he smiles, revealing a gap between his front teeth.

Hoots of laughter and the shouts of young people reach him well before he arrives at the crowded area in front of the club. Social life – meeting friends, having fun, ignoring yesterday and acting as if tomorrow were not on the agenda – is a culture in and of itself in this city, even amongst recent immigrants such as these. Nightlife connoisseurs the world over have commentated on the extraordinary commitment to partying in this warm Mediterranean city. No matter the night of the week, the streets teem with activity, the bars are packed. It's as if the very act of socializing, of drinking and laughing, of dancing with abandon, is, if not actually sponsored, at least condoned by the municipality. It's a young place in a young country.

———

Mariana has come to the Dolphi to let off a little steam after weeks of intensive studying for her matriculation exams. She looks gorgeous as she waits in the queue, standing with her friend Anya. Mariana has long reddish hair, a bountiful, usually smiling mouth and wide, perfectly almond-shaped eyes. Until this night, few people have seen Mariana wear anything but shorts or trousers – usually jeans – but tonight she's wearing a miniskirt. She looks radiant.

An hour earlier, Mariana quarrelled with her father. She had promised her little sister Sophia that she could come with her to the nightclub, but as they were getting ready their father rose from the couch like an imperious genie and forbade it. Fourteen was too young for a nightclub, he'd insisted. Usually Mariana was able to cajole him a little, convince him that things worked differently in this country, change his mind, but not tonight. He wouldn't budge; he refused to even discuss it. Mariana tried explaining that it was completely safe – tonight was a night for teenagers, teenagers like them, from Kiev and Irkutsk, from Moscow and St Petersburg. Everyone would know each other. But her father wouldn't hear of it. She's put the disagreement out of her mind, though, as she stands in the queue with Anya, chatting and laughing. They make plans to get up as early as possible the following morning and spend the day on the beach.

———

Polina is standing directly behind the two girls. She's wondering why the club doors are still closed. They're normally open by a quarter past eleven at the latest. She wonders if it's a deliberate delaying tactic so that the girls who should be allowed in for free before midnight will have to pay.

Such thoughts disappear upon catching sight of the mass of blonde hair and unmistakable face of Anya right in front of her. Polina has known Anya since nursery school in eastern Russia. They'd been learning to talk when they first

7

met; they'd even shared a potty in the local kindergarten. And now they are here, standing next to each other thousands of miles away, wearing make-up, waiting outside a nightclub in a warm country, thinking about boys. They scream with delight. They hug and exchange summaries of their young lives, their chatter bursting into the blue night like flocks of starlings. The crowd surges, and they are separated. Anya is astounded by how beautiful Polina looks, like a movie star or a model.

Dozens of young people are arriving by taxi, by scooter, and on foot from the bus station nearby, everyone edging towards the entrance of the Dolphinarium, coming together, drawing in, like iron filings towards a magnetic pole. Above them all the building's totem, a copper dolphin, sits atop a concrete plinth gazing out to sea.

———

Jan Blum comes back to the club doors and chats with his cousin Sergei. It will be a long, hot night, and busy too, judging by the crowd outside. Jan checks his messages. It's his boss. *What are you doing?*

Out in the front with Sergei.

Go check the car park.

I've done that.

Do it again, there's hundreds of people around.

Jan shrugs and tells Sergei he'll see him later. He goes off to look once more around the car park.

———

Diaz and Viktor arrive on Viktor's scooter. Diaz is one day into his first-ever leave from the army, and he's spent his afternoon playing one of Vik's computer games. His life is crazy. One day he's at work, on patrol with an assault rifle and live ammunition, and the next he's sitting in his best friend's room strafing scores of enemy aircraft in a computer game.

Diaz is eager to do something for his new country, to be a part of it by giving back. His mother is still in Moscow and he calls her whenever he can, begging her to come. This is our place, he says to her. But she won't join him. She's scared; she has a new baby. This new country makes her nervous, but Diaz feels like he belongs in a way he never felt in the country of his birth. He tells her all this, but he does not tell her how much he misses her – misses her so keenly that it makes him feel wretched every day. He doesn't tell Viktor either, or even Natalie, his girlfriend.

Only the woman who runs the shop underneath his flat knows how much Diaz misses his ma. She knows just by looking at him. He goes into her shop almost every day, ostensibly to buy something, but more because she's a woman who knows where he's come from and what he's left behind. She is kind and does what she can to bring some comfort into that tense space between being a boy and a man.

Diaz and Viktor had originally planned to go to a different nightclub that evening, but Diaz insisted that they stop off at the Dolphinarium first because his girlfriend Natalie will be there. Natalie is fifteen and gorgeous. He plans to surprise her before she goes in and then to whisk her off to another club that he prefers, Metropolis. Viktor doesn't want to be at the Dolphinarium; he has a kind of distaste for the place. And anyway, three of them can't fit on his scooter.

———

A young man with fine features, Saïd, moves towards the thickest part of the crowd. He and Uri Sachar – the social worker − are the only people in the immediate vicinity who have no plans to enter the club. For generations, members of his family have owned land, lived and died within twenty kilometres of this nightclub, but neither Saïd, his brothers, nor his father have ever been as close as he is now. He stands alone in the crowd, wearing a stylish kaftan with wide, loose trousers, a tracksuit top and brand new sneakers. His hair is short and neatly cut, his eyes brown and wide apart, his complexion pale. There's a fragile, gentle look to him that the faint black line of his moustache does nothing to diminish.

He is tense.

A man approaches him; his name is Eduard. At twenty-two, Eduard is the same age as Saïd. An army boy in a tough regiment, he's been trained to react to situations that don't look right. Eduard nods towards the case Saïd is carrying: 'What's that?'

Saïd answers. 'It's a *tarbuki* drum. I'm playing tonight. It's going to be a big one.' His nervous expression turns into a confident smile. Eduard, relieved, returns the smile and walks off. Amidst all this noise and excitement, this camaraderie, Saïd feels acutely alone. Everything around him shimmers with that vivid clarity people experience in falling or drowning. He is a young man with a newly minted sense of purpose. It is 1 June 2001, twenty or so minutes before midnight, and he stands alone in the heat of the evening. A mass of young people − mostly teenage girls − chat and laugh without a care in the world.

———

Diaz is unaware of Saïd's presence, indeed of his existence. He is concentrating on re-spiking his hair. Vik told him before they set off that evening that he was wasting not only time but also hair gel, sculpting his hair into spikes that would be flattened by the motorcycle helmet. Diaz didn't care. He can buy as much hair gel as he wants. He's earning money as a conscript in the army. Not much, but something. What does concern Diaz is that he cannot find Natalie on his one night's leave and, at any moment, the club doors will open.

'Give me your phone,' he shouts to Viktor.

Viktor doesn't want to give him his phone. He doesn't want to be at this nightclub. He can see the traffic getting worse and the crowd outside the club becoming so thick that it's impossible to make out who anybody is.

'I've hardly got any credit left,' Viktor replies. 'Let's get out of here.'

Diaz insists. He needs to call Natalie.

Viktor tosses him the phone. Diaz catches it, dials, and Natalie answers right away. Success! He walks away, cooing and chatting.

———

Anya is in the crowd – a different Anya – let's call her the second Anya. She originally decided to stay at home, but then her friend Nadezhda had turned up at her house in tears. She'd been arguing. Who with? Anya had asked. Everyone, Nadezhda had sobbed. Anya knew this meant her mother. Nadezhda wanted to die, she'd announced. Anya had scolded her for saying such a thing, and being a pragmatic sort of girl, she came up with a solution: 'We will go out,' she said.

'We don't have money,' Nadezhda told her.

'We'll go to the Dolphi, it's free for us before twelve.'

Anya had almost enough money for a taxi ride there and back, and they soon found a sympathetic driver and pleaded with him to take them for exactly half the money in her pocket;

theoretically, they decided, someone will take them back for the other half. The driver dropped them at the corner and waved them off with a smile. Who could refuse two teenage girls all dressed up on a Friday night? Even if they were Russians.

As soon as Nadezhda and Anya arrive outside the club they conclude that they've made a good choice: there's graduation to celebrate and a friend's birthday too. Pointless to stay home. They're standing in the crowd chatting away when Anya sees her boyfriend Ilya. Theirs is a proper relationship, not one of those teenage romances. Anya and Ilya are a serious item. They plan to find an apartment as soon as school is finished, and eventually they'll get married.

But Ilya told her that tonight he was going to another club, called Yellow, and that he wouldn't be able to get her in. Why was he here? He had specifically not asked her out this weekend, having promised that they'd go out another time. Anya had told him that she'd spend some time with her ma, but then Nadezhda appeared with all her dramas, and so she'd changed her plan. And yet, here was Ilya, wearing a new top and smart dark trousers.

She doesn't waste time thinking. She walks straight up to him. 'Why are you here? You're meant to be at Yellow.'

'I'll explain later.'

'Tell me now.'

'I told you. I'll explain later.' Ilya slouches off, but before Anya has a chance to process what's going on, he runs back. 'Just remember, I always loved you and always will.' He dashes off, his face flushed with emotion. The girls look at each other. Nadezhda laughs and rolls her eyes. 'It's a soap-opera night tonight – psycho mums, weird boyfriends, black cats crossing roads – we should never have left the house.'

The edges of the sky are stained nicotine yellow with the glare of the streetlights.

Maybe there *is* something in the air – something like a full moon, some catalyst for hysteria.

But the moon is not full.

––––

Maksim is up near the front of the queue. He's determined to be the first inside. He is friends with the doorman. Maksim's been coming to the Dolphi since the beginning and everyone knows him; he's that kind of person. He's also one of the few people who knows why the club is opening late tonight: it isn't a ploy to cheat the girls of free entry – it's a surprise. There's a new room opening and the management is making last-minute fixes so everything looks perfect.

Maksim's best friend Alexei arrives. Normally Alexei's shy and gentle, but tonight he's full of energy and … loose. It's as if he's taken something, but that isn't his style. Nonetheless he's behaving like a completely different person, like someone with nothing to lose.

––––

As Anya watches her childhood friend Polina drifting away in the crowd, she remembers that she has no money on her. Not even a single coin in her pocket. She asked her mother for something but her mother had nothing to give. Her ma is so broke that she was obliged to borrow her bus fare from the supervisor of her medical course. Her mother never would have let her come to a club this far away, but Anya hasn't been entirely honest. She claimed she was going to celebrate the birthday of a friend who lived down the road, which had a grain of truth in it. She will be celebrating her own sixteenth birthday in a few days' time.

But Anya doesn't care about money right now. She's happy to be at the Dolphi, happy to have just seen Polina. There's no point worrying about pocket change; she knows loads of people, and there are sure to be boys to buy her drinks.

———

Saïd watches another couple of men approach. He fortifies himself with a phrase he's been taught, *make ready your strength to the utmost of your ability*, advice from the Almighty Himself. The young men approach and want to know about the drum case. Their accents are thick with the tones of their former Soviet homelands. Saïd explains about the drum. It's the trend in the early 2000s; dance beats with live drums, a cultural cocktail. They are convinced and they leave, wishing him a fun night.

At some point Saïd smiles, thinking of his family. Not only will they be proud, but their debts will be paid off. He has not spoken to his parents for a month, more; he has hardly been home to the apartment he shares with his brother. Recently, his friends, his new friends, have stayed with him night and day. They've talked with him long into each morning. They've told him to make a list of seventy people to accompany him into his glittering future, but Saïd Hotari does not know seventy people. He uses people who have been good to him, even if their names are unknown: a fruit-seller who spoke kindly from behind a pyramid of scarlet strawberries, the owner of the café who asks about his family abroad, one of the teachers in technical college, his elder brother, whose tracksuit jacket he is wearing …

———

Anya is listening to Nadezhda whilst keeping an eye out for Ilya. She sees him chatting with a boy called Roman. 'One of those guys who dates five girls at the same time,' she says. Anya breaks away from Nadezhda and marches straight up to her boyfriend. She is like that: direct, no nonsense. 'What did you mean then?' she demands.

Roman is uncomfortable, but she ignores him. Ilya is brash. 'I was joking, forget it.' At that moment, as if buckling under the force of three hundred young people's yearning, the club doors open. Had it happened later, Anya and Ilya might have had an argument or kissed, but now Ilya is carried away by the current of the crowd, and Anya lets him go. She doesn't understand what he's talking about, but he looks so handsome in his clothes, and sometimes that's enough.

———

Saïd observes the male and female forms move and jostle towards the club doors, all of them in light and flimsy clothes, their pale bodies exposed in a way he never sees at home. One boy is wearing nothing but a pair of bright red shorts and a loose vest, as if he is going to do sports rather than visit a nightclub.

———

Jan Blum is making his way back into the crowd. He needs to be at the front now that the doors are open. There's nothing going on in the car park – not that there's much he could see with all the people milling about. As he's weaving through the masses, he brushes shoulders with Uri Sachar, who's getting into his car to drive home. They don't notice each other. Jan is focused on the busy night ahead, and the next two weeks of uninterrupted holiday with his wife and baby daughter.

———

Saïd watches everyone. He taps the shoulder of a girl in front of him and demands her name. His tone is aggressive. The girl feels uncomfortable. She walks away. This rejection makes it easier for him. He needs to be able to hate these people, what they represent, rather than who they really are: daughters of fathers, beloved children of mothers, sisters of brothers, young people putting their tender feet into the world, just like him. He needs to see them as part of the idea that has made his life, and the life of everyone he knows, hopeless. As long as he doesn't know them, he can do this.

———

The crowd is thick with young people. The doors of the club are open, teenagers funnelling through, young men standing to the side and letting the girls go first so that they can take advantage of the free entry before midnight.

Anya is by the door, for one moment next to Ilya, their arms rubbing against each other, up and down, like boats in a crowded port, sleek young boats ready to sail out to sea. She wants to say something to him, tries to pull him towards her, but he's borne away by the ebb and flow of the crowd. Diaz is shouting to Vik that he can see Natalie. Maksim is inside the club. Alexei is near the door but stuck behind the fence. Ilya is at the entrance now, stepping aside to let girls in before him. Uri's car is pulling out of the car park. Julia and Elena are nearing, laughing about their grandmother's nightly blessing: *God be with you, God be with you.* All around there is noise: laughing, flirting, the music of longing.

———

There are fourteen minutes left of this day, the first day of June 2001, the seventy-seventh International Children's Day.

Saïd mumbles prayers over and over; he flicks a switch; he screams the name of God into the night sky. He has a bomb strapped to his chest. There are ball bearings, bolts, copper screws, and bullets. He closes his eyes and becomes a fiery cloud of hate and destruction.

———

Ilya is killed. Diaz is killed. Jan is killed. Julia and her sister are killed. Mariana is killed. Roman is killed. Uri is killed. Anya is killed. Saïd is killed. Twenty-one are dead or dying. Over one hundred are injured.

The cracked concrete runs with blood.

TWO

What Is Anyone?

I knew their names. I knew each one of their names. I knew what they looked like. If they passed me on the street, I'd probably recognize them: Jan, Marina, Roman, Ilya, Anya, Catrin, Alexei, Irena, Yelena, Julia, Raisa, Netanya, Diaz, Simona, Saïd, Liana, Uri, Maria. But they weren't going to pass me on the street. For the past ten years, they'd been dead. Instead of falling in love, becoming pregnant, raising children, instead of any such things, they were dead. I hadn't met them, and I'd never meet them. They were memories I didn't even have.

I'd never been to Israel. Nor had the slightest desire to go. But now, ten years later, because of these people, because of the massacre outside the Dolphinarium nightclub on the first night of June 2001, I was on a plane to Tel Aviv.

It will take four or five hours to get from London to Israel, but as soon as I board the plane at Heathrow I feel like I'm already there. As I queue for my seat, I try not to stare at the men around me with luscious Abrahamic beards and eighteenth-century frock coats, in black suits and crisp white shirts with long silky tassels trailing below their hips. There are young boys with close-shaven hair and curling side-locks. There are women, too. Young, old, svelte, heavy, dark, fair. Some look as if they've decided to dress up in not-very-well-thought-out disguises. Skirts and jackets in dull materials and muted colours, clothes distinctive in their lack of distinction. Some wear head scarves, some wigs that look more like wigs than hair; a wig worn to hide hair rather than pretend to be hair.

Hats are everywhere: fedoras, broad brimmed, narrow brimmed, high crowned, indented and sloping every which way. A magnificent homburg bulldozes past me, heavy and deep black. Further down the plane there's a pair of broad, circular low-crowned hats with brims, as worn by Clint Eastwood in one of those westerns in which everyone dies. There's all manner of skullcaps – crochet, small, white, satin black, rainbow. The people surrounding me could be anyone from anywhere, but they are all connected by virtue of headwear.

The plane is full. There's a gentleman already sitting in the seat next to mine. He's a good-looking man in his mid-sixties, with a meandering slope of silver-white hair as sumptuous as icing on an old-fashioned cake. He's wearing a smart blue blazer and thick-rimmed glasses of the sort worn by Italian movie stars of the fifties. He seems like someone who takes a few glasses of wine with his lunch.

Before I sit down I open the luggage compartment above my seat. A vanity case is already there, so I push my hold-all on top of it. A youngish man in a double-breasted black frock coat and a particularly wild beard leaps out of his seat. He looks as if someone has thrown a pitchfork of hay at his face. His coat is satin and stretches down to his knees. His pale blue eyes are fierce.

'You can't put your bag there,' he tells me.

'I'm sorry but there's nowhere else.'

'The space – it's occupied, can't you see?'

'There's plenty of room,' I say.

'It's occupied,' he says. I look at him, and it's clear he's made his mind up. I take my bag off his box and push it under my seat. My seat-mate is smiling, almost laughing.

'Ah, well, that was a mistake,' he confides in me, as if we'd been chatting for hours. 'You don't want to be putting any-thing on his *shtreimel*, my friend. Ha ha, fatal.' He chuckles and rummages in his breast pocket and produces a folded skullcap, which he smooths onto his magnificent hair.

'Yes, yes, I know,' he says as I watch him. 'I'm not obser-vant. My wife's family, sure, but not me. One day perhaps …'

He puts his hands over his generous belly. I look at his cream shirt with the faintest pinstripe worn into it. It's well pressed, soft with age, well cared for, just like him.

'Ruthie passed six years this March, but her brother and the family, I visit them all. Of course, I'd like to die there, but I'm not ready to do it. I should move, of course I should, but every time I leave, I miss home. Next year in Jerusalem … you know how it is.'

I do not know. I am not Jewish. I do, however, come from an obsessively close family with an all-powerful mother. In addition, my entire childhood was defined by an ancient and patriarchal religious tradition manifest through doctrinaire education and frequent visits to church. Despite the fact that my mother remains atheist and anti-religious, the cultural and dogmatic aspects of my father's Irish Roman Catholicism were so interwoven with notions of family that my childhood passed without me separating one from the other. Family, truth, love, parents and God were all pretty much one. Good and evil were opposite and absolute. Sunday was for Holy

Mass and Sunday lunch. These were two indivisible but separate sacraments: mass a symbolic meal with a symbolic parent (God), and lunch a real meal with real parents – parents who managed to be both physical and symbolic without conflict. Mass left me contented because it was over for another week; lunch left me despondent because it always came to an end. The bad thing about good things, I learned, is that they finish, but that's also the good thing about bad things.

I'm not suggesting that all – or many – Jewish people will find kinship with me over these influences, but I like to think that some might, if only with the (sometimes challenging) magnificence of my mother. What is certainly true is that from an early stage, I identified with Jewish families: they seemed more like my own than the others I knew, which were smaller, more efficient, modern units. But Jews, like me, came from *families* – families that lived in the shadows of ancient, invisible forces. It didn't matter if God was real or imagined: He was the force that shaped my life, my family's life, and the life of all the Jews I knew. His was the force that 'through the green fuse drives the flower'.*

My neighbour leans over to me.

'You're Jewish, right?'

'Not so far,' I tell him, trying to be smart.

'Not so far? You're converting?'

Had my mother been Jewish, I'd be Jewish; but if my father had been a Jew instead of an Irish Roman Catholic, I could be many things, but I would not, by this fact, be Jewish. There's surprisingly little controversy about the matrilineage of Jewishness, which strikes me as an anomaly. Imagine if Christian, or Muslim, or French, or African-American identity

---

* Dylan Thomas, 'The force that through the green fuse drives the flower', *18 Poems* (1934).

was only passed through the mother? Nevertheless, so it is with the Jewish people.

Historically, it makes some sense. Matrilineage might be the pragmatic response to two realities. People lie about who they've slept with. While almost everyone knows who their mother is, it's been estimated that 1 person in 25 is not born to the man they think is their father. Thus, matrilineage is one way of confirming that at least one parent is Jewish. And then there's the sad fact that for the Jewish people, with a history of pogroms and rape, the fact that Jewishness passes through the mother ensures that even a child born of unfortunate circumstances can still be part of the tribe.

Despite ongoing searches for a 'Jewish gene' it's never been found. There have been supposedly Jewish characteristics manifest in DNA, but most of these are thought to be from geographic isolation and are found in non-Jewish people as well. But why should science be the new omnipotent source? It is, in some ways, just another ideology. A rabbi once told me that Jewishness grows in the soul and passes through the mother *in utero*. The physical world is a reflection of the spiritual world, so the physical connection with the mother mirrors the spiritual connection. Nice, but is it enough?

The fact is, it's undeniable that the *custom* of Jewish identity is matrilineal; but it is not an *innate truth*, as in, say, *the heart's primary function is to pump blood to the brain and body.* Without disappearing into Buddhist definitions of relative truths and Karl Popper's arguments of falsifiability, the heart is a truth on which everyone can agree. Of course, some religiously observant Jews might say that matrilineage is such a truth, but others like me would say it's a custom – a wise custom – brought about because someone, or a collection of people, decided it would be this way. Now that reliable DNA testing exists, indicating parenthood with practical certainty, perhaps a father being Jewish might *also* become a legitimate consideration in defining Jewish identity. It's not impossible: patrilineal descent is already accepted in certain liberal traditions of Judaism.

Citizenship, like matrilineage, is something that is decided, a fluke of birth, the result of a set of causes and conditions that may have nothing to do with you. To be a citizen of the United States of America you need to have US parents, be naturalized, or be born there – or convince authorities that one or more of these is the case. One of my daughters has a fully Italian mother and an Irish-English father, but she was born in New York City so she is now an American citizen. She may choose later to become Irish, English, Italian, or some other nationality. She can convert to Islam, Christianity or Judaism, but as Schlomo Sand, professor of history at Tel Aviv University, points out, within a *secular* context, she can never become Jewish.

What is anyone? Despite my Irish passport, my Irish father and the sincere Catholicism of my childhood, I was born in London, my accent is English, and my mother is English. When I'm thought of in Ireland (if I'm ever thought of) it's as English. In England, it's as Irish. When I think of myself, it's as both, without friction or contradiction.

As I sit on the plane, possibly the only non-Jew for miles, I look at my neighbour. He is entirely unknown to me and yet he is so familiar, so intrinsically part of the London in which I grew up. My family lived a couple of floors above a famous rabbi and his family. We were three boys and a girl; the Gryns, three girls and a boy. Our mothers had gone to school together and the Gryn son, David, gave me some of the best reggae in my record collection: ska, rocksteady, and it must be admitted, a little dub. Like many people who have the benefit of growing up in a city with a significant population of Jews, I had Jewish friends, Jewish enemies, and – praise be to the paradise I hope Rabbi Gryn is enjoying – Jewish girlfriends. Not that I'm any sort of expert on Jewish people. After all, is someone who's friends with a few Londoners suddenly an expert on London?

Nevertheless, despite my stated habituation (the fact that, ahem, some of my best friends are Jewish), there's no getting away from the fact that on this airplane heading to Tel Aviv, I am gazing about like a nineteenth-century anthropologist. Maybe it's the concentration of so many different cultural manifestations of Jewishness: the Hasidic, the Litvak, the Orthodox, the Conservative, the Reform, the Liberal. Or maybe it's something else – it seems to me that people on the plane are becoming more Jewish as we get closer to Israel.

In the airport, as people rushed past us, we were the same as any group of strangers anywhere. But as soon as we are on board the plane there's a noticeable expansion of bustling and chatting, of laughing and commenting, of reaching up and pushing past, of sitting contentedly and watching, or gazing up to the sky, or trying to ignore one's embarrassing parents … all the different kinds of ways people express themselves, but magnified.

Maybe it is just me, because I have travelled and lived in other places and am so often the odd one out: the only Irishman, the only Englishman, the only European, the only Caucasian. There's always a deep relief in returning to my own majority. So I wonder – as I look at my neighbour who is smiling to himself with his eyes closed, if it is this – if all the expressions of Jewishness I have experienced so far in my life have actually been hushed up and this Israel I am about to visit is not just a bitterly contested stretch of land in the Middle East but a state of being, where being Jewish can play at its natural amplitude.

Unlike my neighbour who is deeply lost to another, more restful world, I can't sleep. I fret about how I might find the witnesses from the Dolphinarium that terrible night, find their friends and relations, piece together who they were and what happened. I wonder how I might learn more about Hotari, the suicide bomber, whether I can meet his family and discover who he was and what faith, fury or insanity drove him to annihilate himself and so many others. Since that fateful moment in 2001, the deaths and slaughter have gone on, as they are going on today. Nothing seems to work, neither war-making nor peace-making.

As the plane soars over Greece or thereabouts, and one hour passes into another, I gaze at the young ultra-Orthodox man who insisted I move my bag and wonder what awaits in this tiny patch of land that occupies so much of the world's consciousness. My neighbour wakes up and catches me staring at the young man.

'The Haredi may look like a bunch of crackpots who walked off a cheap film set, but they're increasing in size and popularity whilst every other group is falling apart.'

'Isn't most of Israel secular?' I ask.

'Sure, half the people don't believe in God,' he replies. 'Until someone gets sick.' This amuses him for a while. 'I'm joking of course, some people are as sincerely secular as the Haredi are orthodox, and those people think the rest of us are all mad, but they feel guilty anyway … You do know what a *shtreimel* is, don't you?'

'It's a hat?' I venture.

'A hat? It's more than a hat, my friend. It's pretty much *the* hat.'

I look at him, blank.

'You didn't put your bag on the *shtreimel* itself. It was the box for the *shtreimel*.'

I ask what the problem was. Was I making it unclean in some way?

'Unclean? I don't think so, ha ha, no … not unclean. Crushed is more like it. It's a very expensive hat, the *shtreimel*. £3000 for a good one, and most of the Haredi are not well off, so it's a fortune. He'll have a good one and a less good one – the rain *shtreimel* – which is still no change from a thousand quid. But I'll bet from the way he looked at you that the good one was in the box you covered with your bag. It's an item, a *shtreimel*. Real craftsmanship, a lot of animals, twenty or thirty foxes or something, I can't remember. Ask him to see it. He'd love to show it to you.'

I lean over to my recent adversary, make a joke about our dispute, and ask him if I can see his *shtreimel*. He looks at me as if I'm insane and raises the palms of his hands as if to say *back off*.

My neighbour shrugs. 'Hey, you tried to crush the man's *shtreimel*. What's he meant to do, invite you to dinner?' He cracks up laughing.

'A few years ago, there were mass brawls in the streets of Tel Aviv,' he tells me. 'Different factions of Haredi battling it out on the corners. The aim was not to injure the others but to capture their hats. There were injuries of course, a broken nose here, a scrape there, but the *shtreimels* were the important thing. Later they were exchanged like hostages. Cuckoo in the head if you ask me, but better than missiles and bombs.'

I look at the young ultra-Orthodox man, now knowing the full gravity of my offence.

'They are much misunderstood people,' my neighbour continues. 'They feel very strongly about some things. Actually, they feel very strongly about most things: children, prayer, ritual, hats, scripture, their *rebbe* of course. They see themselves as the only ones living according to authentic Jewish law. The true Jews. They – the ultra-Orthodox – look down on the regular Orthodox, and the Orthodox look down on the Reform, and the

Reform think the Orthodox are fundamentalists, and everyone looks down on the secular. It's like the old joke, you know it? Every Jew has two synagogues: the one he goes to and the one he wouldn't be seen dead in. Where two or three Jews are gathered there will be a disagreement, it's the essence of democracy.'

'So who are the true Jews?' I ask him.

He shrugs. 'The ones with a Jewish mother.'

I think of the wiry Jesuit priest from my schooldays who instructed us that only the followers of Christ could enter the Kingdom of Heaven. But only the *true* followers of Christ: Roman Catholics, not Anglicans, not Calvinists, Episcopalians, Methodists and certainly not Jews.

'Father, father,' a boy asked, hand stretching up and waving. 'What happens to everyone else? To the Protestants and the Jewish people?'

'They do *not* enter the Kingdom of Heaven.'

'What about Gandhi, father, and what about people who are good like the vicar in the Proddie church? Do they go to the Kingdom of Heaven?'

'No.'

'Do they burn in the fiery furnace for all eternity, father?'

'Not always. God is merciful and people who are good but not part of the one true faith go somewhere called *limbo*. Babies go to limbo if they die before baptism.'

'Is limbo nice, father?'

'Yes, Somerville. Limbo is nice, but not as nice as heaven.'

My childhood was shaped by Roman Catholicism, my mind trained like an espaliered apple tree. And although there is rich history, elegance and much good in the Roman Church, what I've since learned of the centuries of corruption, and what I've heard, not to mention experienced, of their sexual abuse of children means that it no longer has credibility for me. Despite advocating confession and penance, the Roman

Church, right up to the last pope, denied its terrible crimes against children – not three times, like St Peter, on whom the church was founded, but time and time again – admitting to the truth only long after its dishonesty has been uncovered. They have now said sorry. But where is their penance?

Astonishingly, given the facts of recent history, the Roman Catholic Church continues to pronounce on what it claims are God's own views about sexual relations between consenting adults. Apparently, God doesn't want you to use a condom or take the pill because although He made sex He made it for procreation. God doesn't want you to be homosexual either, a kind of sex that's been going on within the church for ever – particularly since marriage was forbidden in order to stop priests passing their property to their children instead of the church. It beggars belief.

Limbo was officially retired by the Roman Catholic Church in 2007, and the babies who died prior to baptism, not to mention Gandhi and the saintly vicar from the Anglican church down the road, are now presumably free to enter heaven. It's all too little too late for me.

THREE

MCI

A bomb is a terrible thing.

The first of the young people arrive at the Sourasky Medical Center in Tel Aviv within eleven minutes of the blast. They're drenched in blood but it's soon clear it's not theirs: the blood is from the dead on site, or the injured about to arrive.

Lena, Julia, the two Anyas, Ilya, Jan, Uri, Alexei, Maksim as well as more than a hundred others cease to be individuals with names, personalities, histories, dreams, fears and families. They've become casualties; nameless human forms with fragile flames of life that the trauma units in each hospital will battle to keep alight. They arrive crusted in dust on blood-soaked stretchers, moaning in pain or silent in shock. They are identified by a number and then photographed. Names are not useful in an incident such as this. Many have lost their hearing and are incapable of speaking and any other means of identification – telephones, wallets, clothes – have been incinerated or altered beyond recognition by the force of the blast.

Within a few minutes of the explosion Dror Soffer, director at the trauma centre, declares a Mass Casualty Incident (MCI). This initiates a set of protocols that focuses the entire resources of this and surrounding hospitals on those injured in the Dolphinarium blast. Emergency rooms are cleared and all non-life-threatened patients in the hospitals are sent home or to facilities in other parts of the country. Nurses muster at specific points, radiological support teams assemble, key specialists are called in. Each team has a pre-arranged, rehearsed location; no phone calls have to be made, no people tracked down; a computerized communications system carries out simultaneous calls on a prioritized line. Key section chiefs carry a pager that functions in all conditions, even if the phone networks are jammed or destroyed. Every detail of an MCI has been thought out and rehearsed, down to clearing all parking spaces around the hospital so that arriving emergency personnel don't waste time looking for parking when they could be saving lives.

Dror Soffer is a specialist trauma surgeon and the most qualified person in the immediate vicinity to direct an MCI of this size. He's in his early forties and physically slight, almost elfin. But even though he looks at least a dozen years younger than he is and walks with an athletic springiness, he has a sort of egoless authority, a sovereignty over himself that suggests a much older person. Soffer is a peculiarly intelligent and dynamic thinker with a quiet, decisive gift for leadership. He speaks softly, directing teams senior in age and specialized experience with every implication that there's a big stick behind him. Though diminutive, his presence fills a room. He is a man unafraid of silence in the search for the correct course of action, and he is not someone you want to disappoint. He comes from a tough and practical don't-waste-my-time-with-bullshit mould, which Israel seems to have perfected in its sixty-five years of existence.

Empty beds are stacked up by the roadside where the ambulances are already driving up. Within a five-minute period, twenty-three casualties arrive. A paramedic stops at the entrance to the hospital corridor so that a policeman can search the patient on the trolley. There's always the possibility that terrorists will attempt a second attack by smuggling a bomb into the hospital. Once through, the patient is given a number for identification as a paramedic assesses his condition. The paramedic has about thirty seconds to make a decision based on what she's been told and what she can assess. Her decision is expressed in one of four colours: red, yellow, green and black. Red denotes *Immediate*: the patient needs immediate attention in order to sustain life. Yellow is *Delayed*: the patient can wait for further evaluation without serious threat to life. Green is *Minor*: non-serious fractures or small wounds. Black carries the terrible term *Expectant*: palliative treatment only, not enough chance to make a good recovery, death imminent. Expectant. The word for a pregnant woman.

Leaving an injured person to die without proper care may seem morally wrong, but as Soffer puts it, 'When you have an MCI the rules of the game change. You have to play God and make your priorities.' An MCI is as much a question of logistics as medicine. 'You treat those you can save,' he says. This is why the first stage of treatment at the hospital does not benefit any single individual, but preserves the most number of lives. It's called triage.

Triage comes from the French verb *trier*, which means to sort or select. The concept was developed in Napoleonic times by the great military surgeon Baron Dominique-Jean Larrey. He devised a new intelligence to deal with the hundreds, sometimes thousands of casualties that battles created, by instituting a practice of prioritizing treatment according to gravity of injury and urgency of need, rather than according to what class of society the casualty came from or whether he was ally or foe.*

Few other countries have a better MCI response than Israel, which, in itself, is a poignant indication of the country's recent history. Each step of dealing with an MCI has been worked out and rehearsed, every staff member and volunteer briefed, trained and drilled. The objective is clear: to save maximum lives with available resources. The pursuit of that goal requires sophisticated, sometimes counter-intuitive, prioritization, a high level of medical expertise, logistical planning and the ability to work calmly amidst chaos.

Saïd Hotari has detonated the bomb he was carrying near the densest part of the crowd. Within five minutes of the explosion, there are more than a dozen confirmed dead and more than a hundred casualties, many of whom would certainly die without swift medical care.

The emergency room is thick with medical personnel, their roles identified by coloured waistcoats. Personnel in an MCI may have never worked together before, and so the waistcoats let them know if a person is a student, porter or neurosurgeon. Dror wears short-sleeved scrubs and stands in the centre of activity. His posture is relaxed, but there's a feline attentiveness, an intensity of awareness with no visible emotional reaction. He clutches a piece of paper in one hand:

---

* Non-prejudicial medical care is at the heart of medical ethics, and the Israeli medical system was until recently one of the few areas (along with the judiciary) where Palestinians in Israel would receive equal treatment. By the spring of 2016, it had been widely reported that some Israeli ambulance crews were withholding treatment to Palestinians injured in attacks and the non-partisan approach to triage has been changed by some medical bodies. Yaron Mazuz, a Deputy Minister, publicly backed a change to triage, saying: 'The first priority should be given to the residents of Israel.'

it has numbers scribbled and crossed out, each representing a patient. Though the paramedic gives the patient a preliminary once over, it's Dror who makes the ultimate decisions about which patient goes where and what happens next. It is he who plays God, keeping everything in sight, talking quietly, moving about lightly from one group to another. He does not wear a coloured waistcoat. Everyone knows who he is.

Patient 506 lies on his side, the top part of his torso naked, an arm thrown above his head as if he were lazing in the sun. Just below his armpit, stained yellow with antiseptic, is an opening big enough for an American football to pass through. A surgeon has both hands in the opening and is rummaging around as if searching for a lost key in the upholstery of a sofa. There are five or six other medics around the boy and an anaesthetist at his head. The surgeon with his arms in the boy's chest shouts for a nurse as his smock slips off his shoulders and gathers at his forearms.

A few paces away, casualty 515 lies with her head and neck immobilized by a brace. Other than a wash of blood on her left leg and small red-brown stains dotted on the sheets, she shows no signs of injury. There are tubes in her nose and mouth secured by strips of matt tape. She is conscious, her eyes wide open, terrified.

Next to her there's a mass of coloured waistcoats setting up machines, taking readings, hanging intravenous drips, inserting tubes. Patient 523 is almost hidden by these figures but an incision in her chest is visible, from which a pink strip of lung is being removed.

There is ceaseless activity and intense concentration: it's feverish but not panicked, chaotic but effective. The bleeps from heart monitors and alarms, the background wails of ambulances are punctuated by insistent commands and responses from within each medical team. Smocks of pale blue, jade green and yellow move about. The surgical smocks are split open at the back, revealing jeans and sweatshirts, beneath them sneakers and sandals – the informal uniform of Israelis that seems somehow at odds with their efficiency and discipline.

Soffer moves from one patient group to another, examining, listening, advising, making notes on his crumpled strip of paper. Frenetic activity and raised voices break out around 515, the girl with the neck brace. Soffer must be aware of it, but he doesn't rush over. He listens to the team he's with, gives instruction, and only then moves towards the new crisis. One of the doctors next to the girl updates him. Soffer's eyes flick from the girl to the monitor and back to the doctor. He says a few quiet words and turns away. Immediately the team around the girl stack the monitors onto her bed, pull up the guardrails, and rush her towards the operating theatre. Soffer has already changed position: he's with the yellow-tagged *Delayed* group, checking to assess if anyone has deteriorated to red classification. And then he is back in the mêlée.

A few of the injuries are appalling: multiple traumatic amputations, protruding fractures, third-degree burns. Patients keep coming from nowhere, crises manifest, there's no respite from the pressure. To be a trauma specialist, Soffer says: 'You need to be the sort of person who can run a marathon, cross the finish line, pick up a heavy weight, and keep on running.'

FOUR

Welcome to Israel

The plane lands and I try a friendly nod to my Haredi neighbour as we file towards the exit. He nods back to me and within minutes I step onto the gangway. Always a relief to get off a plane – until I'm pulled aside by an official. The man is fair-haired and stocky, fit and very casual, in a shirt and chinos. He looks like a well-scrubbed county rugby player. He holds a clipboard loosely in one hand and has one eye trained on the passengers still disembarking. He seems relaxed but looks at everyone with keen intent. I feel he's been waiting for me.

There are no preliminaries. He wants my passport, wants to know what I'm doing in Israel, wants my name and date of birth. Where will I be staying, he wants to know. With whom, how long? Where exactly will I go in the next week? What do I do for a living, how long have I done it? His questions are in perfect English, but with a guttural *h*, as if he's clearing his throat, and they are insistent, one followed by another. He conveys the sense that he already knows the answers, but is offering me an opportunity to prove that I'm less culpable than he already knows I am. I tell him what I can.

'Why are you researching the Dolphinarium bombing?'

'I'm a writer.'

'You are writing a book about this?'

'Maybe, yes.'

'Why do you write a book about this?'

I look at him and realize that most of the victims would have been around his age by now. It could have been any of them standing with this job, this clipboard. 'It's complicated. I don't know for sure. I …'

'You come all this way and you don't know?' He has a point.

'Yes …'

'What were you doing in Egypt so many times?'

'Another book, a novel, set just outside Cairo.'

'About what?'

I'm looking at him. The other passengers have gone. He is entirely self-possessed but so young, downy-lipped, I find it hard to believe that he has the right to talk to me in this way, that he can be serious, that he isn't some young guy in a Los Angeles actors' workshop role-playing a security operative.

'It was fiction,' I tell him. 'Made up … a story.'

'What is it about?' he repeats.

I give him the plot in exhaustive detail. He cuts me off before chapter two and hands my passport back.

'Enjoy your visit.'

It's an order. I have been probed, professionally examined. My selection had nothing to do with chance or character. I'd been profiled: non-Jew, passport with Arab stamps. I might as well have been wearing a headscarf and a *galabeya*.

My brief interrogation was probably more of a search for 'deception cues' – physical signals that denote lying – than information. Lying under pressure creates stress in most people. This stress can manifest in gestures, expressions or tics that a skilled interrogator can pick up. Touching or covering the eyes, mouth or nose with the hand; turning the body away from the questioner; or super quick micro-emotions – flashes of worry or alarm, or grins to mask real feeling. All these can be signs of lying, but since false and truthful assertions sit differently with each person an interviewer will often begin by asking banal questions with known answers: what is your name, your date of birth, your nationality. Answers to these establish a control, a baseline for behaviour so that a comparison can be made when more challenging questions are asked. These methods work well on people like myself but are less likely to work with someone highly motivated to conceal, someone who makes a living out of deceit, or a psychopath.

I breeze through passport control where young, physically fit people with no uniforms and clear, quick eyes are at every corner, watching. An official stamps my passport before I can request that she uses a separate paper insert. An Israeli stamp in a passport is a prohibitive liability for someone who visits Arab countries. Then I'm off to wait for my luggage.

The key difference between Israel's airport security and that of the US is not so much sophistication as *intelligence* in every sense of the word. US airport security is run by the Transport Security Administration (TSA), which, since 9/11, has seen a rise in personnel from 16,000 to 50,000 and an increase in spending estimated at 300 per cent. They use a strategy beloved by Parisian taxi drivers, which I call 'equal opportunity rudeness'.

I think it's fair to say that US airport security staff aren't as bad as the taxi drivers of Paris, but in 2011, after tens of thousands of searches, threats and discourtesies to innocent passengers, the TSA managed to confiscate a great deal of face cream and breast milk, as well as an Action Man doll with his four-inch plastic rifle (apparently it was a 'replica weapon'). Amongst their achievements was the discovery of a small charge of C4 explosive carried by an ex-serviceman who wanted to show it off to his family and friends. The chilling irony of the explosive was that it wasn't discovered on the way out from his base, but on the man's *return* trip. Homeland Security is a fear-driven juggernaut. However, the fact remains that, to this day, outside of the wars in Iraq and Afghanistan, more people die in the bath in the US than from Islamic extremist terrorism worldwide.

Israeli airport security is different in almost every way. It's pragmatic, efficient, and very effective. It's built on simple profiling models, which care everything for safety and nothing for accusations of discrimination. Put simply, the profiling strategy is based on whether you're Jewish or not and whether you've been to a Muslim country. Jewish: fine. Gentile: suspicious. Visit to Muslim country: probable threat. Arab: certain enemy. Intelligence doesn't begin at the airport but from the moment an air ticket is purchased. If a person's life history has crossed any of the profile zones, a trip wire of protocols is set off that may require him or her to surrender his or her bags, computer and body for thorough investigation. Although my categorization might oscillate between suspicious and probable threat, I'm allowed to pass into Israel without further impediment. I am surprised about this because although I am not an enemy of Israel I wonder if I'm really a friend.

I forget my anxiety for a moment in the monumental magnificence of Ben Gurion International Airport. Considering the relative smallness of the airport there is a vast hall bisected by broad sloping walkways for those arriving and those departing. Israeli flags, with their six-pointed stars, hang at intervals. Along a wall, there are vintage posters celebrating the independence of Israel and the stunning antiquities that attest to the ancient history of Jews in the land. It's impressive. A beautiful mosaic in the hall has an inscription in Ancient Greek from the Torah: *Blessed shall you be when you come in, and blessed shall you be when you go out.* It's a touching and powerful welcome, but the absence of any reference to the Palestinian people undercuts all this bombast.

Hebrew has different words for 'Palestinian' and 'Arab', just like every other language. But for socio-political reasons, there are many Israelis who refuse to use the word Palestinian, *Palestinai.* Instead, they use only the word for Arab, *Arav.* This choice might be of little consequence, since, after all, *Arav* is used in both Arabic and Hebrew.

But it might be an expression of something deeper. In Hebrew, the word *Arav* derives from the root word *arv,* which means 'to mix up'. I wonder if the refusal to use the word *Palestinai* (acknowledging a people's discrete nationhood) and the insistence on using the word *Aravi* (implying a 'mix of people') signifies that there's no such thing as a Palestinian people but that all people of Arab descent are some sort of mongrel horde out in the wilderness.

The idea of Palestinians as a dispersed, unaffiliated people works well with the Israeli government's narrative that history and culture and infrastructure began only with the arrival of the Israelis. As I walk down the majestic hallways of Ben Gurion, there's no reminder that before 1948 the airport had been called Lydda Airport, after the Palestinian town nearby. I remember an old photograph I saw on the Ben Gurion website of a group of armed men in a jeep. It said only *[Operation] Danny, during which the city of Lod was liberated.*

It's not surprising that what really happened at Lydda or Lod is hidden under the euphemism *liberated*, because Lydda was the site of a terrible massacre. On 12 June 1948 – during the 1948 war – Israeli forces slaughtered 250 civilians, seeking shelter in a mosque, with artillery fire and then expelled the entire Palestinian population of the town, something like 75,000 men, women and children. After a thousand years of history in Lydda, Palestinian citizens were given ninety minutes to leave on foot with whatever they could carry. The 250 casualties in the mosque may have been a tragic accident but the expulsion was deliberate: *The inhabitants of Lydda must be expelled quickly without attention to age*, the Israeli order had stated. Hundreds of Palestinians died on what became a death march, mostly infants and the elderly who succumbed to dehydration and the intense heat on the road. The Israeli writer and reporter Ari Shavit points out that the expulsion of Lydda's population was 'no accident'. It was part of a plan, 'an integral and essential part', which 'laid the foundation for the Jewish state''. It happened a couple of decades before I was born. This is history so recent that one can almost touch it.

I glide along the automatic walkway under the blue-lit Hebrew text that reads, with what feels like real sincerity, *Welcome to Israel.*

It's a mess, a real mess.

---

* Ari Shavit, *My Promised Land: the Triumph and Tragedy of Israel* (2013).

FIVE

Blast

A gruesome scene is being replayed in all the hospitals around Tel Aviv: the Ichilov, Wolfson, Beilinson, Schneider and Tel HaShomer. Doctors are running flat out. Support teams are working at full tilt in complex logistical webs. Cleaners are ready with mops and disinfectants as soon as an operating room or scanning facility is vacated. Nurses and porters keep each trauma centre stocked with dressings, sutures, needles, syringes, IV bags and assorted catheters. High-school students work as back-up porters: these are teenage volunteers who have been trained for this kind of eventuality throughout the year and are on hand to move equipment and supplies, wheel casualties around and even ventilate patients.

For the next four hours casualties continue to arrive at trauma units across Tel Aviv. The patients are stabilized, or, despite the intense efforts of the medical teams, they die. The floors are strewn with debris: plastic bags, surgical gloves, tubes, bunched-up sheets and, above all, blood. It might look like the aftermath of a music festival were it not for the blood.

Dror Soffer is a veteran of MCIs, but despite his steady hands and calm demeanour he has never experienced anything like this: the victims are nearly all teenagers and they're extraordinarily resilient, disciplined and quiet.

Blast creates a peculiarly destructive pattern of injuries on unprotected bodies. A high-explosive blast packed with shrapnel is like the simultaneous firing of thousands of shotguns. Medically, dealing with the effects requires the attentions of a great number of specialists at the same time: trauma surgeons, otolaryngologists (ear, nose and throat), pulmonary medicine specialists, critical care specialists, orthopaedic surgeons, plastic surgeons, urologists and toxicologists, to name a few. Sometimes all are required on the same patient at once. According to Soffer the effect of a bomb blast on the body is like a fall from a cliff, followed by being run over by a truck, before the truck then bursts into flames and the body is shot repeatedly.

At some point, millennia ago, belligerent encounters were conducted with teeth and fists and feet, then clubs, then weapons made of iron and bronze, then steel. Then there were arrows, muskets, canon, rifles, machine guns and now the technology of warfare has become blast. Bullets, of course, prevail, but today's expression of military destruction is as much about blast.[*]

---

[*] A much better-informed expression of the balance between bullets and blast can be seen from the response of Lieutenant Colonel Alastair Rogers who was kind enough to spell out the real situation when I asked him this question via email. I reproduce it in full here – it gives a picture of the high calibre of the modern British officer: 'The need for precision has insisted on the availability of the bullet as much as the bomb – both precision weapons, with their place, neither irrelevant and neither pre-eminent. They are capabilities whose utility is determined by context. A kill/capture task in which certainty is essential needs 'boots on the ground' to assure it. Where

The development of the machine gun changed the balance of warfare: it enables one man to hold off many. But explosives packed with projectiles are a level up from the machine gun: they enable a single person to inflict multi-system life-threatening injuries on hundreds of people in one moment. They allow small, barely trained groups of insurgents to attract the attention of the world's most sophisticated military forces. They allow a levelling of the asymmetry of modern warfare.

The device that Saïd Hotari detonated amidst the crowd of teenagers waiting outside the Dolphinarium was sophisticated for a garage-made bomb. It was hyper-efficient for its size: probably no more than 10 kg of high explosives but surrounded by quantities of metal shrapnel. From the perspective of a weapons engineer, it was a job well done. From the perspective of a parent, a friend, any human being, the damage was appalling.

Blast produces injuries seldom seen outside combat. It doesn't merely wound and kill; it mutilates. The basic

---

that certainty has already been confirmed, a bomb posted through the window causes the required effect and destroys the target, without risk to 'friendlies', but equally with the concomitant risk of 'collateral damage' – something we are increasingly keen to avoid, because dead civilians obviously undermine a campaign's success. Blast is not always successful and even where thermobaric or conventional high explosives are used, people sometimes walk away and an objective often needs to be cleared by soldiers with bullet and bayonet to confirm damage and deal with the aftermath/stragglers. Therefore, neither capability is redundant and neither is of greater value than the other, it depends entirely on context. Where there is a conventional force-on-force engagement in which collateral damage is either irrelevant or controlled, blast evens the odds and is therefore valuable, but clearance of a position (by infantry soldiers) remains an essential component part of holding ground. Blast simply reduces the need for and the risks associated with close combat, but does not remove the need for it entirely.'

functioning of a high-explosive bomb is that the detonation causes a chemical reaction, which creates a massive expansion of volume and an almost immediate rise in air pressure. This rise in pressure creates a tsunami-like wave, a blast wave, which, passing through any air-filled parts of the body – the lungs, the digestive organs, the auditory systems – causes damage known as primary blast injury. Eardrums are blown out and organs are damaged by the violent change in pressure. As Hubert Schardin wrote in the 1950s:[*] 'The blast wave is a shot without a bullet, a slash without a sword. It is present everywhere within its range.' Primary blast damage to the lungs and digestive system is difficult to detect and to treat, and it's often fatal. By detonating his bomb near the curved concrete wall of the nightclub Hotari magnified the pressure wave and maximized the impact of primary blast injury.

On the shoulder of the blast wave is a deadly hail of shrapnel. This destroys whatever is in its path causing secondary blast injury, which accounts for about 85 per cent of the injuries from suicide bombs in Israel. Hotari's bomb was packed with steel balls, the most effective filler for a bomb of this size, as well as bolts and screws, which travel less distance than ball bearings but cause extensive tissue damage. Also following the high-pressure wave that causes primary blast injury is an air blast powerful enough to tear off limbs or thrust bodies against other objects, causing tertiary blast injury. Other injuries, known as quaternary injuries, range from burns to fractures.

In the case of suicide bombs such as Hotari's, many of the injuries caused by shrapnel are also penetrated by fragments of the bomber's body matter. In one attack, the bomber was found to carry hepatitis B, and any victim impregnated with

---

[*] Hubert Schardin, 'The physical principles of the effects of a detonation', *German Aviation Medicine, World War Two* (1950).

such 'organic shrapnel' could theoretically develop the disease. Ever since, doctors in Israel treating casualties with shrapnel wounds from suicide bombs vaccinate patients against hepatitis.

SIX

Beginning

It's cold and grey when I awake on my first morning in Israel – dismal weather for what has to be done. I'd slept badly, my mind flashing with images of blood-soaked tarmac and mutilated teenagers half covered with blankets, the whole display flickering and ringing like the echo of a terrible chorus. There's no point putting off the work ahead by pretending I don't know what it is, so I focus my resolve.

I feel a chill, a shiver. Cold weather in typically hot countries is all the more biting because the architecture is torqued towards coolness. Sunshine is shunned, breezes are courted. But it's raining outside. So I put on a jumper, moss green with a hole in the elbow. I don't relish the whole writer-with-a-hole-in-the-jumper cliché, but it has a hole, so what can I do?

I leave the house and head onwards, towards the scene of the bomb, to see where it all happened. I walk to the nearest main road according to instructions I've been given. The enclave of houses gives way to a suburban artery packed with trucks and cars roaring through the damp morning. There's a man dressed for the Arctic waiting by the side of the road. He has a scarf bandaged around his head and tied under his chin. What skin is visible is darkly brown.

I ask him how to get into Tel Aviv. He's Indian, from Kerala, and speaks excellent English. We stand together by the road waiting for what he calls a 'service bus'. I point out that the place we're standing has no indication of being a bus stop. He gives me the lateral Indian head wobble, which means 'exactly so/perhaps not'. Despite the scarf and the thick down jacket, the man still looks frozen, and every so often he shivers dramatically into his puffa.

I confess my familiarity with Kerala and we discuss the waterways, the Communist Party and the beaches of Southern India. He tells me he is pleased by my knowledge of Kerala, but I can see from his eyes and the way the skin sags on his face that he is exhausted. I ask him about his life and work and he tells me that he has a degree in polymer chemistry but works as a caretaker in an old people's home outside Tel Aviv.

'How is the work?' I ask.

'Bad,' he tells me without rancour. 'Many hours, low pay.'

And his employers? 'Not so kind.'

He spots a minivan amidst the traffic and waves, running up the road to where it stops, its lights flashing like jewels in the drizzling rain. Before long I see my bus roaring up the highway on the far lane. I wave as instructed, the driver pulls over, and I scramble on, repeating the words my Keralan friend told me. I offer a handful of coins and he selects a few and gestures for me to sit down with a quick jerk of his head. I stare out of the window at the grey urban expanse as the bus joins the traffic. The vista is a suburban sprawl like so many in the modern world: a spiritless sea of car parks and cement forms with occasional glimmers of colour from traffic lights, like flashes of tropical fish. There are advertisements, and road signs in Hebrew, Arabic and English that point to the extraordinary, mythic places of my childhood: Judea, Nazareth, Jericho and Jerusalem. The minibus halts at random places on the main road. Before long the street thickens into a city, and we are within Tel Aviv. The bus pulls over and the driver gestures to the door.

I find myself on a residential street lined on both sides with parked cars and not a person or shopfront in sight. I walk in the direction the driver had indicated for the centre of town, looking up at the concrete buildings on either side of me, two- and three-storey rectangular blocks stained dirty cream, teal, yellow and brown. The road is heat-cracked and above it electricity wires criss-cross like cat's cradles. Ahead I see a mall. It looks like any concrete mall you might find in a Belgian suburb or down-at-heel parts of America – a concrete bunker plastered with advertisements and split with a thin strip of window. I'm interested in malls and I want to delay going to the Dolphinarium so I walk in. I pass through a metal detector where an African security guard surveys a screen without comment.

There's something exotic and impressive in the idea of shopping malls: modern bazaars heaving with miscellany, shiny and sleek with pointless items, corridors stacked with sacks of every kind of food, mobile phone shops and boutiques selling soap, entire businesses dedicated to towels and bed linen, toys from China, books from everywhere, hiking shops with high-tech anoraks, hand-pump water-purifiers and pens that work on the moon. I like to imagine they could be modern version of the markets that entranced Marco Polo. But the only similarity to a bazaar is that getting lost is inevitable. This is part of the dark art of mall design. It even has a name, 'the Gruen transfer', whereby spaces are made intentionally confusing, with the idea that this encourages the shopper to make impulse buys. It's a corruption because the real Mr Gruen, an Austrian named Victor, wanted nothing to do with such strategies – his intention was to recreate the bustle and promise of a provincial European city, like the one he came from. Mr Gruen had a nostalgia for the old-fashioned. He wanted to humanize architecture within a shopping mall. Of course, there are fiercely competing ideologies in mall design. There's the Gruen transfer but there's also the 'Jerde transfer' (the full experience of a metropolitan modern city without the crime and traffic) and don't get me onto the theories of threshold resistance ... I find it strange that these complex creative strategies work to make our world homogeneous and dull. It is like staying in a Holiday Inn: whether you're in Delhi, Des Moines or Durham it is unsurprising, similar, undifferentiated. Nevertheless, here I am in the Dizengoff mall. I note that it seems mired in the eighties, the heraldry of global brands flashing on every surface.

I look around, fighting the Gruen transfer by trying to make sense of the backlit Hebrew map of the mall when my attention is snagged by the sight of a teenage girl travelling up the escalator dressed as one of the lizard creatures from the film *Avatar*. Behind her are more perfectly turned-out adolescent lizards: shimmering blue-green body suits, reptilian make-up. One of them slurps the froth of a pink drink through a straw. They're followed by a noisy group of boys, some of whom are Vikings with plastic swords wearing horned helmets with attached blond plaits and impressive metallic armour.

I follow them on the escalator and as they scurry off I continue upwards. A flight above me there is a group of three women in their twenties. They are wearing stylish, casual clothes. Two of them have handbags slung off the shoulder, the third, an assault rifle. The weapon hangs diagonally across her back. It looks real. It is real. Its barrel bounces against her jeans as she chats to her friends.

I arrive at a level that leads to an Apple Store. Other teens in fancy dress are playing games on the different units. The store is a wipe-clean white shell of moulded plastics and curved wood – the same as any other Apple Store in the world – except that here there are alien lizards playing video games with boys dressed as Vikings. An Apple 'Genius' with an Old Testament beard asks if he can help me. I ask him if he knows where the Dolphinarium is. He has heard of it, it's by the sea, I should ask outside the mall. I compliment him on his perfect English.

'Thanks bro, I'm from Santa Cruz, California.' He says it without the *t*, 'Sanna', and I realize that I have mislabelled his facial hair. It's not a religious beard: although luscious and thick like that of the Haredim on the plane, it is in fact very different. It is squared off and has more to do with the hipster bear-trapping archetype than being an authentic Jew, or follower of the Prophet Mohammed.

I remember a British journalist giving a talk and describing how, in his early twenties, he had rebelled against the English liberal ways his Pakistani parents had adopted with immigrant enthusiasm and travelled to Pakistan to attend a strict *madrasa*, a school for Islamic studies. He wanted to connect with his religion and mother culture. With all the intensity of a young man finding his own path he tried to be devout and a good student at the *madrasa*. What bothered him was that none of the other Pakistani students would associate with him.

One day he asked them, 'Why won't you talk to me?' and one of them told him: 'Because you don't have a beard.' He asked why a beard should be so important and was told: 'Brother, the Prophet Mohammed, peace be upon Him, had a beard, so we have beards.' Brought up on a diet of Monty Python, the young, second-generation Englishman could not resist suggesting that maybe the Prophet, peace be upon Him, didn't have a razor. He was expelled from the *madrasa* that day.

When I leave the Dizengoff mall the sun has come out and blazed everything to summer. The streets are filling up with people, increasing numbers of whom are also in fancy dress. The age demographic of costume wearers has broadened and now includes people in their twenties. I wonder if it is being synchronized according to age and if, by evening, there will be groups of septuagenarians walking the streets dressed as pirates and sexy cats. I keep walking and pass a monument of sorts outside the doors. It's a slab of stone polished matt black that seems to absorb the light of the sun and is inscribed with Hebrew letters. A bunch of roses lies on the sloping face of the monument, their pale yellow colour incongruous against the rock. There's an elderly man standing by, gazing ahead with eyes that look like they've been sad long enough to become cold.

Further down the road there's a group of young men dressed as Hasidim dancing to psychedelic trance music. Three are leaping up and down with extraordinary energy, one spinning around with arms outstretched. I wonder if they're costumed as Hasidim or if they're actually Hasidim. Am I seeing a group of ultra-Orthodox young Jewish men ecstatically dancing to trance music, or is this completely illusory? I'm not sure which would be more surreal, and it makes me think of the Chinese philosopher Zhuangzi who fell asleep and dreamed he was a butterfly. He wrote: 'Now I do not know whether I was then a man dreaming I was a butterfly or whether I am now a butterfly dreaming I am a man.'*

I need someone who knows where the Dolphinarium is, so I push open the door of a café. Loud music hits me like air

---

* William Soothill, *The Three Religions of China* (1913).

conditioning in a desert. It's Nina Simone, singing *Birds flying high you know how I feel. Sun in the sky you know how I feel. Breeze driftin' on by you know how I feel ...** There's a woman behind the counter. She has a mole on her face. She's devastatingly beautiful. I give her my best smile and forget about the Dolphinarium. I ask her if I can have a coffee.

'It's a coffee shop,' she answers, without moving any part of her body or face.

'Right. Do you have cappuccino?'

'It's a coffee shop,' she repeats.

'That's a yes?'

She nods with her eyebrows.

'No chocolate,' I add.

'On the cappuccino? We don't put chocolate.'

People are at work on laptops, writing in notebooks, reading or just talking. Paperbacks are piled on every surface. Plants trail and flourish. I like it here. My ice-cold coffee mistress gives me my coffee. It has a palm patterned in the foam.

'You want cake,' she says, making it sound like a statement.

'No thanks.'

'The cake is good,' she adds, turning around like I'm an idiot. She reminds me of the interrogator at the airport, but sexy. Obviously I can't ask her for directions.

The coffee is oily and strong. In fact it's as good as coffee can be. The last place I had a coffee like this was in Naples. I look around for a seat. The sun has reached one of the three tables on the outside, so I follow it. There's a man sitting with a pack of cigarettes, two iPhones in front of him, and a face as stubbled as scorched grass. If this were London or New York I'd guess he works in advertising. I sit next to him, and we start to chat. He tells me he works in advertising. He smells of aftershave and yesterday's alcohol. I rave about the coffee.

---

* 'Feeling Good' by very kind permission of Leslie Bricusse.

'Israelis are obsessed with coffee,' he says. 'If you like coffee, this is the place for you. It's the best in the world, I guess.'

'The world?' I feel affronted for a moment. 'What about Naples?'

'Haven't been there. But we can agree the coffee here is good, no?'

'Yes, the coffee here is good.'

I ask him about the lizard and Viking teenagers, and he nods and smiles a little.

'It's Purim,' he explains. 'A holiday. Everyone dresses up on Purim. Kids play, adults drink.'

'And you?'

'I went to bed at five.' He rubs his eyes. 'The same again tonight, maybe worse.'

I look closer. His dark, unshaven face masks eyes bruised with fatigue. I ask him if it's worth it.

'Worth it? What does this mean? Good? Yes, it's good. It's always good in Tel Aviv … too good,' he says. 'Things are crazy here. Everyone dresses up. Everyone is drunk, even the Haredim. I mean everyone. And here … Once the party starts, it keeps going. Two, three days … Maybe it goes too far. I don't know. People must work a little, you know?'

I ask him what is being celebrated in Purim.

'You don't know Purim?' His eyes flick between his brace of iPhones and me. 'Ha ha, my dad, he'd be so happy if he could hear me now, listen …'

He takes a cigarette, lights it, takes a deep puff, and speaks. 'Purim celebrates the Book of Esther. We are all taught it as children. The story goes that Achashverosh, King of Persia – who is Xerxes … maybe – gets crazy drunk after 187 days of partying and comes up with the idea that his beautiful queen, Vashti, should parade about in her crown and maybe nothing else. She says no way, and Achashverosh gets mad and divorces her on the spot. Achashverosh then makes a competition to find the next lucky woman to be his queen, a sort of Persian *American Idol*. Esther, a beautiful girl from the ghetto, enters the talent show and gets first prize as Achashverosh's new queen. Esther, of course, is Jewish, *but* her uncle Mordechai – who, like most heroes in our stories, is descended from King David – warns her that she should hide the fact that she's a Jew. Outside of Israel, and maybe LA, this has always been the case; hide that you're a Jew. Then, the bad guy arrives: Haman. You make a noise whenever his name is mentioned in the telling of the story, like hissing or stamping your feet ...

'Haman asks the king for permission to kill all the Jews in the kingdom. He's like Hitler – all about hating Jews. The king says sure, go right ahead. Mordechai hears about the Jew-killing idea and rushes to Esther to tell her that her husband's signed off on a massacre. The king doesn't know, of course, that his wife is Jewish. Not that this changes the moral question, but you can imagine things might be a tense around dinner time.

'Anyway, in true Persian style, Esther puts on a big drunken party and invites not only the king, but also evil Haman (you should now be hissing or stamping your feet). There's serious drinking and probably some sexy dancing, and by the end of it, Esther tells the king her secret: that she's Jewish, and that Haman is out to kill her and her people. Haman is put to death instead of Mordechai, and, of course, to ensure the story has a classic Bible ending, five hundred of Haman's tribe are put to death by the conquering Jews, including his entire family, and, I think, his sheep.'

I laugh and drink the dregs of my now cold coffee. The sun shines and the streets fill with people. I like this guy, and I like his story. I ask why it is that so many Jewish narratives are about victimization. He plays me a song on his iPhone. The chorus is: *They tried to kill us (we survived, let's eat!).* More laughter. He tells me it wouldn't be so bad if it were just a joke, but it's history too. My new friend, Two-Phones, lights another cigarette and explains that religion is not the point in Purim. In fact, there's no mention of God in the entire Book of Esther, which is strange for a religious story, but it may well be one of the reasons it's so popular in a place as secular as Tel Aviv. That and the fact that it has more drinking than a Friday night in Donegal.

I wonder if what I'm hearing about here is a late-winter debauch, a pre-Lent piss-up, like Mardi Gras. There's laughter and silliness, masks and drunkenness, frenzied dancing and kissing people you shouldn't; the amnesty that what happens in Purim stays in Purim. It makes sense. Why should teenage lizards and drunk ultra-Orthodox Jews dancing to house music seem more bizarre than an obese and bearded velvet-clad pensioner on a sleigh pulled by a red-nosed reindeer, and the birth of Jesus Christ in a stable?

A silence hovers over our table for a moment. I smoke one of Two-Phones' cigarettes. Somewhere a feeling for this country has taken hold: the dressing up, the dancing, the cute girl, Nina Simone, the quality of coffee, the laughter at the horrors of history and the horrors themselves.

Two-Phones asks me what I'm doing in Tel Aviv, and I tell him I'm on my way to the site of the suicide bomb that killed twenty-three young people. 'You don't have to go anywhere. It was right here,' he tells me, pointing to the shopping centre. 'It was a while ago. I remember it.'

'The Dolphinarium bombing was here?' I ask him.

'No. Not the Dolphinarium, the Dizengoff bomb, right here. I'm confusing them.' He clasps the bridge of his nose. 'The Dolphi is down by the sea. That was a few years after. I remember

---

* 'Jewmongous' by Sean Altman.

it … terrible. I heard it, the ground shook and I thought, "Shit, this again?" But the Dizengoff bomb, that was in the 1990s, in fact, shit, it was today, because it was Purim. Kids died, adults, too, hundreds wounded. There would have been many more if the bomber hadn't seen policemen inside the mall. My cousin Uri was there, he was thirteen. He literally saw bodies flying through the air … well that's what he still says.'

Two-Phones gets up. He has to go do some work, or sleep, more likely. I ask him how to get to the Dolphinarium site and he gives me directions: 'Go if you want, but there's nothing there. Nothing to see …'

SEVEN

Let Us Defeat the Angel of Death

Dror Soffer's ward is an inventory of injuries.

Maksim, the boy who wanted to be first into the Dolphinarium club, has a severe shoulder wound and open fractures on both legs, the bones sticking out. His nerve damage will never fully heal and his two best friends died in the blast. Nadezhda, Anya's dearest friend, has two broken ribs, punctured lungs, burst eardrums, lacerations in both legs and multiple splinter wounds. Anya herself is left with serious leg and head wounds, partial loss of eyesight and a broken eardrum that will affect her hearing for life. One of the last people she saw clearly was her boyfriend Ilya; he was killed immediately. Anya will soon be sixteen years old.

Irina and Igor Shaportov are desperately searching for their daughter Alena. They've been turned away from the Dolphinarium site and directed to the Sourasky, the nearest hospital where Dror Soffer is running the MCI. The Shaportovs run over to the hospital staff and shoot off descriptions of Alena as best they can. They expect their description of her long blonde hair and blue eyes – not the most common features in the Middle East – will immediately fit one of the patients, but there is no girl of that description in the Sourasky. They're shown lists of in-patients from other hospitals, but they don't come up with any possibilities.

Staff suggest the parents look through photographs of all the people yet to be identified. The distraught parents look through the images of scores of injured youths that were taken as they were admitted, but they don't see their Alena amongst the harrowing gallery of digital pictures. Are they *sure* she was actually at the Dolphinarium? Yes. She was there with a friend, Catrin Castenda, and they've since received confirmation that they were there together. The staff tell the Shaportovs that Catrin has been identified: dead. The parents are directed to the Abu Kabir morgue eight kilometres away. They make the terrible trek, but Alena doesn't seem to be there. They spend three hours filling in forms to detail every identifiable mark on Alena in case she, or parts of her, are brought in.

It is 4 am when they are told that the last of the wounded have been admitted across all hospitals, and that no one matching their description of Alena is amongst them. A policeman arrives with a plastic sack full of mobile phones, some charred and bloodied, and asks if they can identify Alena's amidst them. They discover what they believe is her phone.

Meanwhile Irina's elder sister Vika has returned to the Sourasky hospital on a hunch, wanting to add a description of Alena's favourite bracelet. It's this information that allows the hospital to identify a severely wounded young female patient, tagged 129. Alena Shaportov has suffered such serious head and facial wounds that photographic recognition isn't possible. Metal has pierced her skull over her eyebrow all but destroying the left hemisphere of her brain and her lower jaw has been shattered. Since her hair had been shaved off in the ambulance and her blue eyes had been closed, the points of description offered were ineffectual. When her parents see her coming out of the operating room the following morning they don't recognize her. They think there must be a mistake; but there is no mistake.

Alena is very seriously injured and will undergo nine complex neurosurgical operations just to stabilize her condition. She'll have to relearn the most fundamental human functions, how to talk, to walk. At the time of the bomb she'd been a fit and healthy young girl studying for her exams. Now she'll have to struggle for years to reassemble the basic elements of life. But she's alive, and eventually, she'll recover.

Dror Soffer has seen more of the devastating effects of Palestinian weapons of terror than most people – possibly more than anyone alive – but he does not speak of hatred, of revenge, of politics. 'My enemy is death,' he says. 'It's hardest when a child dies, but children die, too. It's part of life. We are here in the valley of tears.' His mantra whispers through the halls: *Let us go and defeat the Angel of Death*. He smiles in a way that seems to recognize humanity even amidst the brutality, and he finds a place beyond despair in which to function.

EIGHT

The Memorial that Isn't

I walk purposefully in one direction as if I know where I am going. Sometimes I imagine that this sort of confidence may get me somewhere, and often it does, but rarely to where I want to go. I ask directions from someone who, instead of replying, spits the husk of a sunflower seed onto the ground and walks away. The next person I ask for directions is helpful. I follow her directions but go wrong and find myself at a dead end where there is a fenced-off building site with what looks like a shepherd's house surrounded by wire fencing. It is hundreds of years old and has faded terracotta roof tiles and is strange amidst the concrete low-rise buildings. On a wall is a poorly graffitied Star of David in blue spray paint. It's faded like an old tattoo. Beneath the Star is a penis and balls in one continual line of spray by the same artist. I double back to where I made a wrong turn and before long I am among people queuing for buses, herding children this way and that, and the horizon opens up to the sea.

EIGHT The Memorial that Isn't

The clouds are dark above the water. The sky is turning black but there's a single strip of ultramarine. A storm is coming. I walk on and find a concrete mass, which, judging by the dolphin statue, is the Dolphinarium. There is no one around. No one's been around for a while by the looks of it. The place is lifeless, a patch of wasteland in downtown Tel Aviv. The roof of the Dolphinarium is faded pink concrete, and beyond is the sea. It has that sadness peculiar to a ruined pier in winter, the burnt husk of a seaside amusement arcade. The walls are covered in graffiti, wooden and metal boards seal the doors, sprouts of dirty grass push up between the grey pavement and the road.

In the seventies, this was a place where people watched dolphins perform. The idea was that it would develop into a unique urban aquarium with galleries into the sea, but then the investors pulled out amidst rumours that it had been used by South Africans as a project simply to get money out of the country. Soon the aquarium plans were shelved, the show petered out and the dolphins died. Now the building looks like a modernist bomb shelter.

It's hard to imagine a huge crowd of teenagers wanting to be here, young people chatting and laughing, massing at a nightclub's doors. It's dismal, deserted. The only thing not lifeless is the graffiti: green and yellow letters bulging like balloons, spelling words I can't even pronounce. The script is fluorescent, the letters like a signature on the building's death certificate.

I'm not sure what I'd expected, but something else, something better. A monument, a garden. Some kind of effort of memory or transformation. How can a site of such particular tragedy be left to rot in this way? Of course there had been so many bombs and deaths in Israel during the second intifada, but something about this one, the targeting of teenagers, the

hundred-plus lives scarred with injury, the shock and grief …
I thought it would be worthy of more.

It sits here, a thing abandoned, a thing that cannot be looked at.

I lived in Paris near a memorial that was erected to commemorate those deported by the Nazis. I walked past it for two years before knowing it was there. One day I noticed a small sign and a stone staircase behind Notre Dame. The stairs led down to the river, to a magnificent, claustrophobic space, dense with the memory of the victims. It was an extraordinary and grimly elegant memorial, and yet it was hidden away like a guilty secret, right in the centre of town.* Hidden, like France's history under Nazi occupation.†

I wander through the empty parking lot towards a fence and find a memorial for the Dolphinarium victims. It's a little smaller than the black stone at the shopping centre, but there it lies, behind the oxidized wire. I walk around to look closer. The names of the dead are inscribed in Hebrew, Russian, and on the back of the monument, English. The text says it's commemorating the many youngsters whose lives were cut off by *murderes in the bloody terror attack*. The word *murderes* looks haunted, jagged, violent. Only later do I realize it's lacking an r, that's all. There are no fresh roses on the memorial, just a bunch of dried-out flowers collapsed against the base of the stone where slabs of broken pavement are gathered. A brown-red mark runs in a thick ribbon down a corner. It looks

---

* Mémorial des Martyrs de la Déportation designed by Georges-Henri Pingusson.

† 76,000 Jews were deported to camps in France under Nazi occupation, of whom 2500 survived: 11,000 of these were children. They were not pulled out of their beds, their homes, by Nazi soldiers but by their own neighbours, by their own police, legal system and civil service, fellow countrymen and women. France denied direct involvement right up to 1995 with President Mitterrand saying they were 'never involved'.

like a bloodstain, but it can't be blood after so many years.

I walk back towards the building by a roughly landscaped stretch of ground where there's sparse grass and ground sprouting with desert shrubs. I follow the iron chain-link fence, rusted almost red by the sea air. A few cats sit motion-less amidst the crushed drink cans and thorny plants, as if they've gathered in silent protest at the brutality of human-kind. On the building is the face of a young man, graffitied in shades of blue, like an early Picasso. The man's chin is raised, his eyes shut. He is dead or closing his eyes to what is before him. I wander around the parking lot and gaze up at the dirty white concrete, on top of which sits the copper dolphin of the Dolphinarium, the sole reminder of the seaside complex's ambitious earliest days. This dolphin looks down across Tel Aviv, just as it did when Saïd Hotari blew himself up in the midst of the crowd.

Too often have I pored over the photographs of the after-math: a teenage boy staggering past, his shirt half ripped off, a tourniquet round his arm, his undershirt scorched and black-ened with blood, eyes wide with shock; a young man carrying a girl, her face paper white, the bottom half of her body soaked in blood like a sodden sponge; haphazard clusters of stretchers scattered this way and that; a girl with part of her face obscured by a bag valve mask, the top of her head blackened with gore; a boy being resuscitated by a young girl, her slender hands on his pale white body. Ambulances, equipment, neck braces, foil blankets, dressings taped to an abdomen, a lake of blood pooling in the cement, ambulance workers with gloved hands stepping over equipment. Bodies covered with black plastic sheets and white tarpaulins with ridged holes. And most chilling, what resembles a pile of twisted bodies. I can't know for sure that that's what the pile was – the darkened corners of the photograph make it impossible to be sure – but that's what it looks like. Bodies. Like the piles of bodies of those pictures in Bergen-Belsen.

I feel sick with myself for being here and sick with the decay of the place. I know so little of this country, but from the efficacy I've seen and the high level of intelligence and confidence of the people I've met, the smooth systematic working of things when they have to be done and the ruthless responses to attack, I expected something else here, something less desultory, less broken. It's like visiting a once admirable friend who's suffered a terrible loss and has become a run-down, unwashed and bitter drunk. You expect him to be rebuilding his life – eating healthy food, exercising, working outside, seeing a therapist – but instead he stinks of piss and despair and lives in a slum of old newspapers.

Ahead of me a bus stops and a group of very young schoolchildren get off. They wear bright orange waistcoats like tiny workmen. I look at them with their funny little walks and their excitement and the way they grasp each other's hands. And they make conscious an ambivalence towards Israel which I'd both buried and somehow justified to myself. Justified because of the politics, because of the way the Palestinians are treated. And I realize suddenly that if I think it is ok to be anti-Israeli then I am against these children. It doesn't help anyone, not the Palestinian people, and not me. It is ignorant, it is part of what killed these teenagers here. I sit down with the words *children should be seen and not hurt* echoing around my head like a chorus and wondering if I will understand anything about this country, about what happened.

A while later, as I'm still trying to pull myself together, gazing towards the bomb site, this abandoned seafront in the heart of a city, I think how broadminded, youthful, hopeful, and yet callous and jingoistic things are here. I look back at this place of terrible destruction, now a monument to denial, and I feel haunted by its savage memories. But no thought can deny the breeze coming across the ocean and the fact that the gathering storm has not even gathered. I can't even read the weather. I put my face into the light wind and walk away along the beach thinking about that great Old Testament prophet Dylan singing *You don't need a weatherman to know which way the wind blows.*

NINE

Survivors

I need to find the people who'd been outside the nightclub that early summer night. Israel is a tiny country, but I'm hampered by an inability to speak the language. Most native-born Israelis speak some English, but those who arrived after the collapse of the Soviet Union tend to speak their native languages (Ukrainian, Uzbek, Russian) and at some point – although not necessarily – Hebrew.

I hear of a documentary called *Empty Rooms*, about the victims of the bomb, but I can't find a copy anywhere. Even the impressive Israeli Cinema Centre in Tel Aviv doesn't have it. So I decide to track down the director, a veteran Israeli-Dutch filmmaker with companies in Holland and Israel, and hope he might help me find some of the people who were outside the nightclub that night or, at the very least, lend or sell me a copy of the film. I go through a few days of phoning and being told to call back later, a frustrating game

I'm familiar with from my days working in TV. Eventually I get the filmmaker on the line.

He tells me he's too busy to meet me and, on top of that, he doesn't have a copy of his film. I ask if he can help me speak with some of the people who'd been at the Dolphinarium that night, or with any family of the victims. He wants to know who else I will be speaking with and I mention that I'll be looking for the family of Hotari, the suicide bomber. He demands to know why I intend to speak to the 'terrorists'. I explain that, whilst I obviously can't speak with Hotari, I hope to speak with someone who knew him, to try to understand who he was and how he came to do such a terrible thing. Why do I want to make the 'terrorist into a martyr?' I tell him that my ambition is to understand the situation, not to make or unmake martyrs. He repeats that he won't be able to see me, but he promises to send me a copy of the film (which he seems to have found) if I email my details, which I do. That's the last I hear from him.

There's something curious about the situation, so I investigate the documentary and find it's been financed by an individual named Michael Chernoy, a businessman 'philanthropist' from the former Soviet states and the tenth-richest man in Israel. I don't have to dig far to find that he's a figure mired in controversy. At a High Court hearing in Britain in 2008 the judge said of him:* 'A considerable amount of evidence has been put forward in relation to [Chernoy's] alleged criminality [...] He is reputed to be a gangster in some of the public press in Russia and there is heavy evidence that this view is taken by some security personnel.' I don't know whether this is fair or accurate – the judge does, after all, use the word *reputed*, and only a few years later, a court in Switzerland concluded that Chernoy wasn't part of any

---

* Mr Justice Christopher Clarke.

mafia. And yet Mr Chernoy remains today on the Interpol wanted list.

Luckily an Israeli journalist gives me a book with testimonies from the victims' families and friends called *Dolphinarium: Terror Targets the Young*, which has also been financed by Chernoy. In the introduction, the editors equate the 'Palestinian terrorists' with 'Nazism ... reborn as Islamic terrorism', and draw parallels between the Dolphinarium bomb and the Holocaust. This isn't the first or last time such comparisons will be made. In 2014 Elie Wiesel, the famous Nobel Laureate and survivor of both Auschwitz and Buchenwald, compared Hamas to the Nazis in *The New York Times*. A year later Israeli Prime Minister Netanyahu addressed Congress, fearing the spectre of peace between the US and Iran. He asserted that the Iranians are guided by irrational leaders with the suicide-bomber mindset; in his *pièce de résistance*, he addressed the much-respected Wiesel in front of Congress, declaiming that he wished he could promise him 'never again', in reference to the Shoah.

Time and time again Netanyahu compares his enemies to the Nazis. In his book *A Durable Peace** he writes that any notion that the Palestinians are 'a separate people that deserve the right of self-determination' is 'borrowed directly from the Nazis'. In 2002 he frames the Iraqis as the Nazis, urging the US to attack Iraq on the grounds that: 'Had the democracies taken pre-emptive action to bring down Hitler in the 1930s the worst horrors in history could have been avoided.' In 2006 the Iranians become the Nazis again: 'It's 1938 and Iran is Germany.'[†]

Shortly after Wiesel's 2014 letter comparing Hamas to the Nazis, three hundred survivors of the Holocaust respond with a letter to the opposite effect, condemning Wiesel and anyone

---

* Benjamin Netanyahu, *A Durable Peace* (2009).
† I am indebted to an excellent article in the newspaper *Haaretz* (3 September 1915) by Peter Beinart for this information on Netanyahu.

who uses the appalling realities of the Shoah as an excuse to oppress others. In their letter they too use the word *genocide* – but as a description of Israel's policy towards the Palestinians. The great philosopher of science Yehuda Elkana, who was imprisoned in Auschwitz from the age of ten, writes: 'While it may be important for the world at large to remember … we must learn to forget."* He sees the danger of his people mirroring the behaviour they had suffered, 'which would grant Hitler a tragic and paradoxical victory'. As one of the spokesmen for the survivors opposing Elie Wiesel's letter puts it in a radio interview: 'Never again, means never again for anyone.'

Chernoy himself writes in *Dolphinarium: Terror Targets the Young* that the bomber had deliberately targeted Russian children in order to halt the immigration of Russian Jews into Israel. He suggests that the bomb achieved the opposite effect to the one intended by Hamas, because now, 'the blood of their children ties them to the land'. He also writes: 'The testimony in this book will break your heart.' This was true for me. It was heartbreaking. But it does not help me find any of the people I'm looking for.

More out of desperation than strategy, I contact an Israeli academic who has co-authored a paper on memory and trauma† drawing on the experience of survivors from the Dolphinarium blast. Despite never having met me, and the paper being a decade old, she comes to my rescue and digs out as many contacts as she can find. Through her efforts, I'm able to call a young woman named Liya who was outside the Dolphinarium the night of the bomb.

---

* *Haartez*, 3 February 1988.
†'Effect of personal involvement in traumatic events on memory: the case of the Dolphinarium explosion' (*Memory* 2010), Israel Nachson and Irena Slavutskay-Tsukerman, Bar Ilan University, Ramat Gan, Israel.

I ring Liya on my new Israeli mobile, aware of the intrusion I'm about to make into this young woman's life. She may have found a degree of peace after months, maybe years of trauma. Also there's the language barrier: what can I say with any delicacy? When I was seventeen I worked as a receptionist's assistant in a grand hotel in Paris. One morning I picked up the phone and an elderly man asked to be put through to a room in which the guest had died the night before. I panicked and tried to pass the phone to a receptionist. It would have been difficult in English but with my limited French I didn't know what to say. She refused to help me (it was Paris) and not having the vocabulary to express myself any better I said to the poor man, '*Je suis desolé monsieur, elle est morte.*' There was a pause and a heartrending 'ahh' from the old fellow, and then he put the phone down.

Maybe this is why I stop my call to Liya and send her a carefully worded text instead. She replies after less than ten minutes. She speaks with a quiet, clear voice and a strong Russian accent. Her English is good but she apologizes for its faults. She says it's hard for her to talk about the bomb but that she'll meet me at a café in a town called Bat Yam outside Tel Aviv. She describes herself as small with dark hair.

I'm staying in Jaffa, the town below Tel Aviv. Jaffa/Yafo was conquered by Saladin in the twelfth century, and before that it had been in the hands of the Assyrians, Israelites, Babylonians, Phoenicians, Persians, Canaanites and European Crusaders. Everyone seems to have passed through, but since 636 CE most of the inhabitants have been the people who call themselves Palestinian. During the fighting between Palestinians and Jews wishing to form a separate state, most of the Palestinian population in Jaffa ran for their lives expecting to return when the war was over. They left food in the kitchen, clothes in the wardrobes, and all their possessions. They were not allowed to return. The few thousand Palestinians who had not fled were imprisoned in a corner of the town, which was enclosed with barbed wire and controlled for the next two years by a military governor.

The vast proportion of properties, some owned for centuries by the same Palestinian families, were gifted to Jewish immigrants, many fleeing the Holocaust, as sanctioned by the new Israeli government. In 1950 a law was passed called the Absentee Property Law, which made this appropriation of property legal. The Palestinians were dispossessed and the streets were renamed with Hebrew names. Those who managed to keep hold of their properties continue to face eviction and demolition threats to this day. It's surprising that there's not more of an undercurrent of tension; perhaps everyone keeps it under wraps for the tourists so that Jaffa can remain the magical place it is.

I ask an achingly beautiful passer-by how to get to Bat Yam and she points up the road saying 'straight, straight … die-rect' with such a splutter of Hebrew pharyngeal or glottal noises that it sounds to my anglophone ears like a multigenerational curse. I board the first bus that passes, pleased to be going in the right direction and to have liberated my dwindling resources from another expensive taxi.

Within twenty minutes we've moved from the contemporaneity of Tel Aviv to what looks like a bustling, Third World linear development populated with Vietnamese, Filipinos, Ethiopians and those from the former Soviet Union – pretty much my fellow passengers on the bus. Tel Aviv's metropolitan sprawl now seems cosmopolitan and affluent by comparison. Here, in what I am assuming is Bat Yam, gangs of boys gather at corners on bicycles, waves of traffic roar forward, open shop fronts hawk plastic toys next to those selling electronics, kebabs, piles of nuts and dried apricots. I find my café on a street corner, a shiny plastic box amidst the cracked concrete.

I look about for Liya. Groups of young men with acned skin and hooded tops chat away, occasionally dashing out to suck at cigarettes. There's a table with three Slavic men in their sixties, all in tracksuits that have never been inside a gym. They remind me of mobsters on *The Sopranos*. In the middle is a table packed with women in bright clothes with bleached blonde hair and thick makeup. They're applying lipstick to a little girl who inclines forward, her lips pursed, an expression as solemn as if she were about to receive a sacrament.

But no Liya.

Seats have been pushed together and tables are crowded with discarded wrappers, coffee cups of all shapes and sizes, frothed milk, cans of coke and mobile phones. There's more than a hum of conversation. People raise their voices, laugh and slap the table to emphasize points. I see a girl a few tables away from me. She has dark hair. I can't tell if she's small, but she's alone at a table for two. I walk up and grin and ask if she's waiting for someone. It doesn't come over very well. She seems repulsed, shakes her head and sucks at her mouth making a disapproving *tut* with her tongue. I retreat, red-faced, to my table. Three smartly dressed women click clack through the door in unfeasibly high shoes, tight black skirts, jackets with zips and ruthlessly plucked eyebrows; outfits thought out to the last buckle and shimmer. They walk up to the ersatz mobsters. One of the women leans over and plants a kiss on the crown of one of the bald heads.

Forty minutes pass. Liya's not in the café. She's not coming. She warned me it would be difficult for her. She must have changed her mind. And then I see an email. *Are you here? I am waiting* ... I realize I must be at the wrong café, or there are two cafés, or ... I call her. I hail a cab. I am in the wrong town. It's a ten-minute drive away.

The café is within a shopping mall and it's deserted. We are completely enclosed. There's no window onto the world; we could be underground or deep in the sea. Liya gives me a brief smile. She speaks quickly, words tumbling over each other. It's soon clear she's not here for herself. It's as if being part of this terrible moment of history has left her with a responsibility. Her sincerity is earnest, heartfelt. There's a quiet respectability about this young woman, a deep sense of value without vanity from which I have the impression she was deeply loved as a child. She carries it with her like a glow.

Suddenly she is speaking about the bomb, like someone plunging into icy water rather than standing nervously on the bank. She felt a boom but thought it was a *napatzim*, a word for which she doesn't know the English. We work out it's a firework. She pauses and looks at me as if trying to articulate her reality or calibrating how much I could ever understand.

'I'm not stupid,' she tells me.

Her mother, her uncles, they are all very intelligent people. She is back to the moment the bomb went off and talking about holding her cousin's hand, but when she turned to look at Etty there was nothing.

I try to find a way to slow her down, there's too much shock and we are at its centre, but she can't hear me. I touch her wrist. 'Liya, will you breathe?'

'What?'

'Breathe a little.'

I take a loud breath. She looks at me. We both take a deep breath and release them together. She smiles. I sit back again and ask her to tell me about her life in Israel. Was she born here? She shakes her head.

'I'm a lawyer now,' she says as if it's an answer.

We chat about the law, and I ask her to tell me about the experience of coming to Israel. She describes arriving from

Turkmenistan a few years before the attack. She came with her sister and mother. They were joining her uncles, but it was a hard landing for her: she didn't speak a word of Hebrew and kids at school called her 'dirty' and 'many bad things'. It was difficult at the beginning, she says. She'd been to see a doctor, a psychiatrist, and this had helped.

This was after the bomb? I ask.

No, she says. This was *before* the bomb. It had been to help her with the bullying. Native-born Israeli kids didn't like the 'Russian' Jews. Israel, I suggest, has not been too kind to her, but she shakes her head vehemently: 'I love Israel. It is my home, the place for Jews.'

I want to know if she remembers anything before the bomb.

It had been her eighteenth birthday one week before, she says. Her face floods with the memory. It had been the best night of her life. She'd had a party for her friends in her uncle's flat. They had sushi and cocktails and it was the first time in her life she'd been drunk. Her cousins Kacy and Etty were there, and then after the party this boy turned up 'from nowhere' and she ended up kissing him. Kacy and Etty liked Russian boys but it was Israeli boys that Liya liked. I asked if there were many native-born Israelis at the Dolphinarium and she shakes her head. Nearly everyone was from former Soviet countries; that is how it was.

'So there would be no boys to kiss at the Dolphinarium for you?' I teased.

Liya didn't mind. Her cousins were her best friends in the world. They called themselves The Three Musketeers. They almost didn't go to the Dolphinarium the following Friday, she explained, because it was Etty's brother's birthday and her father said she couldn't leave until the washing up was finished. The girls begged him; it would take hours to wash up, and then they'd be too late to get in free. 'Not my problem,' he had answered. Liya and Etty burst into tears, which was a technique they'd perfected in theatre club at school. Her uncle was no match for two weeping teenagers and relented. The girls ran off to get ready, and Etty pronounced that they would never forget this evening.

Liya describes her outfit in almost forensic detail: a backless shirt, jeans, platform shoes. It's as if she'll draw herself to any detail but the terrible one before us. Her clothes were birthday presents from the previous week and it was the first time she'd worn them. I ask if she was cold outside the club in a backless shirt, and she tells me no, it was a summer night – even at eleven o'clock it was still warm. Then she stops. 'All the boys looked so beautiful,' she says. Her head drops.

In a moment she's talking about a blue shirt, one young man in a blue shirt. 'Lovely boy … shy.' He'd asked her if he could wait in the line with her and Etty because boys on their own couldn't always get in. The three of them were right at the front of the crowd, near the door on the right side; she, her cousin, and the boy with the blue shirt. She talks of the boy with the blue shirt with all the tenderness of a loved one, laughing at his clumsy efforts to make conversation, then returning to the blueness of his shirt. 'It was like nothing else,' she says, 'so deep, glowing.' 'The terrorist,' she says, 'was different.' She saw him standing on the far left. He was dark. His clothes were dark.

When the explosion came, she'd felt heat on her back, as if someone had thrown boiling water on her from behind. She'd turned around and scrabbled for Etty's hand; and where the boy with the blue shirt had been, she saw nothing. I want her to elaborate on *nothing*. She shakes her head.

'Smoke?' I try.

'Nothing.'

'White? Lights? Fire?'

'Nothing.'

'Darkness, black?' She nods as if grasping at the idea. I think she has agreed to get me to move on. As a child, I would tell people that my nightmares were about monsters and spiders because there was no way of articulating the real terrors. Liya looks at me with wide, insistent eyes and tells me that God was there. At that moment she felt Him, as if He was blessing her with what she described as all of her life.

Her next thought was of her new shoes, and then when she turned back around she caught sight of the boy with the blue shirt, and she understood what had happened: a bomb. There had been a wave of blast, a wind, she called it, which had carried away Etty and him. They scrambled to find each other. Etty was in tears but Liya did not cry. She felt strong, because of God, but her legs beneath the knee were wet with blood. She tells me that she still has bits of metal from the bomb scattered down her calves. Despite the sense of being burnt on her back, she was unharmed, the skin was like a baby's. She's convinced her platform shoes saved her – the shoes and God.

'And the boy with a blue shirt?' I ask. 'What happened to him?'

His hand was missing, she says. And then the memory overwhelms her. She's describing the blood and the shirt and his hand and she's no longer in the shopping mall with me.

'There was too much blood. I cannot forget, never.'

I tell her that this is enough. I call her name and take her hand.

'No, no,' she says, and she's caught in the blood, her own skin so soft and unharmed, protected like an infant by a loving God. She's looking at me, demanding I meet her eyes, demanding I understand. Then the moment is over. She breaks our gaze and leans back in her chair.

'My mother is the most important thing,' she tells me. 'I had one idea after the blast, to speak to my mother, but no one's phone had a signal. The lines always go down in emergencies so that they're clear for the essential services. Etty insisted that we go to the hospital because of my injuries, but I had to talk to my mother, or see her.'

She is explaining to me, and to Etty a decade ago, that her mother will die if she fails to see her. Before anything else, she must see her mother. I don't want to interrupt because she has momentum. It's as if she's not so much talking to me as unravelling herself.

'Another cousin,' she says, 'comes looking for us in his car as soon as he hears news of the bomb. Somehow he finds us and takes us to a local clinic, but it's closed for Shabbat. He wants to drive me to the main hospital, but I make him take me to my mother.'

I ask her to elaborate: why does she want to see her mother before getting treatment? She says her mother only has her and her sister. They are her life. If she was to hear of the bomb and think that Liya had been in it, she would just … die.

This makes me cry. I don't know what it is exactly: the essence of love, selfless protection against suffering, her legs peppered with shrapnel, or the realization that those who love us most are those most hurt by such violence. Liya sees a tear on my face. She points with one finger as if indicating a curious insect. 'You're crying?' She smiles in surprise. When she does finally see her mother, she tells me, Liya faints and wakes up in hospital where the doctors remove as much of the shrapnel as they can.

That was it. The story is finished. We both relax and take refuge in the present.

She asks about my novels and life in Europe. I want to ask if the young man in the blue shirt is the boy she'd kissed at her birthday party. I want to know if it was Alex, or Diaz, or Ilya Gutman. I have pictures of them in my phone, but as soon as

I bring it up, she shakes her head. Her expression makes me understand that she does not want to know any more. 'I am a lawyer now,' she says again.

I feel for her as if she were a child, although she is plainly an adult. And suddenly I am overcome with the sense of being older. Older and melancholic. It's time to go. We hug. I tell her the simple truth, that I'm happy she's alive. I wish I could do something more, but these words are all I have.

———

Somehow I find the number for the Medvenko family. All I know is that Mariana Medvenko was sixteen years old when she was killed outside the Dolphinarium and her father and mother have agreed to speak to me in their home in a block of dozens of identical high-rise apartments on the outskirts of Tel Aviv.

There's a Soviet-era grimness to the municipal apartment blocks in this part of the city. A few patches of grassy greenery sprout out between the buildings, but they seem to emphasize the greyness more than break it up. The Medvenkos live a good many storeys up, and because of the graffiti, I expect the elevators to be out of order; but we're a world away from what I know. This is a new country, and the elevators work perfectly, and no one has used them as a lavatory.

The Medvenkos' apartment is tidy and simple and looks far out onto a featureless urban plain. A TV murmurs from a cabinet. Photographs line the walls: a man in a Russian military uniform with a line of medals on his chest; family trips in the Soviet Union; two girls in a Soviet kindergarten classroom wearing absurdly frilly dresses.

One of the girls from the picture sits in front of me. She has porcelain skin, huge eyes and a dyed blonde bob. A little boy sits next to her playing with a toy parrot. Behind me, taking up most of one wall, is a display cabinet dedicated to Mariana. It houses a large oil painting of her with graceful hands and a frozen smile, copied from some snapshot. Beside this there are photographs, mementos and a gaudy children's clock that looks like a birthday cake, with teddy bears hugging each other and tumbling over a moulded cottage. The hands are somewhere before quarter to midnight. 'It stopped when she died,' her mother tells me.

While we drink tea, Viktor, Mariana's father, shows me videos and photos of Mariana: images of a willowy teenager with friends, in front of posters of pop idols in her room, with her father at what looks like a Christmas dinner. I see Mariana with a group of girls, their hands splayed into innocent teenage parodies of gang-like hand signals that seem to shout out: *Don't fret, we're the next generation.* I see Mariana in a cropped top and high-waisted jeans admiring her newly pierced belly button; with her hair back, poised as a ballet dancer, drinking wine with her little sister. I watch a film clip of her doing a dance for a relative's video camera, wiggling her hips and laughing. It's completely innocent and agonizingly full of life. I watch her at seven years old in a shocking pink meringue party frock looking into the camera like the most sensible of princesses. Even as a tiny girl in a nylon Barbie dress there's a quiet confidence to her, a knowingness in her eyes.

Viktor tells me that his daughter had been a dedicated student, intrigued by robotics and engineering. Going to the Dolphinarium that night was her second night out in months because she'd been studying. She had hoped to bring her fourteen-year-old sister – the young woman with the ivory bob in front of me. Had it not been for Viktor's refusal to let both girls go, the tragedy would have been devastatingly complete, and both girls would have been killed. The sense of this possibility hung in the air, a counterpoint to what actually happened, enshrined in the memorabilia in the display cabinet.

I don't need to ask any questions about the night, or any questions at all. Everything relevant sits before me, the unself-pitying dignity of parental grief, a sister grown up amidst tragedy and knowing instinctively that the best support she can offer is to radiate life. I look around the room and realize I don't recognize any of signs of Jewish culture. Even if they're there, I don't see them. Viktor tells me that prior to the bomb he had not wanted to stay in Israel. He missed Siberia, the landscape and the people. It was the girls who wanted to stay, and so he and his wife agreed they would wait until they were grown up before moving back home. The terrorist bomb was an attempt to drive them away, he explained, an attempt to scare them. 'Now, we will never leave,' he says. 'This is our home now. You won't be able to drag me out of here.'

I've heard many versions of this same narrative. Recent Israelis – some with little or no previous contact with Jewish culture, no tradition of Judaism, no knowledge of the Jewish link in their families – emigrate to provide a better life for their children. When they arrive, they find themselves alienated, not just by the foreign culture and territory but because of a prejudice against 'Russians' that persists to this day. The native-born Israelis responsible for this prejudice have beaten them to the new country by only a generation or two, but their sense of ownership is none the weaker for that. Then comes the very act of devastation that is meant to drive the immigrants away, but instead inextricably ties them to the land. Chernoy got it right in his introduction. These acts achieve the exact opposite effect of what they intend: they forge links between these new arrivals and the land of Israel, drawing this disparate nation closer together.

———

Alexei Neminov had two sisters, Lena, eighteen, and Julia, sixteen. Those were their ages when they were killed outside the Dolphinarium. I've seen photographs of Alexei as an eight- or nine-year-old with his two older siblings, one either side, and another picture of him as a thirteen-year-old with his sisters. This may have been the last picture of them together.

At the beginning of my trip, I called an Israeli journalist and asked if she had any idea how to find the families of the people who had been at the club that night. Now, two weeks later, she sends me an email with a list of numbers and a request for some money. I protest; she never mentioned being paid, we hadn't discussed it. She's put out. What did I think she was doing? She's a professional and I've asked her for a service. She doesn't even know me – of course she wants to be paid! I have an emergency $100 note I've been saving for a year or two in a small folded square in my wallet, so I walk into a post office and mail her the bill. People are straight here, so I guess this is the way it goes.

I text the man named Alexei from the list. There's no reply. I text again. Still nothing. I wonder if my messages have gone through to his phone as a mass of garbled letters via Hebrew or Russian. Or maybe he doesn't want to speak to me. I call him, and he answers straight away. He seems to speak some English. I say that I want to talk to him about the bomb that killed his sisters, and as the words form in my mouth, they feel awkward and wrong. There's a pause during which I hope he hasn't understood me. I hear voices in the background. Then he comes back on the line and says he'll see me, but he'll need his girlfriend to translate. I should come to his work on Allenby Road in Tel Aviv. The name sounds so familiar, so peculiarly English, and it reminds me of something.

Alexei's address on Allenby turns out to be a tattoo parlour. Two middle-aged men, swaying slightly, stumble out of the shop and lurch off down the road slurring at each other in Russian. There's very loud, very hard rock music blasting out of the door, but within it's as spotlessly clean as a private health clinic and surprisingly minimalist and chic. I'm not looking for a tattoo, but if I were, this seems a good place to get one. I ask for Alexei, and after a moment of incomprehension, the heavily pierced modern primitive at the desk turns and shouts for Sasha. He comes out, clean-cut, muscled and serious. The boy in the pictures I'd seen has grown into a man. A large man. He shakes my hand and suggests we sit outside and wait for his girlfriend. His English is much better than he claimed. It's accented with Russian, but precise and clear. We sit on the pavement as cars and buses roar past.

His family had come from the city of Yekaterinburg in the Urals in 1995, he tells me. They – that's his sisters, mother, and grandmother – were all pleased to make the move. Yekaterinburg was an 'ugly, dirty place', polluted and indus-trial. In Israel it was warm, and they were told it could be a home for them, with education, healthcare and prospects. It seemed like a real opportunity for a better life. What parent in the world would not move continents for such reasons? I don't ask whether his family had been culturally or religiously Jewish. He describes himself as Israeli and Russian, and who am I to argue?

Alexei talks about his family as if it's something sacred. He was a single boy among four strong women, and there was a bond of particular closeness. It's clear that even as a young boy, whilst being loved and cosseted, he'd assumed the mantle of the man of his family. He speaks about his work, his mother and his grandmother until the girlfriend arrives. There are a few words between them, but I can't tell if they're in Hebrew or Russian. She sits next to him on the pavement and only then does he begin to talk about his sisters.

Years ago, after arriving, his mother had taken two jobs: one working in a café and the other cleaning an office at night. Yelena, his elder sister, would help her with the cleaning, and Alexei, even as a boy, found a job in the souk making deliveries with a trolley. Yelena, he tells me, had celebrated her eighteenth birthday a few days before the Dolphinarium bomb. She loved to draw and read and had dreams of going to university. Yelena used to have various boyfriends, but a few months before the bomb, she'd begun to date someone more seriously. Julia, his younger sister, was sixteen and more mischievous. She was self-assured and could seem tough – she'd even been suspended from school for fighting. But underneath, she was soft, always ready to help people. The two girls loved going out, they loved MTV and most of all they loved the trance music that Israeli youth had made their own.

I bring him round to the night of the bomb. He looks at his girlfriend who, other than saying hello in English, has not spoken a word. She's so much smaller than Sasha, so slight next to his large frame. She nudges closer to him and takes his huge hand in her lap. I understand that perhaps she's not there so much for translation as for strength.

Everyone was young that night at the Dolphi, he tells me. Everyone felt safe there; they were all from the former Soviet states. He should have been out, but his grandmother had not been feeling well. She, Fania, was like a second mother to him, so he'd cancelled his plans and stayed at home with her watching TV. She told him she was feeling 'nervous', so he'd given her medication. Shortly after, a friend phoned and told him about the blast.

He called both sisters straight away but there was no reply. He picked up his mother and tried to drive to the club, but it was blocked off and they couldn't get near. They spent the night going from one hospital to another trying to find information, looking at photographs. Eventually, around dawn, someone suggested they go to the morgue at Abu Kabir.

And that's where they found his sisters. He tried to help his mother as best he could. He says this simply, and then is silent as the traffic on Allenby rushes this way and that.

Alexei is so stalwart at mastering his feelings and talking in a calm, low voice that I don't perceive how upset he is as he finishes cigarette after cigarette with a sort of efficient precision. When he pauses, I notice a vein pulsing along his jawline. That's all. That and the way his girlfriend clasps his hand between hers.

The terrorist, he goes on, carried a bag with a drum, two bags in fact. Someone Alexei knew was by the front of the club at the kiosk buying cigarettes. He saw the terrorist; he was tanned like a Moroccan with a little moustache and a goatee. The friend asked him, 'What are you doing here?' and the bomber said, 'I'm playing the *tarbuki*.'

'The bomb had bullets in it,' Alexei says quietly. 'Bullets and nails ... I do my best for my mother and my grandmother.' Alexei gets up and stretches. He needs to return to work, he says. He shakes my hand, and the pair walk back into the shop. I understand what Dr Dror Soffer from the trauma unit meant when he said that these Russians are brave.

PART II
Heart

TEN

The Surgeon

A little over five miles southeast of the Sourasky hospital, 52-year-old surgeon Yakov Lavie sits at his desk. Dr Lavie is not a deeply political man; he hasn't paused for such things since he left school. Like most top-level cardiac surgeons, his life has been one of ceaseless training and practise, honing and advancing the intellectual, physical and creative skills needed for heart surgery.

When Lavie left the Tel HaShomer medical centre on the outskirts of Tel Aviv on the morning of 1 June 2001, all had been normal, quiet but for the brisk footsteps of nurses, the intermittent screech of a trolley's rubber wheels on well-polished floors, the voices, beeps, and buzzing – all the professionally contained dramas of a modern hospital. By the time Dr Lavie enters the grounds the following day, the wards of the modern medical centre are overflowing with wounds commonly found on a battlefield, except that most of these casualties are teenage girls.

Dr Lavie is a convincing presence, solid without being heavyset. He has a kind, darkly tanned face, a smile that floods his eyes with warmth, and a large, nut-brown head that looks as if it hasn't known hair for decades and never really needed it. There's a peculiar confidence to him, a confidence that cardiac surgeons often possess. I don't know if this is a quality that draws heart surgeons to the specialty or something that's earned on the way up. Often it's accompanied by arrogance, but not in this case. When thinking or listening Lavie displays an almost palpable force of attention, pressing the forefinger of his left hand into his temple, particularly on a difficult telephone call, as if to concentrate the thought or support his heavy head.

On the day after the bomb, Zev Rothstein, the hospital deputy director, gives a press conference during which he says: 'The attack was characterized by wounds from screws,' and that his staff have 'never seen injuries like this'. Many of the young people admitted to this hospital have what is called a multi-dimensional injury pattern. These include impact wounds from the penetration of shrapnel and other matter, and burns from the ignited gas and blast effects. They require brain surgery, orthopaedic surgery, abdominal surgery and treatment for burns, but the one thing that none of the young people require, in this instance, is cardiac surgery.

The halls are swarming with activity, but Lavie is in his office. He's not used to this. Cardiac surgeons are accustomed to being the nucleus of attention – the divas of the medical drama, to put it bluntly. For the latter four decades of the twentieth century, cardiology has attracted the best minds and the best hands; people with a fusion of high intelligence, dexterity, intense studiousness and the confidence to make life-or-death decisions under extreme pressure. Heart surgeons like Lavie are not accustomed to sitting about in a crisis twiddling their well-coordinated thumbs. But in this particular crisis, there's nothing for him to do. He was not on the list of specialists called into the MCI, and he is not needed now.

Heart surgery is predominantly a peacetime activity. There are, of course, cardiac surgeons in the military, but they spend more time dealing with overfed generals and chain-smoking captains with cholesterol than with patching blast casualties on the battlefield, which means that despite the urgency and the demand on the medical personnel during this horrific MCI, there's no role for Yakov Lavie. In this rare moment there is nothing for him to do but allow the emotional impact of this attack on unarmed teenagers to soak into him.

Lavie sits at his desk jamming his forefinger against his temple, deliberating the damage to these young people. He knows better than most the impact of death on a family; he knows the impact of injuries like these on young lives. If Lavie were pushed to define his politics, he would describe himself as a left-winger, aware of the mistreatment of the Palestinians and sympathetic. But right now Lavie sits in his office and experiences what he will later describe simply as *rage*.

As much of Israel stands still in the aftermath of this attack, Lavie scrambles for something to distract him. He marches through the corridors teeming with activity until he reaches the hospital's small ward of end-stage heart-failure patients. The ward is quiet, filled with his patients closest to death, the most severe cardiac cases for whom there remains only one treatment. The most traumatic and radical procedure modern medicine has to offer, a treatment only performed when all other avenues are exhausted.

A heart transplant.

ELEVEN

There Are No Jokes

I head back up Allenby after speaking with Alexei. The street is longer and wider than any other road in the city, so my mind starts to wander with my feet and the answer surfaces. Allenby was the British general in the film *Lawrence of Arabia*, and also in real life. Edmund Allenby was T.E. Lawrence's commanding officer when Lawrence convinced the Arab tribes under Prince Faisal to work with the British to liberate Jerusalem in 1917, after four centuries of Ottoman rule.

The general sent all the right signals when he arrived at the gates of Jerusalem. He dismounted from his horse and entered on foot to show the British Empire's great respect for the city. In his first pronouncement as conquering hero, he guaranteed Jerusalemites that under British governance all would be free to practise their own religion, and all shrines and modes of worship would be equally protected. However, in light of recent history, I'm not sure how liberating he was. Behind the scenes, the British had secured Prince Faisal's help through Lawrence by promising that they'd support an independent homeland for Faisal's people. What even Lawrence didn't know was that the British made a similar declaration to the Zionists in the well-known 1917 Balfour Declaration, in which Britain committed that they'd *view with favour* a homeland for the Jewish people in Palestine – despite the fact that in 1917 only 10 per cent of the country's population were Jews.

Promising the same land to both the Jews and Arabs was like the trustee of an estate telling two members of the same family that the lands belong exclusively to them. The Balfour Declaration is still widely used as part of the legitimization of the State of Israel, but less so the part of the letter that insists it must be 'clearly understood that nothing shall be done which may prejudice the civil and religious rights of existing non-Jewish communities in Palestine'.

My mind is still in 1917 when this woman stumbles towards me – hardly a woman, a girl – in a wedding dress. She pauses after each step like a computer trying to reboot. The bodice of white lace is splattered with blood and a part of her skull is missing, showing a grey and pink mass of brain. There's no time to do or say anything because a few steps behind her staggers a young man dressed in a button-down shirt and a clip-on tie. He looks as if he might work for a chain of exhaust fitters or suchlike. One hand holds a clipboard; the other is a bloody stump. Behind him are five girls dressed as nurses holding trays with slippery piles of bloodied organs and bandages and bloody sponges. An entire surgical team follows in scrubs brandishing severed limbs. The traffic has stopped. Young men in white T-shirts drenched in red, with chalk-whitened faces and blackened eyes lurch forward with the same halting step. One has an axe embedded in his head. A soldier with an eyeball hanging out of its socket walks by chatting to a porcelain-skinned girl with one side of her skull open as if exposed by a can opener. It's a macabre procession of blood-drenched casualties, like extras from a horror movie. It's as if I've just walked into my own nightmare.

Then, I notice the bottles of beer.

I'm hollowed out by my interviews. Alexei, the Medvenkos and Liya are good people who've had the precious core of their lives ripped out and burnt in front of them. Imagine what it is to lose a child ... two children ... all your siblings.

I watch this bloody procession and think how, only a decade before, people like Mariana Medvenko, Alexei's sisters, Julia, Polina, Anya, Viktor, Nadezhda had been soaked in real blood. They'd been targeted not only because they were Israelis, but because they were the new immigrants from the former Soviet Union. They had told me how they found themselves derided by other Israelis as second-class citizens, Jewish enough to immigrate to Israel but not valued in the same way as the European Jews and earlier émigrés. Despised by so many Israelis, hated by so many Palestinians.

I remember my friend Uri's mother, a ninety-year-old woman in an old people's home in Tel Aviv. She explained that after World War Two people in Israel felt a sort of tight-lipped distaste for those Jews arriving from the Shoah. The new émigrés weren't encouraged to speak of what had happened 'over there', and if they did, they weren't believed. I asked her when this changed. She said, 'It was the trial of Adolf Eichmann.' The survivors of the concentration camps gave witness on live TV broadcast to the world. This changed everything.

Hamas had wanted the Dolphinarium bomb to send a clear message to the new immigrants, that this was not their land, that they were not safe here. But it did the exact opposite. It made the ex-Soviets, even those without Jewish ancestry, feel part of the new country in a deep and powerful way. And not only this, it forced many second-generation Israelis to question their prejudices surrounding these new immigrants, and work to integrate them more fully.

I'm still gazing in dumb surprise at the procession, because history, even recent history, seems so far from what I'm seeing. It all feels so wrong, but I can't deny that these people are enjoying themselves. Many of the costumes and wounds are bound with jokes and many are professionally intricate. It's clear that these are costumes but they're far from the *Avatar* lizards, sexy cats and muscle-suited superheroes I'd seen at the beginning of the festivities.

I ask someone if this is some sort of final Purim parade and receive the beery reply that this is Tel Aviv's first Zombie Walk. The incongruity of the whole occasion is overwhelming, especially in the context of my last few hours, but even more so for these young people who live under the constant shadow of such violence. This Halloween-like masquerade is of course a joke, but as that great Ashkenazi sage taught us, 'There are no jokes.'* Maybe there's a strange alchemy at work. Sure, it's driven by laughter but there's an exorcism as well, a reversal of the expected, an inversion of normality so that real-life horror is transformed through playfulness and humour. Nietzsche spoke of maturity as the seriousness of a child at play.† This procession is serious play, and perhaps that is what Purim is, serious play.

It was the Russian philosopher Mikhail Bakhtin who decoded carnivals as a revolt against order.‡ He showed how since times predating Christianity and Judaism, the carnival allowed people to parody and, for a day or two, subvert the

---

* Sigmund Freud, *Jokes and Their Relation to the Unconscious* (tr. 1960).
† Friedrich Nietzsche, *Beyond Good and Evil* (1886).
‡ Mikhail Bakhtin, *Rabelais and His World* (1965).

forces of dominant power. The ruled could do the ruling. It was a release valve, but it also helped keep the people in check for the rest of the year. As I watch the zombies stumble past, it's clear this is not just a celebration of a Jewish feast, or an excuse for a pub crawl (although it's both of these, too); it's a march against nihilism, against fear. It is the 'laughing truth' that Bakhtin believed could 'degrade power'.

I wonder if this is a demonstration against history, against the bloodshed and death that haunts these young people every single day. Violent death – not just a neat bullet wound here or there, but mutilation, limbs hanging off, faces blown away, skin burnt off. This is what they, their neighbours and friends, are threatened with every day. But it's much worse than that: not only are these young people the potential victims of such mutilating violence but they're also being prepared to become the future perpetrators of the same offences.

I let the parade pass and head into the nearest bar to do what everyone else seems to be doing.

TWELVE

Heart Disease

Dr Lavie enters the ward of end-stage heart-failure patients and sees Yigal Cohen lying in his hospital bed. In his mid-forties, Cohen is a thickset man with a broad chest and a strong jaw, still burly despite his illness. Not the sort of person you'd want to join in a boxing ring.

Originally he trained as a technician but he took a job as a salesman for L'Oréal, peddling products to hairdressing salons. It wasn't an obvious step* for someone whose main ambition was to 'get rich', but it was a job and he had two children and a

---

* L'Oréal, the cosmetic company, was one of the post-war success stories of French business. This was despite the owner and founder's overt collaboration and support for the Nazis during the occupation of France and financial backing of an extreme right-wing, anti-Semitic French political party. Like so much of history that is uncomfortable to the accepted persona of France as a nation it was brushed under the carpet of history. L'Oréal completely rehabilitated themselves in Israel and their past associations with the Nazi forces have been effectively absolved.

wife to support. His father was a pioneering Israeli, his mother was from Bulgaria, and he was one of four brothers, one of whom was his twin. He grew up, led an active life and was a stranger to illness.

Then one day his twin collapsed during a heavy bout of influenza. He was taken to the hospital where it was discovered that he was suffering from cardiomyopathy, a disorder that affects the heart muscle and tends to run in families. Since Yigal was his infirm brother's identical twin, the hospital insisted that he, too, come in for a check-up. Yigal had no symptoms, so he refused, but the hospital persisted. Eventually, he succumbed to a full examination and was informed that he had a similar condition to his brother's. Yigal decided to adopt a strategy familiar to many people, particularly men, in situations of medical threat: denial. He ignored the problem and hoped it would go away. Yigal's twin deteriorated and was told that his only hope lay in a transplant. He was placed on a waiting list and quickly received a new heart.

Before long, it became clear that this was a prescient reflection of the condition of Yigal's heart, as the cardiologists had warned. Yigal was soon no longer able to deny his own symptoms, his breathlessness and fatigue, and was obliged to seek medical help. He was advised to stop working, and within months, he too was placed on a transplant list. Naturally, Yigal supposed getting himself a new heart would be as swift as it had been for his brother. However, he wasn't so fortunate. Months after being placed on the list, Yigal became a long-term patient in Lavie's end-stage ward – a ward from which there are only two ways out: a new heart or death.

Yigal has seen the beds around him empty, and knows that if a heart doesn't appear soon, his bed will empty too. He begins to scour the pages of newspapers, guiltily hoping that something might happen that could grant him a chance of life. A multiple car crash, a small-scale disaster ... anything that might bring him a healthy heart. Strangely, just such a tragedy occurred exactly a week before the Dolphinarium tragedy: the floor of the Versailles Wedding Hall in Jerusalem collapsed during a crowded event and sent a packed mass of guests crashing through two floors of the building onto the ground. More than a hundred people were injured and twenty-one died. Terrorist involvement was suspected, but it was soon established that this was entirely a civil disaster – the worst in Israel's history, but no one to blame except the building engineers and those who ignored the regulations. A prominent rabbi at the time, Reuven Levi, announced to the press that the cause of the floor's collapse may have been the 'licentiousness' of men and women dancing together 'punishable by a divine death sentence',* thus putting into focus the similarities between fundamentalists, be they Muslim, Christian, or Jew – each being closer to other fundamentalists than they are to the reasonable majority.

Yigal Cohen yearns for life and has the courage to admit to it. His desire is an essential impulse, one that unifies not just humans but possibly all living beings: the desire to live. More than four hundred years ago the great (Jewish) philosopher Baruch Spinoza, looking for a factor that links all living things, articulated this as Proposition Seven: 'It pertains to the nature of a substance to exist.' Yet Yitzhak's hope for a heart from the Versailles wedding tragedy comes to nothing. It's been exactly a week, which means it's been too long to hope for a heart.

Israel in 2001 is a depressing place to be waiting for a heart. Not because of the quality of medicine – the Israeli transplant centre offers world-class, state-sponsored treatment – but because the organs themselves are so hard to come by. The first issue is one of numbers: there are only 7 million people in Israel. Unless they're fighting a war and losing, that's only

---

* Jpost.com (*The Jerusalem Post* newspaper online edition), 1 June 2001.

about 60,000 natural deaths a year. It's not enough. In the US, there are 2.4 million deaths a year, and yet there are still only about 2500 donor hearts available.

The second issue is religion: people do not want to sign up to be donors. It's an issue of religious conviction, specifically, for the Haredi Jewish community, the ultra-Orthodox. They do not recognize brain death as death. Some go so far as carrying an anti-donor card that reads *I do not give my permission to take from me, not in life or in death, any organ or part of my body for any purpose.* Nevertheless, people from this religious tradition demand that they should be eligible to receive donor organs should they need them. They insist that, although their religious practice forbids them from providing organs, it would be prejudicial to block them from receiving a life-saving organ. The Haredi people are not responsible for the shortfall in organs. It's an international problem related to altruism, education, attitudes to death; but within Israel, they make up about 10 per cent of the population, and in 2001 their willingness to take but not give certainly contributes to the shortage.

The third issue is location. In other countries, like the UK for instance, neighbouring territories like France or Germany may provide a heart. Israel's neighbours, however, are more likely to send ordnance than organs. Of course, Israel's smaller population means less heart disease; nevertheless, despite available funds, there are not enough hearts. Incommensurate with the country's size, there's an acute shortage of hearts.

So Yigal Cohen waits and waits and tries to reassure his wife and children that he will continue to be in their lives, but each day that passes he knows his grip on life slips. It's just after midnight on 2 June 2001 when he hears ambulances screeching into the hospital. He's aware straight away that a significant event has occurred, and the thought occurs to him that from all these people, there might be a healthy heart for him. As Cohen lies in bed hoping that this tragedy might give him a chance of a new life, TV sets are playing the news footage. Experts and eyewitnesses are analysing every angle; radios, newspapers and news channels repeat information. People watch and re-watch and read and re-read the same story over and over. They have a desperate hunger to hear again and again what happened in the hope of finding new facts, understanding, shifting the impact of the narrative from despair to something other than fear and fury. The facts they seek are not in the newspapers or on TV or to be heard on radio. The facts lie in the Sheba or Sourasky medical centres; the facts lie embedded in the cracks of the road outside the nightclub, or compounded with shreds of clothing in the rubble. The facts are carried off in the beaks of unquestioning gulls.

Of course, there's more to this event than the packaged news stories, more than the remains of the young people, more than the injuries of the children bleeding into hospital beds. There are historical dimensions, forces played out over centuries, political machinations over decades, strategic elements over the past few years. Different positions make different truths of all the factors of the narrative.

But …

Nothing can deny the wanton destruction of someone's daughter or son. Parents despair; politicians go about their daily business; the organizers of the bomb rejoice and hide; Dr Soffer takes command; Dr Lavie checks on his ward; Yigal Cohen longs for a heart. Vaporized traces of a desperate 22-year-old man turned suicide bomber coat the charred palm fronds of the date tree outside the nightclub, scraps of his humanity fused into the blue paint of municipal lamp posts. The physical remains of the young man, Saïd Hotari, dry on the verdigris of the copper dolphin outside the entrance, becoming dust in the sunlight of another day.

THIRTEEN

Another Innocent Man

When Mazan Al-Joulani gets into bed in his small apartment in Shuafat, East Jerusalem, each night and settles next to his beloved wife Maha, he does not think, *I hate Jews*. And when he wakes each morning – perhaps disturbed by the impatient cries of Lotfi, the youngest of his three children, or by the agitations and pressures of his daily life, which are many and which six hours of sleep can never put to rest – his first thought is not, *I hate Israelis*.

No, he is no less a human being than you or I. He thinks of his children, his wife, the lines around his eyes, his job. He asks himself whether he'll go to the bathroom before or after his coffee; he considers an irritating colleague at work; he tries to remember what it was that his wife told him not to forget. Mazan Al-Joulani thinks of the hand-drawn picture, a soldier and a blazing bush of barbed wire, that his son thrust into his hand, and the rainbow his daughter drew so as to be included.

He thinks about his children; he thinks about how much he loves them; and he feels it like his own blood moving through him. He feels it like an ache. And then, almost simultaneously his mind flits to the coffee. Should he use the last of it or leave it for Maha? After all these things, he might think of Israelis. But perhaps not.

It is 2 June 2001, not even a year into the second intifada, which is not an easy time to be a Palestinian in East Jerusalem, let alone work and raise a family. Mazan Al-Joulani is a 33-year-old pharmacist, and on the morning after the suicide attack outside the Dolphinarium nightclub, Mazan is getting ready for work. Ignorant of the bomb that exploded before midnight, for the moment he is not connected in any way.

Breakfast is a noisy affair with a five-, four- and two-year-old. Feeding and wiping little faces, laughing, perhaps a brief burst of tears. Sometimes there's eggs, bread, coffee, jam, falafel. Often Mazan cannot stay long, because for a Palestinian during the intifada, even one with a privileged blue Israeli identity card, it's impossible to estimate how long the commute to work might take. Travelling a few kilometres might take fifteen minutes or three hours, depending on the permanent barriers, which slow down the entrances and exits to each Palestinian neighbourhood, and the 'flying check-points' set up by the Israeli military, temporary obstructions in the passage of vehicles and civilians that pop up in unlikely places. They're meant to be security, but, to the Palestinians, they're another form of punishment.

Mazan leaves his house and begins the arduous drive to work. His focus is not how to injure an Israeli, how to over-throw an occupying military force, how to defeat injustice. Despite the fact that, at this point in the intifada, Palestinians have suffered 450 casualties and Israel has suffered sixty-six, his focus is the same as yours or mine, how to get through another day, how to get to work on time, how to take the children safely to school, how to buy food for the family.

As he makes his way to the main road Mazan gathers as much information about the route to work as he can. Where are the delays, the new checkpoints, the demonstrations planned? He greets the man selling newspapers who gives him the latest updates; calls a friend in the Sheik Jarrah neighbourhood where he works to ask what's going on there; questions a young man getting off a bus. In a very short time, he puts together not only a detailed report of the checkpoints and closed-off routes in his area, but also a variety of options to circumnavigate all the deliberate obstructions: which roads to cut through and which buses have changed their routes to take paths through the hills. He might learn that a benevolent farmer has cleared Israeli military cement blocks to the side with his tractor, or that the back door of a shop has been deliberately left open so people can detour around a checkpoint.

The news of the bomb the night before has caused a bigger shock than anticipated, reaching across the world and of course creating a dramatic increase in the Israeli military presence all over the Palestinian areas. The deaths of young people – hardly more than children, so many of them girls – has caused a grim fury amongst the Israeli troops. For the past few years, they might have laughingly shot in the direction of those evading checkpoints, or thrown a rock or two. It might have been boredom, orders or simply the culture of hatred that saturates this land. But the day after the Dolphinarium atrocity, there's a quiet, murderous rage. For once, young conscripts are more determined than nervous. The same young fingers rest on hair-trigger automatic weapons, but today it's not just fear that might pull the trigger, it's fury too.

There have been demonstrations across Israel and attacks on Palestinian businesses. In Jaffa, the historic bakery Abulafia, loved by Israelis and Palestinians alike, has been set on fire. However, unlike on other occasions, there has been no Israeli military counter-attack on the Palestinians in the West Bank. Ariel Sharon learned his lesson when he was publicly criticized by Israeli papers for ordering (US-built) F16 strikes in the West Bank and Gaza after the Netanya mall bombing – not because of the civilian casualties amongst the Palestinians but because he didn't 'give their public relations apparatus enough time to exploit the terrorist bombing'.

He's now testing a new strategy of restraint, a strategy to exploit media support in the international battle for sympathy. Many Israelis disagree. They believe currying international support is a waste of time. They feel that anything less than an eye for an eye, than Palestinian rubble and corpses, is a weak response. But Sharon's spokesman puts it directly, saying: 'It would be unwise to give into the desire for revenge and at the same time destroy favourable international opinion.' His strategy is paying off. Messages of profound sympathy have already arrived from the leaders of most of the non-Arab countries of the world, and some of the Arab ones as well. This reaction stands in sharp contrast to the response of some Palestinians in the West Bank and Gaza. Celebrations are visible. Spontaneous street parties are thrown in the home-town of the bomber Saïd Hotari. Signs have been posted, trumpeting slogans such as *22 and counting*, after the twenty-second casualty, a teenage girl, succumbed to her injuries. The father of the bomber, Abu Hotari, makes a statement that pours acid into the wounds. For Palestinians familiar with such rhetoric it hardly registers, but for all those Israelis and their supporters who think the Palestinians barbaric, it fulfils expectations. What he says is: 'I wish I had seven such sons to carry out seven such attacks.'

FOURTEEN

The Old City

I'm off to Jerusalem, another minibus, almost full and ready to leave. Shabbat falls today, and the Jewish parts of Jerusalem will close like a giant clam. Not the best time to be taking any sort of journey, but better than elbowing through crowds in Tel Aviv for that last bottle of Galilee chardonnay.

I've been invited to Shabbat dinner by an Orthodox family, relations of my friend Saul who lives in New York City. Most of the people I've been getting to know around Tel Aviv have been liberal and secular, which is, I suppose, because I'm liberal and secular. Saul's told me that his family is 'more observant' than he is. I'm worried about this because Saul is the most observant Jewish person I know. I don't think his family will be in eighteenth-century frock coats and fur hats, but it's quite possible that the men might be in dark suits and the women in wigs and tan tights. I've never been to an Orthodox Shabbat dinner, and I feel myself beginning to fret over what might go wrong.

I've the last seat in the minibus, behind the driver – the seat people avoid because of the chore of passing bus fare change around. Next to me is a ginger-haired man in his early thirties wearing a skullcap. He gathers his bags from my seating area as I approach and hunches over the screen of his phone. His face is pale and close enough to the broad screen of his phone to catch its glow: glaucous, I think that's the word for such a light. He has thick freckles like shadows and the sort of mad scraggy beard favoured by young religious men of Abrahamic religions. His trousers are festooned with pockets, pouches and loops for tools, or perhaps for weapons. His hips are broader than his shoulders, which despite the tool-pants and beard give him a sense of femininity. I think of Akhenaten, the most radical of the great pharaohs of Egypt, who in the space of a couple of decades introduced monotheism, built a new capital city and married Nefertiti, the most gorgeous queen in all of history – all this with the slim shoulders and broad hips of a particularly curvy woman. Of course, Akhenaten lacked the wiry orange beard of my neighbour and none of the statues or portraits show the pharaoh wearing thick hiking socks and all-terrain sandals.

As the minibus untangles itself from the knot of Tel Aviv traffic and breaks into the country, I can smell, almost taste, the faintest trace of orange blossom in the air, and I remember for the first time in so many months that there is more to existence than concrete and exhaust fumes. We're passing orchards in full flower, plains hazy with sprouting crops and hills combed in even lines of freshly leafed vines. The sun's light is loosening, becoming golden, and the promise of spring is in the air. We're out on the broad motorway, and I'm happy to feel the space expanding around me and within my head. In less than forty minutes we enter what must be the beginning of Jerusalem. I see crowds of strict-Orthodox, the Haredi, rushing about all spic and span in satin coats and hats like fur turbans from the days of Marco Polo. The bus has stopped and a beautiful young woman is gesturing to me. Her face is caramel brown like a Spanish teenager at the end of summer. Her eyes are enormous and she wears a long dark skirt with black buttons down to the hem. She looks as though she may be strict-Orthodox but I wonder in a flash of erotic possibility if she may be signifying interest in me – but no, her gesture is telling me to get off the bus before it heads into its garage.

I disembark on the dusty street and hail a taxi, which takes us towards Old Jerusalem. Riot police muster on the stretches of grass outside the city walls. Young men strap on body armour, flex muscles, swing clubs, pick up shields, check equipment. It occurs to me that they're readying for the sort of battle that might have happened outside these walls a thousand years before. My driver – a Palestinian in his mid-thirties with an unshaven face and the corpulent body of a once physically fit man who does a lot more eating and sitting around than he used to – tells me that today an Israeli policeman stamped on the Quran and now there will be riots.

'For what?' I ask.

'For the insult to Allah,' he explains, as if it were obvious.

'Would it not be better for the people to leave insults against Allah for Allah to sort out?'

He sighs. 'Of course ... but men are men.'

He leaves me outside the Gate of the Flowers, which was built during the reign of Suleiman the Magnificent over a breach in the walls that the Crusaders had made five hundred years before. Beyond this gate is the Old City, and I'm soon lost in a knot of passageways circumvented by walls and narrow, looping, covered alleyways that have confounded the greatest travellers and most seasoned pathfinders.

I find myself in a food market. Everyone here seems Jewish, rushing to and fro in the last moments of shopping before the sounding of the Shabbat horn signals a commercial whiteout. The atmosphere is urgent. A group of bearded men in cream satin dressing gowns mass around a vendor whose produce I can't see. Their hats are extraordinary, thick haloes of brown fur. A woman walks by with dozens of bags on each arm, a stroller in front of her and four wide-eyed children with heads shaved but for two glistening locks. All around me food is being inspected, vegetables held up, assessed, derided, bought or tossed back. Piles of melons, pickled fish, small green cucumbers, hills of cooked rice with strands of macaroni, cooling mounds of slow-cooked aubergines glistening black, pyramids of strawberries, mountains of *challahs* still warm from the oven exuding their yeasty scent like shameless cats.

Young, ultra-Orthodox men gather at corners offering with evangelical zeal to tie black prayer boxes, *tefillin*, on the heads and arms of passing men. They crowd around takers like Three Card Monte hustlers egging on a new mark, cheering them on with ecstatic delight. The men are straight out of Appalachian moonshine tales: exuberant facial hair, big hats, wild eyes. I'm beginning to understand that whether Jewish or Muslim, if you want to make any absolute theological claims you need an impressive beard; and obviously, you have to be male.

I walk on, winding my way through the vaulted alleyways, dodging children on bicycles, passing stalls selling sunglasses, mobile phones, batteries, shawls, wall hangings, plastic buckets, rolls of linoleum and rubber under-flooring, postcards, spices, women's shoes and sneakers, one tied to another like an eccentric mobile, turning this way and that as people rush by. I find myself in the Islamic quarter. Strangely, the rooftops of some of the buildings are crowned with high metal fences, with barbed wire and towers clustered with surveillance cameras.

It's a curious sight to see buildings with security fences on the rooftops like high-tech zoos, especially when everything else is so ancient. There are clusters of Israeli flags atop the fences. A small group of people is on one rooftop, a man all in white – extravagantly bearded of course – a white *kippah* on his head. This particular roof terrace is bedecked with flags like the UN headquarters, except that all of the flags here are Israeli.

Just as some Israelis continue to expand into the West Bank (in settlements deemed illegal by the UN) extremist groups have been quietly establishing a Jewish presence in the Muslim quarter of Old Jerusalem ever since the mid-eighties. These groups have enjoyed either overt or covert backing from the government, and never more so than today. Prime Minister Benjamin Netanyahu went on CBS's *Face the Nation* in 2014 to say that he was baffled by any criticism of this particular case: 'Jewish residents of Jerusalem bought apartments legally from Arabs in a predominantly Arab neighbourhood,' he complained, 'and this is seen as a terrible thing.' It was countered that the purchases had not been made by Jewish residents of Jerusalem as the prime minister had claimed; according to Palestinian residents the apartments were bought by a Palestinian frontman called Farid Hajj Yehiya who claimed to the owners that the apartments were to be used for Muslim pilgrims visiting Old Jerusalem – whilst secretly in the employ of a right-wing settlement organization known as Elad whose stated aim is to overtake the Muslim areas of Jerusalem with Jews.[*]

I leave the Israeli flags in the Muslim quarter behind and see a sign for the Church of the Holy Sepulchre. This is the holiest church in the whole of Christendom, the place where Christ was crucified and resurrected, the spiritual epicentre of the first half of my life. I follow the signs and find a small

---

[*] Public Radio International, October 2014.

square. The church itself is surprisingly diminutive, as if it's been squeezed into a corner in an effort to save space in this crowded city. It's a curious hodgepodge of Romanesque and Byzantine styles in bits and pieces, a chaotic fusion of ancient afterthoughts. Any idea of design has disappeared amidst repairs, fires, destruction and rebuilding.

Despite the church's small and haphazard exterior, it's enormous within. There are levels and cavernous subterranean chapels, a labyrinth of arches and corners with chandeliers and lanterns on long loops of cord. It's ancient and colossal, like those engravings of fantasy prisons by Piranesi. I'm astounded that this is the place where Jesus, the real Jesus of Nazareth, was crucified and buried – and in which, I was absolutely certain from the age of four, He rose from the dead.

The church is spookily cool. I watch people come and go and, in the moments between, I sit and listen for God, but hear only the various guides with their Russian, Scots-English and Japanese accents. From the Scots-English guide I learn that I'm standing in the Chapel of the Holy Prison, where Jesus was kept before being crucified. It's dark and heavy, like a damp cave. Whilst I'm praying that children may be safe, and for peace in the Middle East – in case there is a God – a group of Eastern Orthodox priests in black hats and ornate robes usher me out so that they can perform a ritual involving singing, lighting candles and chanting Greek prayers.

I head to the tomb itself, the Holy Sepulchre, under the main dome of the church. This is the holiest place in the church and indeed the *raison d'être* of Christianity, because it was here that Christ rose from the dead. Other religions have their miracles and prophets, but only Christianity has a son of God coming back to life. A swarm of pilgrims are trying to get into the tomb, which looks like a marbled garden shed plonked under the cavernous arches. I join the throng and wait in a line that seems to ebb backward and forward. Time passes, but I move no closer to the door of the tomb. Meanwhile groups of priests and bishop-types file in and out of the shed with jewelled books, precious staffs, ceremonial crosses and clouds of incense. Every twenty minutes or so, a new group arrives in different robes with different sacred objects. Only a dozen pilgrims are allowed to enter in between the groups, creating the impression that this holy place is for sacred professionals only.

I learn that this church is a *simultaneum mixtum*, meaning that the building is shared amongst different Christian religions, in this case the Roman Catholics and Eastern, Oriental and Greek Orthodox Christians. This might reasonably be thought of as a concrete example of religious tolerance, but here in the Church of the Holy Sepulchre, any tolerance is wafer thin, and when it cracks, brawls erupt. During a ceremony in 2004 Orthodox priests noticed that a door to the Catholic chapel had been left open. This they interpreted as a sign of disrespect. Forgetting the instruction to love thy neighbour, they charged in like warring gangs for an ecclesiastical punch-up with the Franciscans. Another priestly brawl erupted on Palm Sunday 2008 in which dozens of monks and police were injured. A few months later, Armenian and Greek priests had a fist fight at the entrance to the Sepulchre itself.

The only group all the denominations seem to listen to is an aristocratic Palestinian family known as the Nuseibehs, which traces its lineage back to a man called Sheikh Ghanim ben Ali ben Hussein al-Ansari al-Khazrajy, born near Nablus in 562 CE. The Nuseibehs are inheritors of an agreement made between Saladin and Richard the Lionheart in 1192, which gave them the job of maintaining order in the church, governing an alliance between the sects known as the 'status quo'. As far as I know, this treaty may be the longest-lasting agreement between any religious groups in the Middle East. Even today you can see the Nuseibehs' men marching about the Church of the Holy Sepulchre, broad-shouldered, often blue-suited and invariably wearing fez. They carry thick brass-tipped staffs and the sort of stern expression that teachers in tough schools acquire after decades on the educational front line.

Some reflex of Roman Catholicism stirs and I make my way out of the church down the Via Dolorosa, the path Jesus took carrying the cross to his slow death. There are fourteen sites on this path that are venerated by Roman Catholics, Orthodox and other Christian sects. The Catholics call these sites the Stations of the Cross. 'Doing the Stations' was a frequent ritual in my childhood involving pausing in front of sculptural reliefs of scenes from Jesus's crucifixion and repeating prayers. Perhaps there was some unseen merit to such activity, but at the time the strongest feeling I experienced was a longing for it to end.

The discovery and veneration of Christian sites in Jerusalem began in 326 CE with Helena the mother of the Holy Roman Emperor Constantine. In her eighties – so the story goes – Helena decided she must locate the True Cross on which Jesus had been crucified. She travelled to Jerusalem, and on arrival gathered all the rabbis of the city into one place and informed them, with all the zeal of a shining convert to a newly minted religion, that unless they told her where she could find the tomb and the True Cross, she would have them all burnt. These learned men were part of a religious tradition that had already survived two thousand years of conquerors including the Assyrians, Babylonians, Persians, Egyptians and pretty much anyone else with an army, so they agreed, immediately producing an individual called Judas (no relation) whom they assured her knew precisely where the sacred site was but was under strict orders not to tell anyone. Helena informed this poor soul (so the legend goes) that he would be starved to death until he told her what she wanted to know. On the seventh day he revealed that the tomb of Christ was beneath an old Roman temple dedicated to the goddess Venus.

Whether or not Judas had chosen the authentic spot, the place he indicated was topographically expedient. Here was a site on which Helen could project her son Constantine's beloved ideological vision: replacing old Roman religion with the fresh ideas of Christianity. The old temple was destroyed, the True Cross was duly discovered, and the Church of the Holy Sepulchre was built on the foundations of what was once the Temple of Venus.

This is part of church lore, but whether it is actually true is another thing altogether. Eusebius, Bishop of Caesarea and historian of the early church, was (likely) in Jerusalem at this time. He was the friend and biographer of Constantine and his mother Helen. One would expect that the discovery of the most important relic in the Christian narrative might have aroused sufficient interest to have made it into his writing, but he doesn't mention it. Nor does he mention Helen's other supposed discoveries such as the Three Holy Nails, the Holy Tunic and the location of the Old Testament Burning Bush. This lively tale may well have been woven centuries later by church historians, along with the convenient detail that Judas (he of the secret) was so impressed by his Christian captors that he converted from Judaism and eventually became bishop of Jerusalem.

By the fifth century Jerusalem was controlled by a branch of the Ottoman Turks who made life difficult for the Christian pilgrims. Out of such misfortune, a monastery in Bologna created a sort of Jerusalem Experience on its grounds. It's possible that this new pilgrimage theme park was the embryonic form of the now standardized Stations of the Cross, the idea being that Christians could re-experience Jesus's execution without having to go to Jerusalem.

As I make my own way through the actual places that the Stations commemorate, I begin to see that there might be a correlation between the topography of the Stations and the positioning of the souvenir shops. Whether or not all the places indicated commemorate the actual pilgrimage of Christ, the places seem, at least to my untutored eye, to be in places ideally positioned for commerce. Regardless of the facts of history, real estate along the last walk is precious. I'd later find out from a historian staying in my guest house that, at a certain point before the fourteenth century, there had been two opposing factions of the Catholic Church with churches on different ends of the city, each insisting that the only route Christ had taken was the one that went past their church.

There's a simple reason that so much of the narrative that makes up the Stations of the Cross is debated: it's not mentioned in the scriptures, because the stories were invented hundreds of years later. There may or may not be a God, but I wonder, has not His religion *always* been fabricated? Like all things made, it develops, expands, fades and changes; it becomes unmade.

This comes into focus as I stand in front of Station VI, where Veronica wiped the face of Jesus Christ with her most precious cloth and an image of his face remained on the material. Tourists meander about. Groups of devout Russian women, younger women than in the church and all in floral print dresses, clutch crosses and follow lean charismatic priests with fierce Slavic eyes. The fiercest of these, a doppelgänger for Rasputin, storms past me, ahead of his flock, as if leading them to battle or at least a fairly determined sit-in. Were I in a bar in Donegal, he would be just the sort of person I'd like to have a few pints with, but not here on the Via Dolorosa. I step back to let him and his group pass. He has a beard, of course, and he looks like he's slept in a stable.

And I remember that I did spend an evening in a bar with a priest. It was in Donegal and on St Patrick's Day. He had returned that very afternoon from 'the missions' in Malawi in southeastern Africa. A once-every-five-years leave, so I was told, back to the village of his childhood. He was not wasting time catching up with old friends, siblings or a favourite aunt. He sat at the bar on a corner stool on his own, and before my eyes drank twelve gin and tonics, one after the other. He did not budge from his seat, hardly even moved his head. Straight into Conway's Bar and twelve gin and tonics down him. The man seemed unaffected except for a few beads of sweat glistening on his forehead in the dim light of the burning turf. I thought those gins must have been putting out some terrible fires. A group of American pilgrims bustle me back to the present as they stomp past in liveries of Gap: T-shirts, sweatpants and baseball hats. Among them is a man with a belly hanging over his khaki trousers like a sack of cement. He's carrying a wooden cross, large and heavy enough to crucify him. They pass, and before I can advance, I'm in a party of West Africans. The day has become desert hot but the Africans aren't taking any chances: over the colourful splashes of their traditional clothing they wear winter coats and woolly scarves. I nod hello to a man in a thick cable-knit jumper and bright baseball cap, and he grasps my right hand with both of his and bellows 'hello my brother'. He tells me he's with a group from Abuja in Nigeria, on pilgrimage with their pastor. They're elated to be in the place where 'Jesus Christ our saviour walked'. Their faith is as solid as the walls around the city, their joy infectious, and there's an empty space when they stride away.

Flocks of nuns pass in white or grey or black, behind them Franciscans with brown cassocks and rope belts. Two Jewish

Orthodox boys walk side by side, their black suit jackets pressed, tassels poking from under their shirts at either hip, their shirts pristine, fedoras perched jauntily on the backs of their head – perhaps a coded manifestation of rebellion for an Orthodox teenager.

I'm mystified by the cruel beauty of the beaver hats and the archaic elegance of the frock coats on the ultra-Orthodox men. I imagine it's the English in me but I find something mad and brave about this unsuitable clothing in a country that is mostly desert. Decades ago, I went to see the great salsa maestro Tito Puente play in a nightclub in London. It was summer and the weather was hotter than it had been for a century, and soon the air conditioning broke under the strain of the heat and the crowd's frenzied dancing. Tito and his band had come prepared for the weather in England and they wore heavy three-piece suits. The band played and danced until the tide marks of sweat blackened the whole of their suits, and steam gathered about them like auras lit in the stage lights. Scores of bare-chested men and flimsy-skirted girls were carried out of the club with heat exhaustion but not one of the band loosened their ties or undid so much as a button of their thick suits.

My guest house is behind Station III of the Cross. The area around the marker is packed with curiously quiet Korean pilgrims listening to a priest on wireless headphones. The church at Station III is from the nineteenth century, small and unprepossessing, with the strange name of Our Lady of the Spasm. I wonder if there's been a translating error but no, this is where Jesus, having been beaten and crowned with thorns, is said to have met his mother, the Virgin Mary. Christianity lacks a mother goddess like Tara, Quan Yin, Aphrodite, Isis or Shakti. The idea of Mary as mother of God was only developed five hundred years after the death of Christ. Our profound human yearning to worship a female deity had to find a manifestation, and it did through the Blessed Virgin Mary. I think about the word *spasm*, which sounds strange to me, bringing to mind fits and a certain amount of drooling. Such translations of the Latin *spasm* would not have received high marks from my Latin teacher. I suspect he'd have preferred *swoon*, but then he was a Jesuit and a great man, which is why I still remember his lessons. *Swoon* is what Jesus' mother did when she saw her son bloody and battered, staggering to what they both knew was his death.

I look up at the relief above the church door of Mary seeing Christ. This Mary is distraught, gazing at her son. She is *swooning* and as a part of me is thinking pedantically that this is another scene not actually mentioned in the New Testament, I realize looking at her face that I'm missing the point: it doesn't matter if the historical Mary, wife of Joseph, father of Jesus of Nazareth, stood on this spot and caught sight of her son on his way to execution. What is true is that somewhere this is happening now. All the times I'd repeated the prayers of the Stations of the Cross as a child, all the times I'd passed them in churches as an adult, it had never occurred to me, not once, that this was meant to be about life. I'd thought it was *religion*, something separate, something grimly sacred, something that happened before anyone's time, in a church somewhere distant, something that had nothing to do with me. But standing here I suddenly see this Station is a memorial to a woman. A memorial to a mother witnessing the suffering of a child and I realize that somewhere a mother in this world is standing by as her child suffers. Somewhere right now, maybe up the road in Hebron, or a few kilometres away in a settlement, in the Congo, Syria, the US, Ireland, somewhere a mother is witnessing the body of her child being destroyed and there is nothing she can do about it. Of course I think about those mothers of the teenagers outside the

Dolphinarium, and then what comes to me is the suffering of my daughter's mother as she watched our little treasure in discomfort and pain, confined to hospital for seven months after she was born, and I realize that such suffering is named and made sacred here at Station III and tears are streaking down my cheeks, cutting through the filth of this city. And it occurs to me that this is what the fabrications and the myths of religion are for.

I squeeze my way past the Korean Christians, and dodge the Israeli Jews running this way and that with shopping bags, and pass the Palestinian shopkeeper sighing and looking at the darkening sky, and I make my way to my guest house.

FIFTEEN

Making a Martyr

Mazan walks past what were once posters advertising washing powder, Coca-Cola, and the latest car. On this morning, they're plastered over with cheaply printed notices emblazoned with photographs of Palestinians who have died in the conflict with Israel. *Shaheed*. A word whose closest English equivalent is martyr. Saïd Hotari's mother will be known as *um shaheed*, Mother-of-the-martyr, and his father Father-of-the-martyr, and his brothers too – even the street Hotari lived on will become known as Street-of-the-martyr.

The posters are colourful. There are quotations from the Quran pointing to the bombers' virtues and the paradisal afterlife that awaits them. Most of the pictures have an image in the background of the Al-Aqsa mosque in the Old City of Jerusalem. Al-Aqsa is invariably cited as the third-holiest site in Islam, and although this is true, the description can be misleading. If there were a gold, silver and bronze placement for holiness then yes, it is the third-holiest site. But there's no feeling of *we have Mecca and Medina let's not worry about Al-Aqsa.* Al-Aqsa is as sacred to Muslims as the Virgin Mary is to Roman Catholics.

Unfortunately, Al-Aqsa shares ground with the Temple Mount, Judaism's holiest site, and nowhere in all the disputed territories is the situation between the religions so delicate. When Ariel Sharon visited the Al-Aqsa compound in September 2000 he was accompanied by a battalion of heavily armed soldiers. In his speech he said the words 'this is our land', and in doing so unravelled whatever peace process remained, becoming the most salient catalyst for the second intifada, which went on to kill more than five thousand people, four-fifths of them Palestinian.

Growing up as a Roman Catholic educated by Jesuit priests, the concept of martyrdom played a significant role in my young imagination. From the age of seven, I was taught about Catholic heroes who were put to death for the Church and so gained a special place next to God. We were taught in great detail about the manner of their killing, the precise tortures they endured for the Holy Roman Church. We recoiled and delighted in stories of the fiendish torments concocted for these men of God. I remember brooding about what it would be like to be skinned alive and then crucified upside down like St Bartholomew, or grilled over hot coals like St Lawrence. Because my school was part of the Catholic minority in England, a great favourite was the story of the martyrdom of St Edmund Campion in London. He was told in 1581 exactly what would happen to him: '[You'll] be hanged and let down alive, and you're [*sic*] privy parts cut off, and your entrails taken out and burnt in your sight; then your head to be cut off and your body divided into four parts.'*

---

* Richard Simpson, *Edmund Campion: a Biography* (1867).

However exotic and terrible their deaths, Catholic martyrs earned their martyrdom by being killed, not by killing other people.

I used to imagine that *shaheeds* were more like kamikaze pilots, becoming martyrs by killing any enemies of their cause as well as themselves. But I've since learned that being *shaheed* doesn't require killing anyone else: a baby killed by an Israeli artillery shell is a *shaheed*, an old woman crushed by a bulldozer is a *shaheeda*. Saïd Hotari blowing himself up amidst unarmed teenagers is also a *shaheed*. To be a *shaheed* is to die for your faith or your home; and even if you are secular, dying for Palestine is to die as a *shaheed*.

Our word *martyr* comes from the Greek meaning *witness*. It's used many times in the New Testament but only to mean *witness*, never to describe one who dies for an idea. A *martyr* was simply one who brought *witness* of the good news of the New Testament – no death or killing was required.

It's fascinating that in Arabic the word *shaheed*, via an etymological route unrelated to the Greek, also derives from *witness*. It's almost enough of a coincidence to make you believe in God. *Shaheed* is used in the Quran time and time again to mean *witness* – again, no death required. Long after the death of Jesus, Christians (in the histories of the Apostolic Fathers) and Muslims in the Hadiths (authenticated recordings of the sayings and life of the Prophet Mohammed) began to use *martyr* and *shaheed* in terms of death. According to the Hadith, being killed for one's faith – or dying of plague, abdominal problems, drowning, or falling off a building, as long as it's in the cause of Allah – is enough to be considered a *shaheed*.[*] It's even mentioned that 'whoever is killed protecting his property then he is a *shaheed*'.[†]

---

[*] *Sahih al-Bukhari*, 4:52:82.
[†] *Sahih al-Bukhari*, 3:43:660.

There's a persistent and so-called explanation of *shaheed* in the West that focuses on suicide bombings and other violent acts as expressions of salacious erotic yearning for sex after death: seventy-two virgins, the voluptuous *houris*. These famous seventy-two virgins have become divinely inflated sex dolls who will satisfy a frustrated suicide bomber's every desire. Although the celebrated group of seventy-two virgins is mentioned in one of the 'weak' Hadiths, they are not mentioned in the Quran – not once. The Quran is also explicit about forbidding suicide. Like the Bible the Quran has deeply sensuous passages, but focusing on the erotic in trying to understand suicide bombing throws little or no light on why people actually destroy themselves and others. Indeed, the spotlight shifts conveniently away from the real issues – issues we would do well to understand – to instead illuminate a racist stereotype of an Arab *other*, ruthless, sexually depraved and dangerous. Such an image is still prevalent and sometimes lurking under the surface of Western narratives. It is a stereotype no less inaccurate than the anti-Semitic caricature of 'the Jew' as a voracious money grabber. Like all racist caricatures, the image created is deliberately dehumanizing so that the notion of oppression, and even extermination, becomes morally possible.

While *shaheed*, like 'martyr', was originally used to mean 'witness', the root of 'martyr' might well derive from the Sanskrit word *smarati*, which means 'remember'. It's worth considering that the hundreds of *shaheed* posters that Mazan Al-Joulani walks by on 2 June 2001 are not so much a callous celebration of death and violence as an act of remembering. They are memorials to the deceased, ways to give meaning to families and grieving friends – to show that the empty desks at school, the spaces in the marriage bed, and the missing chairs at the family dinner table are not for nothing.

Martyr posters were ubiquitous during the second inti-fada, not just for combatants but for everyone who died in the intifada. Many Israelis and people in the West see images of Palestinians walking by such posters – or smoking a cigarette on a fire escape plastered with them, or working alongside them on the walls of hospitals – and they shudder. We see schoolchildren in a classroom with these posters and we're led to believe that the children are being trained to be suicide bombers. But to people in the West Bank, the reality is that these posters are primarily people remembering their dead within the context of a conflict.

It's possible that even within such a short time Mazan Al-Joulani sees Saïd Hotari's face looking down from one of these posters. It's possible that he's pleased by Hotari's terrible act of resistance. It's possible that he's appalled by it. It's likely that the slaughter recalls the day in 1998 when his own sixteen-year-old cousin was shot in the head by an Israeli sniper in Bethlehem.

I don't know Mazan's view of the Dolphinarium bomb. This book is meant to be non-fiction but I have recreated the events in the last few pages from what I have heard or could pick up. All I know is he was a pharmacist with a young wife and three young children, a man who was not involved in the resistance, other than in the sense that every Palestinian is, merely by existing, by getting on with life.

What I know is this: Mazan Al-Joulani is a man walking to work. He has no idea that his handsome face will soon be pasted on martyr posters showing his head hovering spec-trally before the Al-Aqsa mosque, just like those he's passing between the mobile phone supplier, the overflowing rubbish bins and the Royal Fried Chicken shop.

At some point in the morning Mazan arrives at his work-place. He spends the day with prescriptions to fill, papers to file, people to advise, stock to organize – a day like that of any other pharmacist. Perhaps Mazan calls around to other outlets tracking down a less common medication that someone needs. There's little doubt that people come in talking of the bomb attack in Tel Aviv the night before. For many it's a victory, for others it's a step too far; for some a tragedy, for others yet another manifestation of the internecine relationship with Israeli Jews.

While Mazan goes about his professional life, Maha his wife is on the move, taking the older children to school, buying food for the evening, picking them up from school, washing clothes, cleaning children, sweeping away household dust and childhood anxiety, preparing meals ... As any parent knows, three young children is hard work, but with the added forces of oppression and intifada, just getting through another day is an achievement.

By the time Mazan leaves his pharmacy, martyr posters of Saïd Hotari are on every corner of the West Bank and Gaza, and in parts of East Jerusalem too. He has a nervous smile that makes him look more like a young man on his first day of work experience than a terrorist who has slaughtered two dozen unarmed people. Mazan may well pause in front of one of these posters to put a face to the stories he's been hearing. What is certain is that he decides not to go straight home to his wife in Ras Al-Amoud, but to meet friends at the Al Salaam café at the Shufat camp junction.

At the café, men sit outside in the warm evening sun discussing the day and drinking tea and coffee until the evening news comes on and they move inside to crowd around the TV. Mazan remains outside. Perhaps he has been listening to people retell the news all day and has no need to hear it again. Perhaps he just wants to savour his tea and the evening light. Whatever his reasons, it costs him his life.

BEAT

A car pulls up and a man gets out. An Israeli settler. How can one know? A beard, a gun. Most people in the province of Ulster, where I used to live, can assess the religion and political sympathies of a man passing in the street with little more than a casual glance. It's a question of tribes, and 'settler' is the consensus of those who see the man. The settler – this man – gets out of the car, points his gun towards Mazan, and shoots him through the neck.

SIXTEEN

The Day of Rest

I'm about to step into the shower when the siren comes on. It's as if the high-pitched scream has been waiting for the puerile action of my pinging my underwear across the room with a flick of my foot. I assume the siren is an air raid and freeze. The Israeli air force describes itself as one of the world's most powerful; the Palestinians have no planes. Who could it be? Iranians? One of those Iraqi Scuds that never materialized? Whatever the source, I'm concentrating on getting my trousers back on whilst reassuring myself that the Israelis are bound to have an efficient bomb shelter close by. I look out the window and notice the shopkeeper opposite me calmly gazing upwards, as he's been doing for the last hour. It's not an air-raid siren at all, I realize. It's just signalling the beginning of Shabbat.

When I leave my guest house, I find the streets hushed, as if the soft pedal of a city-sized piano was being held down. I

think of the marvellous book *Asterix in Britain* in which, after
the horn for teatime is sounded, every ancient Briton puts
down his weapon mid-battle and sips his beverage, allowing
the nefarious Romans great advantage. But things aren't as
calm as they seem. There are knots of soldiers everywhere; the
way to the Western Wall is blocked. I pass a man surrounded
by soldiers. They stand around him like toughs in a school
yard. I watch until he produces his ID papers, and then they
let him go, one soldier patting him on the back. I presume he's
a Palestinian so I follow him around the corner and ask what
happened.

'It's nothing,' he tells me with a quick shrug. 'It happens all
the time because I look like an Arab. When they find out I'm
Israeli we laugh about it.' As he speaks, he is looking directly at
a Palestinian man selling sports socks from a cart right in front
of us, but what he sees does not make him question what he is
saying. It reminds me of Ralph Ellison's *Invisible Man*: 'People
refuse to see me … when they approach me they see only my
surroundings, themselves or figments of their imagination –
indeed, everything and anything but me.'

I leave the Old City via the Damascus Gate. Because it's
now Shabbat there are no taxis, so I walk around until I find a
Palestinian driver. I give him the address of Saul's family, and he
takes me to a quiet residential area with tree-lined streets. It's
peaceful here after the 'golden goblet of scorpions' – a phrase
that the tenth-century traveller and geographer Al-Maqdisī
used to describe Old Jerusalem. People stroll about pushing
prams and chatting on street corners. There's an atmosphere
of Levantine bonhomie rather than the tripartite loathing that
saturates the Old City. Here, there's one single tribe. A thousand years ago, in the days of Al-Maqdisī, the city was a great
deal more culturally mixed than today. Today, Palestinians are
unfamiliar with this part of town, and my driver leans out of

his window and asks a huddle of pram-pushing adults for directions.

My friend Saul told me to be at dinner by 7 pm, and I'm already late. I'm becoming anxious. It may be the fact that the formative part of my earliest years was spent under the Sauron-like eye of an English nanny, but the idea of going to someone's house for dinner and doing the *wrong thing* horrifies me. Normally, I know what the wrong thing is, but this is new territory for me. I've brought tea from my favourite shop in Paris as a gift, and I start worrying that it might not be kosher. Not only will I be late, but I'll bring a pollutant into the family home. For all I know, *I* could be the pollutant.

The front door of the building is open but I ring the bell anyway. Then I worry about ringing a bell on the Sabbath. Is it allowed? Is anyone allowed to open the door for me? I've seen refrigerators with a 'kosher mode', but I think this has to be about the light, not the door. Surely people have to be allowed to open doors.

I'd looked into what I could and couldn't do on Shabbat, but the information came in a huge range of observances and prohibitions. I learned that some Jewish people feel they observe the Sabbath by doing nothing other than eating and spending time with their families, but others have no problem driving to the synagogue, picking up the phone and turning the lights on and off. The Orthodox law sets out thirty-nine prohibited acts that relate generally to 'work', but defining what work is has proven to be difficult. For example, electricity is not in itself a problem but illuminating a light bulb is too close to lighting a fire, and lighting a fire is on the list of prohibited things. The divisions in themselves are subtle, with many subdivisions discussed and disputed. Combing one's hair is not permitted, but using a soft brush is fine. If you're eating cherries, picking out the rotten ones would break the

Sabbath but selecting the good ones is fine. Writing with a pen on paper is breaking the Sabbath but writing in the sand with a stick is fine. It sounds crazy, but as is so often the case with Jewish lore, there's a logic. The issue with writing is one of making permanent marks. However, should you feel the need to write with a pen, there's a special Sabbath pen that uses disappearing ink. With this, one can make notes on paper as one normally would, photocopy them after Shabbat, and later the disappearing ink will vanish, leaving the photocopies for all eternity.

An industry worth tens of millions annually exists in creating Shabbat-safe devices, which use technology or ingenuity or both to get around religious law. Groups of rabbis sit on boards to decide if a new product is acceptable under rabbinical law. There are ovens and refrigerators, telephones, elevators, even cappuccino machines that can be used on Shabbat without breaking the rules. At the simplest end of the spectrum there's a lamp that has a cover that can be turned to block a light that remains lit throughout the Sabbath. More complex is the KosherSwitch, which allows electricity to be turned on and off using technology that circumvents the sacred laws. I don't have enough of an understanding of the interplay between rabbinical law, divine law and the physics of electric switches to understand what makes this acceptable, but it's something to do with creating a gap between the action and the actioner – and a concept called Halachic uncertainty.

It all comes down to interpretation and definition. To my mind, if writing on paper were truly making a *permanent* mark, then every piece of writing ever written would still be extant and all book conservators would be out of a job. Writing in sand is only *impermanent* because of the tide, wind, and animal tracks. If writing in the sand were sufficiently protected, it would remain as long as engraving onto granite. So whilst the invisible ink ruse is clever, it also seems a delightfully absurd way to outwit an omniscient being. But what do I know?

What we can agree on is that for Jews, and Christians as well, Shabbat is meant to be a day of rest. The Christians borrowed Shabbat from the Jews, because the first Christians were Jews. Since the Jewish Shabbat was a Saturday, the Christians chose Sunday. If Jews celebrated Shabbat on a Sunday, you can be sure that the Christians would have been certain that God told them the Holy Day was a Saturday, or any other day except Sunday. And there would no doubt have been quite a few martyrs eager to die in a host of slow and grisly ways for this very point.

For some Jews, and for some Christians, it's about the day itself. God made the world in six days, and on the seventh, He rested. But for most, it's not about the day, and it's not about God either. Even if God weren't part of the equation, such rules are made by humans to define and differentiate one group from another. The nuances are about differentiation. For Orthodox Jews, these rules *are* God's Law and keeping them is part of a personal relationship with the Almighty. But beyond that, there's an inherent unification in refusing special foods, wearing particular clothes, cultivating long beards, shaving your head this way not that. What are all these but ways of putting a marker between you and another community?

That I can even express criticism of Judaism and Christianity and even make jokes without fear of violent reprisal is for me a point in favour of these two older branches of Abrahamic faith. Islam is hypersensitive to any criticism – much like the Roman Church of five hundred years ago. Nevertheless, like the Roman Church, Islam is a religion that has been under attack. People like to focus on the most intolerant adherents of the religion as representative of the entire practice and history of Islam. Any serious historical study of the past two

millennia shows that, over time, there's been much more tolerance towards other religions in Muslim-conquered territories
than in Christian-conquered territories. Tolerance is inscribed
in the Quran, especially towards Judaism and Christianity:
'To you your religion; and to me my religion!' (Chapter 109).
Jews, Christians and Muslims lived in peace for hundreds of
years under the Ottomans. The image of the Muslim with a
Quran in one hand and a sword or bomb in the other is part of
a centuries-old effort to discredit the religion. In researching
this book, I've spoken to an astonishing number of bigots who
attribute all sorts of subhuman qualities to Muslims. I've stood
by whilst educated Christians decontextualize violent passages
in the Quran and wave them about as a moral basis for their
prejudice whilst ignoring the historical barbarities in their
own Old Testament. I've heard people take ghoulish pleasure
in the worst excesses of sharia law or a pornographic delight
in the latest gory outrage from ISIS, heralding aberrant funda-
mentalism as proof of the inherent evil of a religion that is the
cherished belief system of 25 per cent of the world's population. I am no scholar, but I've travelled much of the world and
lived in places with people who call themselves Muslim, and
at the risk of being obvious, this isn't the way the vast majority
of Muslims behave.

That being said, although millions of people have been
slaughtered in the name of Christianity, you're unlikely to be
killed for criticizing Christianity (or Judaism) today. And there's
no getting away from the fact that an astonishing number of
Muslim people today believe that criticism of their religion
merits extreme violence, even death. A poll of British Muslims
after the *Charlie Hebdo* massacre of French cartoonists showed
that 85 per cent disapproved of the idea that 'organizations
which publish images of the Prophet Mohammed deserve to
be attacked', although 27 per cent had 'some support' for the

motives behind the attack. I found it particularly telling that the BBC reported that *Most British Muslims oppose Muhammad Cartoons Reprisals* whilst *The Jerusalem Post* (as well as a host of UK publications) chose the headline: *1 in 4 British Muslims Sympathise with Charlie Hebdo Gunmen*. Both headlines are somewhat supported by the above polls, but each report uses the numbers that best suit its aim.

Non-Muslims should at the very least become aware of the Islamophobia in our culture today, made blatant by the cloddish slurs of Donald Trump, though present also in more nuanced forms, thanks to the centuries-old attempt to discredit the religion. However, not one moment of this history of prejudice has been as effective in discrediting Islam as the actions of a minority we in the West helped create – a minority of extremist Muslims who believe it is acceptable to kill in the name of God.

Of course, as soon as any religion – or even ideology – is powerful enough, schisms appear, and, if the stakes are high, there may be bloodshed. There are schisms in Christianity, in Judaism, schisms in communism … and there's a schism within Islam, a schism beyond Shia and Sunni, a schism that can be simply expressed as between those who believe there should be no compulsion in religion and those who think it's fine to slaughter people who don't support your views. Regardless of our religion or culture we should be coalescing into a united front against radicals and warmongers, whatever banner they hide behind.

In the harsher biblical days, when Judaism was the same age as Islam is today, breaking the Sabbath was punishable by death. In the short-term present, standing on a stairway in the outskirts of Jerusalem, my biggest fear is tardiness. All of which to say, after debating the legality of opening doors on Shabbat for too long, I decide to let myself in. I'd scanned the list of thirty-nine acts prohibited on the Day of Rest: sowing, ploughing, reaping, threshing, selecting, grinding, sifting, kneading, bleaching, dyeing, spinning, stretching, meshing, separating, knotting, sewing, tearing, scraping, marking, cutting, writing, erasing, kindling, carrying, finishing … but there was no mention of opening a door. This is my safest option.

It's dark in the hallways, and when I shine my mobile phone (definitely not permitted for Shabbat) on the apartment doors looking for the name Rosenberg, I see that the names are in Hebrew. I stare at them, hoping they might suddenly become legible. I walk to the top of the stairs and listen at a few doors for any clues. I'd been given instructions as to which floor and which side, but I've forgotten them. The only thing I can remember is that the Rosenbergs have a dog. I love dogs, which is why the information stuck in my mind. I have this idea that dogs sense my love, which gives me a special affinity with them, which gives me the right to put *good with dogs* on dating site profiles, as I once did.

I ascend the stairs and walk up another hallway, coughing now and then in the hope that the aforementioned dog will hear me and bark to reveal my destination. It is, I feel, a clever plan, but it produces no result. An age passes, during which time I meet a guilty-looking fellow on the stairs who's a relation of someone else on the block but has never heard of any Rosenbergs in the building. I knock at a random door and a surprised Orthodox woman in a black wig answers, two small boys peeking round her legs. She tells me she arrived from New York City an hour before and knows no one. Time passes. I am now definitely late. Finally, I hear a dog barking, and in a moment, I'm there.

Eight people are seated on assorted chairs, waiting. I'm sorry and embarrassed to be late, but my discomfort is driven away by eight warm hellos: my host and his wife, a teenage son and two daughters, grandparents and an old family friend. The youngest girl has a mass of hair as red as a sunset and the sweetest, most joyful smile I've ever seen. There are no dark suits, no clumsy wigs, no eighteenth-century frock coats, no exotic rituals, just a peculiarly kind and agreeable group of family and friends between the ages of seven and seventy-five who are evidently very happy in one another's company.

Just as I'm allowing myself to relax into this reality, a door flies open and the family dog bolts towards me, barking and growling. There's an edge of desperation to its violence. It seems the animal believes that unless I am savaged to death, the entire family will perish. I'm tempted to leap behind one of the slower-moving grandparents, but I remain motionless, pathetically holding out my hand. My host and one of his children dive on the frenzied beast and manage to drag it into another room, lapping and snarling in protest. 'He's the sweetest dog really,' the mum shouts over the growls. 'He's just mistrustful of strangers.'

As we sit at the table, my hostess explains that there are ceremonial rituals and prayers that they'll do for the Shabbat meal and that I can join in or not, as I wish. A song is sung about heaven, then a poem by King Solomon is read in praise of wives. I ceremonially wash my hands at the kitchen sink, and the angel-faced little girl stands by offering me a towel and a delighted grin. The last time I washed my hands like this was before prayers in a mosque, but there was no cherub-faced girl to smile and give me a towel. My host's parents then place their hands on the head of their adult son and bless him. I'm moved by the sight of an elderly couple putting their hands on the head of a fifty-year-old father of three, but not as moved as when the parents do the same to each of their three children. It's a profound and deeply moving act, and I'm struck by the straightforward sincerity of what's happening. How can one not feel part of something bigger and more important than one's self with this link between generations?

There are more prayers, a ritual breaking of a loaf of bread, and then dinner begins. There's much family chat, questions, and passing of dishes of food towards me. The grandfather, who must be nearing eighty, is a grouch, or more likely enjoys pretending to be a grouch, pointing out all the things he doesn't like in the world, which are many, weighing in with a *bon mot* and, for this evening's private joke, bringing all conversations back to the subject of herrings, which, at least to me, is very amusing.

'We went to the Purcell and Telemann concert in the Jerusalem Theatre,' someone says from the other end of the table.

'Argh, I hate baroque music,' the grandfather comments.

'What do you like?' I ask.

'Schubert, Shostakovich,' he answers immediately.

'Schuman?'

'That's right anything with *Sh* in it … Sheethoven, Shozart.'

'Shach?' I suggest.

'I hate Bach,' he says.

'What about Shakira?' Angel-Face asks, rescuing me and causing an eruption of laughter. Talk flows to *Desert Island Discs*, the radio programme in which famous people choose their favourite music. The grandfather wants us to know that he's had his top pieces of music ready for more than sixty years. They're the records he and his wife kept and listened to during the time of the Nazis.

There it is, the family's link to the terrible history. There are not many families of European Jews whose history wasn't in some or every way torn and polluted by the rabid anti-Semitism of the Nazis. I remember a moment in the documentary *Shoah* where an inspiring historian with thick, horn-rimmed spectacles was sweating – perhaps from heat, perhaps from the terrible intensity of what he had to say. He explained that the Nazis had not been the first with their grotesque caricatures. Nor, he explains did they create anything new with their laws stealing Jewish property, or forcing Jewish people to identify and mark themselves out … this was part of a historical process going back generations. What *was* new, their one act of 'creativity', was the Final Solution. This moved the history of prejudice from *you cannot live amongst us* to *you cannot live*. Although Zionism predated the Nazis by half a century their terrible act of creativity was the catalyst for the foundation of modern Israel.

Here we are in Jerusalem, in a country whose neighbours are Lebanon, Syria, Jordan and Egypt: Middle Eastern countries, but everyone around this table looks European. Why? Because they *are* European. The family pulses with that peculiarly European intellectual and cultural sensibility, which has produced so much of what's best about Europe. One person here is an archaeologist, another a paediatric anaesthetist. There are excellent minds around this table, but other than their religion – which is as Middle Eastern in origin as Islam, as the Christianity of my childhood – there's nothing Middle Eastern here. Sitting next to me is my host's 21-year-old daughter with the looks of a teenager and the poise of someone much older. She tells me that she's chosen to work on a kibbutz growing organic vegetables instead of doing military service. We don't discuss politics. I don't want to. What could we say? Palestinians are not once mentioned. Family, culture, philosophy, history, prayers, rituals, humour – but not the Palestinians.

I like this family; I feel something not far from love for them. Their way of being with each other, their unaffected intelligence. By looks there's little you might think of as Semitic, and yet their commitment and total immersion in the prayers and rituals derive from this part of the world 3500 years ago.

Surely this is an authentic bond to the land? This and the horrors of the Shoah. But just as surely, their powerful, ancient narrative is missing the history of just under twelve million Palestinians. Does one have to negate the other?

The plates are cleared and dessert is served, sweet crunchy homemade things along with grapes and sorbet. 'What kind of sorbet is this?' the grandfather demands to know. 'It tastes of cheese. Who ever heard of sorbet tasting of cheese?'

There's so much in this family that reminds me of my own family. I ask the grandfather if he knew our neighbour Rabbi Gryn when he lived in London. He and the rabbi would have been comparable in age. Of course he knew who he was, he tells me, but 'we didn't associate with that lot'. I ask him what the problem was, and he explains to me that the Orthodox didn't feel the Reform Jews lived properly as Jews.

When it's time to leave, my host takes me to the street. It's a quiet, prosperous area with large nineteenth-century merchants' houses. I ask about the history of the houses and am told, 'They were once Arab.' And so the Palestinians finally appear.

SEVENTEEN

A Beating Heart

Mazan crumples to the ground as his assailant drives off in a direction described by the witnesses in the café as 'towards the Pisgat Ze'ev settlement'. An ambulance is called. It's been a quiet day for the emergency services in Jerusalem, a lull after the terrible storm of violence the night before in Tel Aviv. The paramedics are quickly on the scene and take the unconscious Mazan to the nearest hospital.

The standard of emergency medicine is high in Israel, particularly for gunshot trauma. Medicine, like the legal system, is one of the few areas of civil life where Palestinians considered 'Arab Israeli' – those permitted to live within the borders of Israel – have equal rights to Jewish Israelis in practice as well as theory. If a Palestinian with a blue identity card needs medical treatment, she or he is likely to be given the same standard of care as a Jewish Israeli. Why is this the case? Because, until recently, many medical personnel in Israel, just like many involved with the law, insist upon benefits being available regardless of race, nationality or religion.

Baron Dominique-Jean de Larrey, Napoleon's chief medical officer and the instigator of triage, was remarkable for providing medical treatment to enemy troops as well as his own. He, like many doctors who've taken the Hippocratic oath, had a real commitment to relieving suffering. Buddhist philosophy sees the practice of such compassion as the Great Vehicle, which alone is enough to transport you to enlightenment. The Dalai Lama puts this in even plainer terms: not only is compassion good for the person you help, but it is also good for you. This is what he describes as 'wise selfishness'. As fate would have it, Baron de Larrey's non-partisan compassion saved his own life. He was captured by a patrol of enemy Prussians and was about to be shot when a passing sergeant recognized him as the doctor who'd saved the life of a high-ranking Prussian officer. De Larrey's life was spared, and he was later released back to France.

Doctors and nurses particularly see the fundamental unifying truth in their work, that regardless of race, nationality, or religion, people are the same. None of us want our loved ones to suffer; none of us want to suffer ourselves. We bleed the same way whatever we believe. The same heart beats within all of us, and Mazan's heart continues to beat with vital force as he lies unconscious in the hospital.

Mazan's family are gathered by his bedside: Maha and the children, his mother Raoufi, his father Lotfi and his younger brother Majdi. Mazan's neck is a mass of dressings and bandages, but his head and face are untouched. His skin is pink and the rhythmic hiss of a respirator breathes air into his lungs. His heart function is now stabilized. His family can touch him, hear the regular beep on the heart monitor, and see the green cursor cresting and dropping. Other than the dressings padding his neck, he looks intact. He's in a spotless, modern hospital surrounded by machines and bustling attention. There should be hope.

A doctor waits outside with two nurses. She enters and explains that the bullet in Mazan exploded on impact causing massive trauma to his neck and to parts of his brain stem. It was a dumdum round.

'How long will it take for him to recover?'

'He will never recover.'

'Will he be in a wheelchair, will he be able to work at all?'

'He will never recover.'

'Not fully, but a little?'

'He will never recover.'

Mazan's brain, she explains, is no longer functioning. It will never function again. There's not even the faintest possibility.

She shows them the MRI images of his brain next to those of a healthy one. Mazan's brain is a cloudy suspension next to an image of complex and vibrant circuitry. She nods towards the respirator. He is only breathing because of mechanical support. Without this, his breathing would stop.

'But his heart – his heart is beating.'

'I am very sorry,' she says, 'but Mazan is effectively dead.'

These words mark the moment the family's life will be different. This is the turning point that will change everything.

'But his heart …'

It's true that Mazan's heart is unaffected by his brain damage. The human heart is almost unique in the body in the way it functions independently of the brain. The heart is an autonomous pump. It doesn't need the brain to coordinate function. It's an exquisite machine. It's true that, if maintained, Mazan's heart could pump for another half century. But it's also true that Mazan is, according to the arguable but most accepted and up-to-date medical definitions, dead.

The Israeli police conduct a brief investigation into the murder. They don't find the gunman. They don't find any accomplice. And they don't find the car. They find nothing. Nevertheless, unlike the eyewitnesses at the café, they are able to conclude that the perpetrator was not a settler, not an Israeli Jew, but in fact, a Palestinian. They release a press statement stating that the shooting was a criminal act relating to a Palestinian feud.

Mazan's heart continues to beat, its activity reflected by a tiny green dot by his bedside, its relentless beep counterpointed by sobs of grief.

EIGHTEEN

An Exquisitely Difficult Task

Mazan Al-Joulani's mother, his father, his wife and his brother fill the spaces between the machines that maintain what life he has: machines that drip fluid into his veins, depress syringes, measure pressure, heartbeats and electrolytes. Machines that pump air into his chest. Machines that suck up his waste. Thick cables of information and electricity link stacks of technological intelligence into a web of life support. There is quiet, or gasps of shock, or fury, or weeping at the injustice. Each family member is numb or raging at the senseless annihilation of this man. Each of them absorbing, according to their different capacities, the now undeniable narrative that a man unknown to them could have deliberately and randomly destroyed this intelligent, peaceable and most of all beloved part of them.

Outside the room a person waits, a professional faced with a challenge almost overwhelming in its delicacy. The job of a donor coordinator is precarious and demanding; success and failure is no less than a matter of life and death. Finding a heart that can be transplanted is rare – only a single per cent of all deaths offer even the possibility of a cardiac transplant. When a suitable donor has been identified, the coordinator has a very short time to try and acquire the organ from the grieving family.

Part of the problem for the coordinator is that the decision-maker within the donor family – be it husband or wife, mother, father, or partner – has only recently received the news that there's no hope for their loved one. Another part is that the prospective donor may well, like Mazan, appear to be living. Mazan's skin is pink, his hair and nails grow, his heart beats. To even ask of his family that his chest be opened and his heart be removed is, at the very least, counter-intuitive. It would be much easier to wait for a week or two so that a vegetative state could be observed first-hand, so that the terrible news of death could sink in. If this were possible, a donor coordinator would wait. However, unlike kidneys, livers, intestines, bones and corneas, a heart transplant cannot wait. It must be done with a healthy functioning heart. It must be done with what is called a *still beating donor*.

For the donor coordinator waiting outside the ward room, the facts are straightforward: Mazan Al-Joulani is brain-dead, but his heart is strong and healthy. A man called Yigal Cohen in a hospital forty minutes' drive away has a healthy brain but his heart is failing. Mazan is the same blood group as Yigal; his heart is compatible in size. It's an ideal match; a life-saving opportunity. These two men are of similar age, born within twenty-five miles of each other, both with a young wife and young children, and, according to the law of the land, both are citizens of the same country.

But whereas Mazan and Yigal both carry identity cards defining them as citizens of Israel, under the category *Nationality*, Yigal's says *Jewish* and Mazan's says – not *Palestinian* or even

Muslim – but *Arab.*[*] Yigal Cohen, of course, is Jewish, but is Jewish his nationality? Yigal's mother is Bulgarian and his father a first-generation Israeli from 1948 when the state was founded. And surely *Arab* is not Mazan Al-Joulani's nationality any more than *Muslim*? Palestinian culture goes back millennia – and the Al-Joulanis themselves have lived on this land for centuries. On the one hand, it is true that the modern nationality of *Palestinian* was constructed in response to the idea of modern Israel. On the other hand, whilst records of Jewish culture in this area go back even further than Palestinian, there were no *Israelis* before 1948. All these labels, these notions, that people believe separate them importantly enough to kill one another, are not of course nothing, but neither are they fixed and essential – they change and flow with the ebbs of history.

Twelve years before the Al-Joulanis gathered around Mazan's hospital bed, another Palestinian family had faced a similar dilemma. A young man, Mohamed Nasser, had been shot by an Israeli soldier during a funeral for a fourteen-year-old boy. Nasser had been twenty-one and unarmed, only two hundred metres from his front door in Nablus, when a bullet entered his head. He was rushed to the hospital. The so-called plastic[†] bullet was lodged in the right side of his head, and he was pronounced brain-dead.

---

* Mazan is from the group of 160,000 Palestinians who were given Israeli identity cards as long as they could prove they had been continuous residents inside the new borders of Israel between 1948 and 1952. This was to differentiate them from the 600-750,000 Palestinians who had been expelled or fled during the 1948 war. Under law in Israel, this gives Mazan theoretical equal rights, but in practice, in areas such as employment, education, the right to buy property, a Palestinian with an Israeli ID card is a second-class citizen.

†Plastic bullets fired from M16 automatic weapons were composed of 70 per cent metal, 20 per cent glass and 10 per cent plastic. They were used widely in the intifada by the Israeli army and police against

His youth, brain death and blood type made him a potential donor for an Israeli named Yehiel Yisrael, forty-six, who was near death after a failed heart operation. Yisreal's family attempted to negotiate for the heart through political leaders and Palestinian religious figures; they even offered a large sum of money. As his brother put it, they 'tried everything'. But the Nasser family refused. Jamal Nasser, the boy's father, said: 'From a human standpoint, it was possible to consider giving his heart. But the way they came with money ... That, after the soldiers shot him. We could not give it up.'

Sadly, no other heart was available and Yehiel Yisreal died. Mohamed Nasser was later buried along with his healthy heart. As a left-wing Israeli politician explained after the event: 'We shoot them and then [want to] use them ... what would you do?'

Although the Yisrael family felt they'd done *everything* by contacting politicians, community leaders and offering money, they didn't do the one thing that might have most affected the Nasser family: speak to them directly. This was not due to malice but an unfamiliarity that lies at the heart of the problem between these two cultures. As was confirmed by a member of the Yisrael family: 'There was never any direct contact with Arabs. We would not have known how to go about it.'*

Yigal Cohen is dying and the only hope for him is beating in the body of Mazan Al-Joulani. The transplant coordinator standing outside the hospital room knows that her approach

---

the Palestinians and an updated version is still in use. Their effect is similar to any other round but calling them plastic or rubber allows perception as a non-lethal round. They are deadly. Between September 1988 and April 1989 a single community clinic in Gaza treated 617 gunshot wounds from 'plastic bullets'. 54.8 per cent of the victims were under eighteen. All were civilians. (*Physicians For Social Responsibility Quarterly*, March '92, vol. 2, number 1)
* *Los Angeles Times*, 1 February 1989.

to the family is critical and that their decision will be the difference between life and death.

The odds of a successful request aren't favourable in peacetime circumstances. But here, in this violently disputed land, in these morbid, vengeance-filled circumstances, the task is exquisitely difficult. The number of heart donations from Palestinians to Israelis has been precisely zero since the intifada began; in fact, the two cultures have perhaps never been further apart than on this very day. In the normally ultra-liberal Tel Aviv, demonstrations following the Dolphinarium bomb vent fury against the Palestinians. One demonstrator goes on record to say: 'We have to make a border ... close them in so they will die inside.'* In Qaliqilya, the West Bank, hometown of the Dolphinarium suicide bomber, there are celebrations and ghoulish banners as the death toll of young Israelis mounts.

In short, at this moment, at this time, in this place, the enmity between Israelis and Palestinians makes being in the same building, let alone asking for a heart, a delicate matter.

---

* *Jerusalem Post*, 3 June 2001.

NINETEEN

An Eye for an Eye

I'm sitting in a bar with a large whiskey. I returned from my Shabbat dinner on foot and made it back to the Old City, full of the evening's conundrums. My hosts and their lovely family define themselves as part of the Jewish people living in Israel, which defines itself as the Jewish homeland. And yet, only the youngest children were born here; the rest are from the UK, Germany, Russia or Poland.

I'm told often by those who oppose the Palestinian attempts at statehood that Palestinians didn't exist until Israel was declared. Some people tell me Palestinians are 'Arabs who could have gone anywhere but as soon as we created Israel they wanted a piece of it.' Golda Meir said so memorably, 'There were no such thing as Palestinians … They did not exist'.* And of course many of the Jewish people who believe that Israel is exclusively theirs need to believe it, because

---

* *The Sunday Times*, 15 June 1969.

otherwise the appropriation of homes and land becomes transparently immoral.

On my walk back, the extraordinary writer Al-Maqdisī – or 'the Jerusalemite' in Arabic – came to mind again. He was born in Jerusalem in 946 CE, and even as far back as that he considered himself Palestinian: 'The master stonecutter asked me: Are you Egyptian? I said: No, I am Palestinian."* As evidenced by this conversation with an engraver in Shiraz, Iran, Al-Maqdisī had no doubts about his homeland. This, despite the fact that the Maqdisī family were likely to have been Palestinian for no more than two generations, since the writer's grandfather was the architect of the great fort of Acre. Further back, it's possible that the Maqdisī ancestors came from Iraq since they were part of the Abbasid empire. Yet Al-Maqdisī considers himself a native of Palestine just as my Jewish host's children consider themselves natives of Israel. In the words of Professor Sand of Tel Aviv University: 'History is the shifting of collective identities.'

I entered the Old City through the Jaffa gate, which Jewish and Christian pilgrims once used to access the city. The walls are particularly magnificent here, and next to the Jaffa gate stands the Tower of David. Hundreds of years ago, that very stonecutter told Al-Maqdisī that the people of Jerusalem 'carve stone like they carve wood', ending with the beautiful words, 'Your stones are malleable and your craft gentle.'† What was it about poets and stones in the Middle East? Hafiz, the great Sufi poet who came from Shiraz four hundred years later, wrote: 'Stones are longing for what you know,'‡ and Rumi, another Persian (although that part of Persia is now Afghanistan) wrote to his artisan lover that he yearned to 'be

---

* *Rihlat Al-Maqdisī, Ahsan al-taqasim fi ma'rifat al-aqalim* (Beirut 2003).
†*Ibid.*
‡Daniel Ladinksy, *The Subject Tonight Is Love* (1996).

in the arc of your mallet when you work'.* The atmosphere of Jerusalem is heavy with stones outliving the lies we tell of our past. King David's tower was not built by or for King David. The towers and entrance are Islamic, other parts are from the Hasmonean rulers, other parts Roman, others Christian.

I'm chatting with my neighbour.

'There's been violence at the Western Wall,' he tells me. A riot had broken out just after I left, and, about the time I was eating my sorbet, there had been violent clashes. 'No one was killed,' he tells me, 'but two Palestinian boys have extensive eye damage.'

'Two separate eye injuries?' It seems a bizarre coincidence. He shakes his head and explains that eye damage like this is common. Rubber bullets are steel bullets with rubber coating. They are deliberately aimed to blow out the eye orbits of Palestinian demonstrators. There are dozens of young men and kids who've lost their eyes this way. I must look unconvinced because he begins pointing and insisting that in one recorded three-month period, the St John Jerusalem Eye Hospital received forty-two patients with eye injuries from so-called rubber bullets.[†] It all seems far-fetched, because – although a study in *The Lancet* by Israeli doctors[‡] urged a banning of rubber bullets – my understanding is that they are not accurate, and I worry that my new friend is drunk and unhinged.

'How do you know so much about eye injuries?' I ask him. He tells me he's an ophthalmic nurse and has just returned from treating the two boys. Now he's treating himself in this bar.

'I'm just back from pilgrimage,' he says.

'From where?' I ask.

---

* Jalal al-Din Rumi, (tr. Coleman Barks), *The Essential Rumi* (2004).
† T. Lavy and S. Abu Asleh, 'Ocular rubber bullet injuries', *Eye* (2003).
‡ *The Lancet* (vol. 359, p. 1759).

'Lourdes.'

'You live in Jerusalem and you're going to Lourdes? Isn't there enough holy stuff here?'

'I'm Roman Catholic,' he tells me. 'A Palestinian Catholic. I was a heroin addict and Jesus Christ saved my life.' It's like this city is a giant blender where information, history and religion is pulped into an indecipherable mush. I get a little drunk, and when I stand up to go, my new friend yells after me that shooting for the eyes is official policy for the Israeli police. I don't know what to believe. Has the cold Old Testament morality of an eye for an eye shifted from symbolic to literal? A Palestinian Catholic in Jerusalem visiting Lourdes. Things take on an unworldly glow as I walk out the door.

Jerusalem is a city full of people living in a past and planning for a future that doesn't include their neighbours. Religious belief is more than belief here; it's ancient politics dragged into the present. As the Israeli poet Yehuda Amichai wrote: 'Religion hangs like a cloud of pollution over this city' – not just the polarizations of Islam and Judaism but also the many Christian sects. For all its longevity, Jerusalem is a brittle place, shivering with a tension that threatens to shatter any minute.

Even archaeology is political in Jerusalem. History is jealously guarded, wantonly appropriated and blatantly stolen, like land. The Israeli artist Zvi Goldstein told me: 'There is no contemporary in Jerusalem.' Perhaps it's this that attracts such an unmatched band of misfits and aberrant religious fundamentalists. Jerusalem has hundreds of sects, self-appointed messiahs and fistfuls of prophets. Most are vehemently opposed to each other, united only in the belief that some sort of apocalypse is just around the corner.

There are people who believe that the purpose of Israel is for the Jews to fulfil a scriptural prophecy that would allow for the Second Coming of Jesus Christ; others suggest

Christians must convert Jews to Christianity. I overhear two Americans in a passionate debate about the precise shade of the hide of a heifer that had been born recently outside the city walls. The colour of this beast is (I later discover) essential because if the young cow is the right hue of red and 'without blemish', its very existence will pave the way for the rebuilding of the Temple in Jerusalem. There's also talk of a 'crimson worm' and a priestly belt that must be made from this worm in order to prepare for the apocalypse, or the Second Coming, or the rebuilding of Solomon's Temple. It's not entirely clear to me. The depth and enthusiasm of competing narratives about the Almighty in Jerusalem – the number of interpretations of what God requires in the way of prayer from his followers; the food, outfits, hairstyles, singing, artworks that He sanctions; the debate over the days He requires His followers to take off – is quite extraordinary. One thing everyone agrees about is that all the narratives originate from the same source, Judaism. The Prophet Mohammed was a follower of the Prophet Abraham. Jesus was a Jew. Judaism is the great mother, or father. The beginning of all of this.

The actual ideological differences between Islam, Christianity and Judaism are less pivotal than their differences from Hinduism, secularism and Buddhism. In theory, the three Abrahamic religions should get along fine. But rather than accept their massive similarities, Islam, Christianity and Judaism fight amongst themselves like a dysfunctional family. Freud might put this down to what he called the narcissism of minor difference: 'It is precisely communities with adjoining territories, and related to each other in other ways as well, who are engaged in constant feuds.'* Perhaps it has nothing to do with faith, ways of living, or God. I wonder if it's no more nor

---

* Sigmund Freud, *Civilization and its Discontents* (1930).

less than the narcissism of people wanting to keep the good stuff to themselves, using religion as the screen onto which these conflicts are projected.

Think about Ireland. It was never really about religion or philosophy; it was about tribes. It was about power, control and fear of annihilation. If God is Christian, is it possible that S/He is either Catholic or Protestant? If there is one God and Allah is His name, and Mohammed is His prophet, is it possible that He is either Sunni or Shia? The differences are about men and who is in charge and who controls. Control and fear of annihilation. Control and fear of annihilation.

TWENTY

Mercy

As the donor coordinator prepares to approach the Al-Joulani family, she knows that she may encounter distress, anger, denial and aggression. She knows that people process sudden bereavement in different ways. She knows that she has to support the family regardless of its decision. But she also knows that this heart is needed, and as soon as possible.

Because of the acute shortage of donor hearts throughout the world, studies have been carried out to analyse how best to achieve consent for heart donation. The key finding is hardly surprising: allow sufficient time between news of brain death and request for organ donation. But of course, time is the very thing that donor coordinators don't have. The family of the prospective donor will live the rest of their lives with the loss of their loved one, but their window to donate an organ is brief. It's a fine balance. If the request is made too early the response can be irrevocably negative; if too late, the heart may no longer be usable. Potential donors are typically people who die suddenly and without warning, since donors who've been sick for long periods of time don't generally have a healthy heart to provide.

The factors that cause any family to agree to a donation are so delicately poised that an ill-advised word or negative image can destroy the possibility of a positive outcome. In 1980 a documentary aired on the BBC reported an example of a rare error in the declaration of brain death. This one moment of TV caused a catastrophic fall in donor rates that impacted the availability of organs for more than a year. Even in non-conflict situations half of all requests are denied, but the donor coordinator is aware that Mazan Al-Joulani was known to be a kind man, a father of three with the sophisticated medical understanding of a professional. Most importantly, from the point of view of securing his heart, he had already offered one of his own kidneys, as a living donor, to his brother who had been on dialysis. This offer would indicate that Mazan was positive about organ donation. However, offering a kidney to someone in your own family is very different from giving your heart to the very tribe that has just destroyed your life.

The donor coordinator is ready to walk into the room and explain the situation to the Al-Joulani family. Giving a heart involves sacrifice, and it requires a profound altruistic impulse. It is a gift likely never to be externally acknowledged. In this case, the request being made to the Al-Joulanis would bring a cruelly accelerated acceptance of the death of their loved one. Not only this, but it would require the Al-Joulanis to give his beating heart to save the life of an enemy, during the thick of the intifada, when there's a social contract demanding complete non-cooperation with Israelis. On top of this, only three years before, the Al-Joulanis' sixteen-year-old cousin from the Aida refugee camp in Bethlehem had been shot in the head by the Israeli army a hundred metres from his home. On that occasion, the family had donated the boy's kidneys.

From the comfort of an armchair far from the cold corridors of the hospital, one might say that if Mazan is brain-dead, he's dead anyway. And indeed, medical specialists in most of the world have successfully convinced most people that brain death is, simply, death.[*] However, the reason someone looks like they're alive even after being declared brain-dead, is because, well, they're alive. Yes, without a ventilator making a brain-dead person breathe, the patient would stop breathing and die by all definitions, but as long as the ventilator functions that person is still alive. Just because a machine is keeping someone alive doesn't mean that the person is dead. If so, people with pacemakers or on kidney dialysis would similarly be considered dead. If one considers death to be a complete and irreversible cessation of life, brain death is not death. Hair and nails grow, the heart beats. Brain death is a cessation of consciousness as defined by brain activity – a definition of 'death' that was created in great haste months after the first-ever heart transplant, specifically to define a state in which a healthy functioning heart might be removed from a body that otherwise would be considered alive. A definition created to enable an advance in medical practice while avoiding the accusations of murder encountered by some of the first transplant surgeons.

Let me put it like this: I am a donor, but I don't believe I'll be dead if my heart is beating and my nails continue to grow. Is a tree dead just because it doesn't have a brain? That said, I don't believe there's any quality to my life without brain function, so my choice is to offer what life I do have to someone with an opportunity of consciousness. This is my reasoning. I don't know what went through the Al-Joulanis' minds other than grief. I don't know what brought them to their

---

[*] Japan is a notable exception.

decision, or what they discussed amongst themselves. I know only what the transplant coordinator told me: that they had already decided, there was nothing for her to say, no begging, convincing or rationalizing necessary – the Al-Joulanis simply offered their son's heart. Despite all the factors that might lead them to a place of anger and hatred, they occupy a place of compassion. Thomas Aquinas described this space centuries before: 'Heartfelt sympathy for another's distress, impelling us to succour him if we can.' He called this quality 'mercy'.

Mazan's mother Raoufi, who is soon to celebrate her seventieth birthday with the gift of a son shot through the neck, puts it simply: 'It is nothing to do with politics or war when it comes to saving a life. You are a Muslim, you are a Christian, you are a Jew. The most important [thing] is to save a life.'

TWENTY-ONE

Out West

It's a Sunday, midday in Jerusalem. The *muezzins* are calling out '*Allahu Akbar*' and church bells are ringing all over the Old City. In Jerusalem they have some of the loudest, lowest bells I have ever heard. One, near the Austrian Hospice, is so vast it sounds like the ringing of a bronze mountain. Nearby, another ancient colossus is cracked: its ring stops as if abridged with an axe. There will be some sort of story around that crack, it's always the same thing with bells, they are magnets for narrative. The *muezzin* calls are neither in harmony nor discord with the bells. One *muezzin's* singing slides up and down in complex scales and arpeggios, and for a moment there is a counterpoint with the toiling bells. Cacophony in Jerusalem. In Cairo the sound of competing prayers is like a city of orchestral instruments all playing different melodies but here in Jerusalem the different calls to prayer seem to compete and argue in a civil fashion; sometimes, for a moment, they complement each other.

I mooch around Jerusalem, meeting contacts and trying to organize interviews with people on the other side of the wall who may have known Saïd Hotari. Most enquiries lead me nowhere. Then I get a lead, and I find myself on my way to Ramallah. The problem is I don't know where Ramallah is. I'm told to leave the city and head north, but I've never been certain where north is, or south or west for that matter. Luckily, a taxi pulls up. '*Salaam Aleikum.*'

'*Aleikum salaam.*'

'Taxi?' he asks.

'Ramallah?' We drive away from the Old City with its walls the colour of pale honey and crenellated towers like the drawings of castles I used to make when I was a child. A busy grey highway, packed on either side, takes us towards Ramallah: cars and buses, trucks and motorbikes roar and stop. It could be Egypt or Morocco or the outskirts of Athens until, towering to the side of us, appears another wall, recently built. The separation barrier … 500 miles long, 25 feet high, and tens of thousands of tons of concrete.

Maybe the walls of Jerusalem looked this menacing to the Jewish, Christian and Muslim inhabitants when Suleiman the Magnificent built what we see round the Old City today. But somehow I don't think so. The walls of Jerusalem have the magnificence of a fortified city, and the separation barrier is like a prison with queues of Palestinians waiting to show their papers to young, heavily armed Israeli guards. This wall isn't fortification, it is what it says, *separation.* There are towers, thick columns of concrete and razor wire, sealed in with thick bomb-proof glass. One thing I tell myself: this wall will not last five hundred years.

As we skirt the corner of the wall, a colourful portrait of Yasser Arafat stretches the height of the barrier with the words *FREE PALESTINE* emblazoned on the side. The chairman's features have been tweaked into heroic good looks by a graffiti artist in the great tradition of court painters. How far this is from the images of Arafat's last days, shuffling about in a tracksuit, his hair fallen out, ravaged by nausea and diarrhoea, aware that his enemies in Israel were circulating the rumour that he was dying of AIDS. The real culprit, it is alleged by former Knesset member Uri Avnery, wasn't the terrible virus that killed more than thirty million people, but the now infamous poison called polonium, administered on the orders of Sharon himself.* French prosecutor Catherine Denis as well as Russian experts disagree: they claim that the high level of polonium discovered by Swiss experts in Arafat's clothes were of an 'environmental nature'. Next to Chairman Arafat is a mural of a young man in Palestinian green with a catapult stretched back away from the wall. Instead of a stone, there's a red heart in the catapult and beneath are the words *From Palestine with love*.

The traffic slows and edges to a halt at the checkpoint, and I think about what I have to achieve inside the West Bank. Most importantly, I need to understand what drove one young man to blow himself up amongst a crowd of unarmed teenagers. I want to find his family and speak to them about their son. All I have is a phone number and the knowledge that the Hotari family lives in Qalqilya, a West Bank town that used to be a centre of agricultural produce but has now been cut off from much of its land, markets and water supply by the separation barrier. A town that is also, I've been told, a Hamas stronghold known for 'active resistance' to the Israeli occupation. I don't know if it's safe for me to go there or to speak with Hotari's family who are under the protection of Hamas. I'm not even sure what it means, in practical terms, that the family is *under the protection of Hamas*.

---

* Uri Avnery, 'If Arafat were still alive', guardian.co.uk, 30 January 2007.

This is the totality of my 'plan'. It's so simple it doesn't even exist. I don't even know where I'm going to sleep. I just know what I want to achieve. Find out about the man, not the myth of the *shaheed*, the terrorist, the freedom fighter. Find out who Saïd was and how he came to do what he did. We arrive at the checkpoint and I hand over my passport to a heavily armed young Israeli woman with sunglasses and no expression. My purpose for going to the West Bank? Tourism. This seems acceptable, and I'm through.

My friend Thomas Collins advised me never to eat at any place called Mom's.* I can't remember if he told me to never take a hotel recommendation from a taxi driver, but I've since insisted that he add this to his roster of wisdom. The taxi driver drops me at a 'hotel', which sits on the second floor of an otherwise empty concrete building. There's no one around until two burly hulks materialize at what might be the reception. They're fit as athletes and don't look like any hotel worker I've ever seen. The desk behind which they stand is made for normal sized people and fits them like a child's suit. One asks me for my passport with all the confidence of a ham-fisted amateur doing a read-through on a script.

After the preliminaries are concluded, I prompt them for my room key. For a while, they have no idea why I should want such a thing, and then they don't seem to know where to look for one. I point out a board with hooks and numbers behind one of their colossal thighs. They're not unfriendly but this doesn't stop them from looking like undercover paramilitary operatives.

---

* Later he told me that the advice had come from the great American writer Nelson Algren who wrote *A Walk on the Wild Side*. Algren didn't mention hotels but his other advice included not playing cards with anyone named Doc and not having sex with someone whose problems were bigger than your own. Nelson Algren was born Nelson Alghren Abraham, and his grandfather was a Swedish convert to Judaism.

'How should I pay?' I ask.

'After, after …' they insist, waving me upstairs to my room. I ask for my passport. 'After, after,' they wave me on. The door to my room isn't much thicker than the taut paper seals that cover the jars of instant coffee. It is so implausibly flimsy that I could run through it leaving a cartoon silhouette of my body. Inside, the room is unremarkable: a bed, a side table – no Bible, that's a first – a padded chair, a grey industrial carpet, a radiator, and a window half shaded by a diaphanous orange and pink nylon curtain, which casts a bubblegum glow over the room. Beyond this a window, a road, and a mosque.

I sit on the bed, becoming aware of a smell I imagine to be the musk from an elephant in rut. I look about like you do in a train when you realize the only other person sharing your carriage has years before eschewed all forms of washing. I stand up to better examine the bed sheet. It's disgusting. A team of teenage boys with all their fervent secretions couldn't render a sheet this soiled. (I spent ten years in a boys' boarding school so I know more than I need to about dirty sheets.) This sheet is repulsive. It's rigid with matter and laced with so many tightly curled pubic hairs that it looks like the contour map of a mogul field. I push open the window but the smell is too strong. It cannot be ignored.

Downstairs, it takes a few minutes of charades to explain the sheet problem to the pair of unlikely receptionists. One of them reappears with folded linen. I take it to my room and peel off the offending sheet, bundle it outside the room and remake the bed. On inspection, I see the issue: illogical as it is, the clean sheets are not, in any way, clean. They're folded and ironed and yet unwashed. I fret that only a workforce made up exclusively of people who don't really work in the hospitality trade could do this. It crosses my mind that the very idea of staying in a hotel might be antithetical to local notions of hospitality.

Certainly, my Egyptian friends in a village outside Cairo were offended when I suggested staying in a hotel. They'd resisted in the strongest terms, as if I were suggesting I was decamping to a brothel. I remember insisting, claiming that I had business in the city. Eventually they agreed and dropped me off at the hotel in the evening and, unbidden, turned up first thing in the morning to take me away. It was futile to struggle against such a force, and anyway, smart international hotels are the same wherever you are, homogeneous hinterlands where space is designed to be precisely the same regardless of the geographical positioning. Mind you, the sheets are generally clean.

I leave my room to look around Ramallah before dark. I cross the main road where an old man is digging a thin patch of ground outside his house with one of those tools that's somewhere between a pick and a shovel. He stops and looks at me as I near.

'Welcome, you are welcome,' he says lifting his hand.

I explain that it's my first time in Ramallah. He seems pleased, repeating his welcome. A police siren wails from the road behind me. He nudges my shoulder and indicates I should look. A group of police cars and motorbikes clear the road so a motorcade of black 4x4's with opaque windows can charge through unimpeded. 'America,' he says. I recall there are peace talks going on.

'How are things in the West Bank?' I ask. He shakes his head. I asked how the talks are progressing.

He shakes his head again. 'Not good ...'

'Why?'

He points to a cluster of buildings on the hill. I look towards them. 'Is-rah-ayel,' he says. There, on the hill overlooking the city, are concrete buildings: the water towers and barbed-wire fencing that make up an Israeli settlement. I can't see much of the structures, but there are enough radio masts to monitor a space rocket. I'm surprised there's a settlement right over the Palestinian capital.

'Is this legal?' I ask.

I hope he doesn't understand me. Israel grudgingly acknowledges that some of the settlements in the West Bank are 'unofficial' outposts, but under international law, they are all illegal.* The reality is, illegal occupation of what's left of Palestinian land continues unabated as an unofficial policy of the present government. Whether the old man understands my question or not, he shrugs, looks down into his hole, and repeats that I am welcome.

I walk on toward the centre of town, past hardware shops and mechanics and through a small fruit and vegetable market with stalls piled high with strawberries, onions, grapefruit, vibrant green bushels of parsley and giant sage-coloured cabbages so big and heavy that a man could just about carry one with both arms. I duck in and out of the shade thrown by umbrellas with multicoloured panels that dot the market.

Everything seems normal. I could be in a bustling town in any southern European or Middle Eastern country. Cars beep and buses lurch forwards on clouds of black smoke, whilst children, men and women bustle this way and that. There's little exotic or strange except for the Arab headdress some of the men wear. On the other side of a roundabout, I'm surprised to see there's even the green and white livery of a Starbucks. I squint and notice it's actually a Stars & Bucks. The devil is in the details – or maybe that's where God is.

---

*http://www.jpost.com/Opinion/Op-Ed-Contributors/The-settlements
-are-illegal-under-international-law-336507.

TWENTY-TWO

Stranger than Fiction

Yakov Lavie is back in his office. It's small. A wood and plastic half-horseshoe desk takes up most of the room allowing space for Dr Lavie's chair and one more for a visitor. The walls are decorated with certificates and awards from hospitals and academic institutions around the world. There are photographs of ex-patients running marathons and climbing hills, and a whiteboard with the week's schedule so packed with numbers and arrows and notes that it looks like an astrophysicist's unresolved equation.

Lavie is still. His head is in his hands. Under normal circumstances, he would be at the centre of things, conducting one of the operations indicated on his whiteboard. But the MCI caused by the Dolphinarium bomb overrides every hospital schedule, occupying operating theatres, X-ray and scanning equipment and beds in intensive care for all but life-threatening emergencies. There is, for the moment, nothing for him to do.

BEAT

A cardiac surgeon like Lavie is accustomed to activity, trained to resist emotional reactions and replace them with well-informed action. Lavie isn't used to lingering amidst the impact of savagely wounded young people. But this MCI, this moment of death and destruction, has demanded a pause, a break in the accustomed rhythm of things.

We call the sound of the heart a 'heartbeat', but it's not so much a beat. It's the sound of something there, followed by the sound of interruption, the sound of something not there. The first resonance in the double beat of the heart, let's call it 'lub', is in fact the closing of the tricuspid and mitral valves within the organ. The second sound, let's call it 'dub', is the closing of the aortic and pulmonary valves, which are the gateways to the aorta and pulmonary arteries. It's a cutting off, an absence. Caesura is from the Latin word *caeseus*, a derivation of the root verb *caedere*, meaning to chop, as in wood. Virgil, that great Irish-Roman poet, used *caedere* to describe a brutal murder. *Caedere* would not be apt for a knock on the head with a rock or a neat wound with a stiletto. It required dismemberment. Hacking – as my old Latin master would insist – into not less than three pieces. The young people scattered about the wards are victims of the brutal trauma of modern blast injury in which whole areas of their bodies have been blown away, and multiple double and triple amputations have become the standard. Blast weapons don't discern between combatant and civilian and don't merely wound or kill. Blast maims. It is, by its nature, indiscriminate.

Caedit: it hacks into pieces.

Julia and Lena Nalimov, the two young sisters who had been waiting in the queue outside the Dolphinarium, are only identifiable by their jewellery and the green polish Julia had painted on her fingernails just before going out. Mariana Medvenko with her perfectly almond-shaped eyes and long red hair is missing much of the left side of her body. Alexei Tupelo has shrapnel wounds in his ear, stomach, chest, and right arm …

Dr Lavie sits motionless, awash with the horror around him. The telephone rings.

It's Tamara Ashkenazi, the head of the Israeli Transplant Unit. She tells him that they have a heart, a good heart, and it's a match for Yigal Cohen. Lavie straightens up, galvanized by the possibility of constructive action. He listens as Ashkenazi conveys all the details demanded by transplant protocols. Then he hears: 'There's one other thing – the heart is Palestinian.'

Lavie, like most people, has heard about the pharmacist shot outside the café in Shufat. It's part of the daily news. But the authorities put it to bed when they released a statement saying that the murder had been Palestinian criminal activity (even whilst AP news, the *Washington Post* and other international publications – as well as the witnesses on the ground – reported that the gunman had been an Israeli settler seeking revenge for the Dolphinarium bomb).

When Ashkenazi tells Lavie that the donor is the Palestinian pharmacist shot by the Israeli settler, the doctor's actual words are: 'You've got to be kidding.'

TWENTY-THREE

Open Sesame

I have two leads in Ramallah, if that's not overstating the case. The first is a phone number that may be the home number of Abu Hotari, although I've been warned not to call myself because the '*shaheed*'s father' speaks only Arabic and a call from an English-speaking stranger would not be welcome. The second is the contact for a filmmaker who, it turns out, is currently working on the Palestinian version of *Sesame Street*. I don't know anyone else, so I call the filmmaker.

Despite never having met or talked to me before, the filmmaker apologizes within a few seconds for not inviting me to stay the night at his home. There's no room at the moment. He's busy right now, he tells me apologetically, but if I want to speak with him, I can come along to a *Sesame Street* production meeting that he's attending that evening. 'It's the only way we can meet, since the crew is about to start shooting the TV show.' I agree to find him at the bar where the production meeting will be taking place.

If I were a foreign correspondent seeking an interview with the father of a suicide bomber, the process would be much more straightforward. I'd have a list of fixers, or I'd get names of fixers from a colleague or from the local office of my newspaper. The fixer would be contacted, briefed about the job, a day rate would be agreed upon – something like $250 – and then, soon after, I'd be taken to the relevant place and my wishes would be fulfilled. I've met a number of fixers in different parts of the world, and they're a diverse bunch: often dynamic, intelligent individuals, who, if they lived in a more stable country – one not torn by war, natural disaster or corruption – would be successful entrepreneurs. They're clever. They have to be. They need to be able to stretch through all the different sides of a conflict, and parse all opinions, however diverse or dangerous. But as much as they're access points *for* information they're also tools used by political and paramilitary groups to propagate their messages.

What I mean is this: the comment that the father of the suicide bomber Abu Hotari made to the press at the time of the Dolphinarium massacre – 'I wish I had seven such sons to carry out seven such acts' – would have not only been cleared with Hamas beforehand, it may even have been written by them. It's not only governments and big businesses that are aware that the conflicts and struggles of today are being played out within the constructed fictions driving public opinion. Hamas, Hezbollah, Islamic Jihad, Fatah – as well as the different concentrations of power within Israel – manipulate the foreign media for their own purposes. It's a game played across the globe. Political parties, governments and media conglomerates, as well as individuals, scratch each other's backs to exploit resources or sell their products or dominate situations so as to hold or win power. I'm not cynical, or worse, a conspiracy theorist, but there's little question that the media's own opportunism is never to be underestimated. To put it simply, stories about people finding a peaceful way to live together do not sell papers or attract viewers. The academic Gadi Wolfsfeld summed it up: 'While the news media make an extremely important contribution to the cause of war, they contribute almost nothing to the cause of peace.'*

To understand an act like the terrible bomb outside the Dolphinarium nightclub, one must recognize that a critical element of terrorism is theatre. The IRA bombing campaign in the UK didn't threaten the safety of the British public in any significant way, just as al-Qaeda's handful of successful missions in the West – including the destruction of the World Trade Centre – did not make life more dangerous for the average American; and the more recent and less sophisticated attacks in Europe, however appalling, have not made life any more dangerous for the average European. Terrorism derives from the Latin *terreo*, or 'I frighten'. Its essence is performance. It seeks a narrative of drama and fear, and to exist, that narrative must not only be narrated but heard. This performance aspect is always present. This is the fact of terrorism: it is a two-handed play of victim and aggressor, audience and performance, media and public. Without an audience, the exponential force of terrorism becomes negligible, and its efficacy doesn't go beyond those directly affected. In short, without an audience, terrorism is just another crime.

At the time of the Dolphinarium bomb, both the Israeli and Palestinian sides were fighting a covert media war. This was played out most notably with two stories. The first: a young Palestinian boy, Mohamed al-Durrah, who was shot in

* Gadi Wolfsfeld, 'The News Media and the Second Intifada', *Palestine-Israel Journal of Politics, Economics and Culture*, (vol. 10, no. 2, 2003).

cold blood by an Israeli army sniper whilst his father tried to protect him. The second: two young Israeli conscripts, Vadim Nurzhitz and Yossi Avrahami, who were beaten and lynched by a mob of men after they'd mistakenly driven their truck into Palestinian territory. The narratives were accompanied by images that created the stories as much as illustrated them. Much of the world saw TV footage that showed a terrified child cowering from Israeli gunfire behind his father and then slump as a bullet hit him. Equally iconic is the image of a Palestinian man showing his bloodied palms to a frenzied mob in front of the body of one of the young Israeli conscripts, suspended out of the window by his ankle.

The narratives and images to which people flocked were manipulated by each side, not to mention by the media. What actually happened is another story altogether. Evidence from a German documentary analysing firing lines and angles suggests that Israeli forces may not in fact have been responsible for shooting Mohamed al-Durrah. The pictures only showed half-truths. The brutal deaths of the young Israeli soldiers, however, remain uncontested. Regardless, both sides used the images to incense their own people, and to manipulate international support.

The character of Saïd Hotari painted by the international media after the Dolphinarium bombing was a caricature of a fanatic Islamist terrorist. His father's comments about seven sons neatly supported this extremist image of an ideologue. I've seen propaganda posters of Saïd Hotari standing with his father. Saïd is wearing a martyr's bandana and brandishing, in one hand, an automatic weapon, and in the other, the Quran. Saïd's father has his arm proudly around his son. The poster exists, but the photograph was never taken. It's Photoshopped, as manufactured as a movie set; even the guns were probably wooden replicas.

After the tragic theatre of a suicide bombing, the organization responsible for the attack has a set of stage directions for the bomber's parents, and in return, they offer protection and adulation. This is how Hamas may have worked with the Hotari family. The family's debts would have been cleared and the surviving family made secure. Hamas would have publicized the 'sacrifice' as something to be remembered forever.

After a bomb such as this, foreign correspondents, following similarly unwritten stage directions, arrive at the surviving family's home for a comment. The paramilitaries' message is communicated to the family, who communicate it to the journalists, who communicate it to the world. The comments Abu Hotari made were expected, if not demanded by Hamas. It left Israelis with the message: *These people don't mind if they die, even if their children die, as long as they kill Israelis. Israel may be more powerful, but these Palestinians will stop at nothing.* And it left Palestinians and their supporters with the message: *At last, a counterattack.* And it left most of the world with the message: *Alas, more dead children in an internecine conflict.*

Fixers are resourceful, useful and sometimes brave, but they are also vehicles of information for all sides and frame any interview within the established genre of a journalistic performance. For this reason, I'm keen to secure my own meeting with Hotari without going down this route. For my purposes, contact with the bomber's father needs to be personal and unofficial, rather than a vehicle of news. But I've not thought through how to actually organize myself.

Which is how I find myself interrupting the pre-shoot production meeting for Ramallah's version of *Sesame Street.*

———

A taxi takes me to a bar squatting under a concrete low-rise. The building is squeezed between a Sheraton hotel and an office block. There are few people on the streets but inside the bar is full, every table occupied. Most people have pints of Heineken in front of them – or, to be precise, they have Heineken glasses but the beer is more likely to be Taybeh, the excellent West Bank beer. Everyone's involved in chatter, but there's surprisingly little noise. Vibrant yet hushed; a new experience for me. I'm waved over to a table.

The *Sesame Street* production meeting is in mid-swing. The table is littered with pads and printouts and pens and pints. I shake hands with a man who introduces himself as Mohammed, and with his wife; I nod to the other five people and the meeting continues. The following day's shoot is being reviewed item by item. There's a discussion about who will buy the cabbages for the counting game. It reminds me of the daily meetings from my own first job on a TV breakfast show. No one wants to spend an extra second in the meeting, but if anything is forgotten, the repercussions will be much more difficult to deal with the following day. I listen and wonder how anyone can carry more than one of the cabbages they have here.

Then my beer arrives. I like having a pint in my hand. It may be indicative of a flawed relationship with alcohol, but a pint of beer feels like ballast to my being. I take polite sips, and eventually the meeting is over. The conversation turns to chat, and I ask how this quirky American institution has found its way to the West Bank. They tell me that *Sesame Street* has a huge non-profit arm and runs versions of the programme in a number of countries. 'The aim,' someone says with a smile, 'is to spread the efficacious ideals of *Sesame Street* to the world. A world where counting, literacy and personal responsibility are all a child needs to survive.' I can't tell if he's being cynical, but I can tell that the people around the table are articulate and bright. Mohammed seems to be running the show, although there's little evidence of social hierarchy and a great sense of bonhomie. They say they're pleased to have the work, because it's work, and work is rare – not to mention the fact that there are few enough programmes for children in Palestine. Most, I'm told, are focused on religion and a long way from fun.

The main frustration they have seems to be an inflexible rule to keep the programmes strictly 'apolitical'. For example, they say, they're obliged to change a puppet's green dress because this is the colour of the Palestinian flag. Someone points out that to be 'not political' in Palestine is itself a political statement. Someone else wonders if it's crazy, or even immoral, to be making a programme dedicated to the letter S and how to tell the time, when more than 70 per cent of boys in Gaza have just told an opinion poll that their main ambition in life is to die in a suicide mission. Someone suggests that it's the Jewish vote in the US that keeps it apolitical. Someone counters that the rules are the same for all the *Sesame Streets* including the Israeli one. The Palestinian *Sesame Street* is actually called *Shara'a Simsim*. This is somewhat ironic, because the US show, which got its iconic title just before it began in 1969, was named not for the aromatic seed, but for the password, Simsim, used by Ali Baba to gain entry to the thieves' cave in the original French translation of the Arab-Persian fairy tales we know as *1001 Arabian Nights*.

When Mohammed asks me what exactly I'm doing in Ramallah, my plans suddenly seem too far from this bar and this meeting. I don't want to bring a decade-old bombing into this arena. It feels like reinforcing the stereotypes that these people are working to disrupt by leading normal lives. But of course I'm not in the West Bank to talk about the letter S or the virtues of punctuality. I'm here because a suicide bomber killed himself and a great many other young people.

If my motivations seem conflicted it's because they are. In the 1990s I headed a team that made a special weekend of programming for MTV Europe on young people in the war -ravaged area of Bosnia Herzegovina. The young people had a consistent message: they didn't want to be seen as victims, they wanted to be seen as normal. Yes, they were living in appalling conditions in a war where 200,000 people had already been killed, where 50,000 women and girls had already been raped, but they didn't want the world to see them as victims of violence or rape. They wanted the world to see them as they saw themselves, as young people just like the other young people in Germany and Holland, the UK and America: people who loved the latest music, who looked forward to pizza on a Friday night; girls and boys who yearned for a dance, a kiss, for a world that was truly theirs. For a moment I wonder if I'm letting those people down by doing what I'm doing now. Still, I have to say something. I explain that I'm writing a book and hoping to interview the father of Saïd Hotari. I tell them that I don't have a fixer, don't speak Arabic, and need someone to call this number I have; and if the father of the *shaheed* answers, I need someone to convince him to talk to me.

There's a fair bit of chat around the table before Mohammed turns to me and explains that they'll try to help. But, he says, none of these people need any trouble in their lives. Is the situation just as I say it is? I say that as far as I know, it is.

After more chat, a young man with an open face, and eyes that would make most girls' knees buckle, approaches. He tells me that it's been agreed that he'll be the one to help. He needs to know exactly what I want, and I'm about to respond when he shakes his head in an undramatic way and says:

'No not here, let us talk outside.'

It's dark on the street. The quietness, interrupted only by an occasional passing car, makes me uneasy. I explain again what I want to achieve, hushing my voice against the silence of the night. He listens and asks me if this is political. He doesn't want to be involved in anything political. But he says he'll help me because I'm a friend of Mohammed's. I feel a little guilty at this, but I suppose Mohammed has presented me as his friend, and I'm grateful for such hospitality. I start blabbing that I'm not a journalist, or an academic, and conclude by saying that if there's danger waiting for us, he should tell me.

The truth is, I don't know if there are political implications to what I'm doing, or whether I am getting into contentious territory. He says Ramallah is quiet these days; I shouldn't worry too much. He asks me who's behind the family of the *shaheed*, and I tell him I suppose it's Hamas since they claimed responsibility for the bomb. I ask if this is bad. He shrugs and says Hamas, like all things, changes. Today it is not the same as in 2001, but Hamas is Hamas. It's fine, it should be fine, but I should be careful. Things are calm now, but this, he says, can become a dangerous place very quickly. He smiles, holds out his hand for my phone, and says let's get it done.

He dials the number and is soon speaking in long and mellifluous phrases. I wonder what he's saying. I want him to succeed, but a part of me also wants him to hang up and tell me it's impossible and I should return home. The conversation goes on. I wonder how it is that my new friend can speak so intently to someone he's never spoken to before. The idea that the whole thing is a set-up flashes into my mind ... *Yes, do whatever you like with him. He's absolutely clueless and a particularly worthless example of an infidel. No, he has no back up, no idea about anything. It couldn't be easier. He'll just turn up and you can do whatever you like.* He returns the phone, lights a cigarette, smokes most of it in a few draws, and smiles. It's good news, he tells me. The father of the *shaheed* will meet me tomorrow. He tells me that he likes him, and writes down the address.

I ask if I can buy him a drink, but he refuses. I thank him, and as we go back in I ask why he was the one chosen to help me. 'They say the way I speak is beautiful,' he tells me.

The crew back at the table are pleased at our success, but not nearly as interested in me as they are in having another beer. No one allows me to buy a drink. When it's time to go, Mohammed and his wife offer me a lift to my hotel. We chat in the car, and I wish I were staying with them, because they're the sort of people I'd like to pass time with, working out the meaning of life over a bottle of whiskey.* When they drop me off, Mohammed looks up at the building and asks: 'This is a hotel?'

And then they drive away.

I find myself alone on the street corner. Pools of yellow sodium light brighten the otherwise dark city, the bulbs like giant fireflies. My stomach is sour from beer, and empty, because it's been one of those rare days when food has not been my focus. I walk down the street towards a row of shops and buy some unappetizing fried chicken from a fast-food outlet. When I return to my room, I'm unnerved to find that my door is open, but I can't remember if I left it unlocked when I'd dashed back in to get my notebook. I go to bed and try not to think of the many unwashed men with whom I'm sharing linen.

---

* Years later, I had the pleasure of being their guest and fulfilling my earlier ambitions. Mohammed and his wife have since had a child and their home has become a hub for cultural projects in Palestine.

TWENTY-FOUR

A Life for a Life

Every moment prior to the removal of the heart is critical. To put it in medical language: 'Prolonged maintenance of brain-dead individuals results in deterioration of organ function."* But the cardiectomy is just the first step. Once a heart is out of the body, timing is even more important: a life-or-death countdown, known as ischemic time, begins. Every extra minute of ischemic time reduces the probability of a successful heart transplant.

For many liberal Israeli Jews in 2001, the Dolphinarium bombing marks the beginning of despair. For so many Palestinians, this despair has been daily life since 1948 – a hopelessness that's intensified further in recent months as the promise of conciliatory measures has come to nothing. The Viennese psychiatrist Viktor Frankl explained it with simple but effective clarity with the equation, D=S−M (despair equals suffering

---

* *Heart Transplant Protocol,* Loma Linda University Medical Center, California.

minus meaning). Despair is a state where life is hardly a better choice than death. Despair is passive and dangerous. It is a profoundly unhealthy state for an organism. Rage, on the other hand, is more dangerous to others than the self. Dr Lavie described his reaction to the Dolphinarium bomb as rage. Rage is preferable to an organism than despair, but it is not in itself an antidote. *Action* is an antidote to despair. Action provides meaning. The possibility of a heart transplant provides Lavie with just this possibility, and he stands and leaves his small office to find Yigal Cohen.

Cohen isn't far away. He lies attached to a drip alongside the other end-stage cardiac patients. After months of hospitalization, Lavie and Cohen have come to know each other. Cohen is a typical *sabra*, a tough cactus that grows in the least hospitable parts of the desert: hard and spiky on the outside, soft within. This is a nickname for a certain type of native-born Israeli, but Cohen's tough edge has started wearing away. His heart is now so weak that it could fail at any time. The slightest effort, walking a few steps, even sitting in a chair, exhausts him and leaves him panting for breath. He sees Lavie come in but has 'no confidence at all'. And then he hears Lavie say they have a heart for him.

Lavie explains that he can't be certain the heart will be suitable, but the signs so far are positive. He tells Cohen that he should inform his family without delay and prepare himself mentally for the transplant. It's early evening on 3 June. If the heart is right, they'll begin the transplant as soon as it arrives sometime before dawn.

Cohen calls his wife who arrives with their two children. One is eleven years old, the other three. He tells them that he's going to get a new heart. They're tense and frightened for their papa. He'll be fine, he reassures them; it's like a new engine for an old car. He'll soon be well, just like their uncle.

But Cohen doesn't feel the confidence with which he speaks. He fears that the heart may never come, and he also fears that it will. 'It is', he says with characteristic *sabra* understatement, 'a difficult time.'

In Jerusalem, Mazan Al-Joulani continues to receive intensive medical care, but it's no longer for his well-being. He is officially dead. The interventions are uniquely focused on his organs, keeping them in an optimum state for harvesting. He gets three litres of fluid per day mixed with dextrose and salt, via intravenous drip. Often a form of diabetes can occur as a result of brain inactivity but treating it can have adverse effects on kidneys that are about to be harvested so treatment is kept at a minimum. Al-Joulani's body temperature is similarly monitored as it's likely to go haywire without his brain.

A cardiologist arrives to evaluate Al-Joulani's heart with an echocardiogram. This involves no more than putting a special gel on Al-Joulani's chest and placing a sensor at different points on his torso. It's non-invasive and offers a three-dimensional image of the heart. One of the top cardiologists in Israel, Rafael Hirsch,[*] describes how, in evaluating a potential donor's heart, he feels a conflict unlike any other in medicine:

> It's our duty as doctors to work to the benefit of every patient in everything we do. When I'm called to do an echo to assess a heart for transplant, there's a part of me that feels like I'm taking advantage of a patient's vulnerable state. We are trained, above all, to help the patient in front of us, and it's difficult, I find it difficult … I feel I should apologize. Actually, I make sure no one can hear, and then I speak to the patient. I say: 'I came to do an echo. I'd rather help you to get better but I can't so we're going to use your heart to make someone else better.'

---

[*] This is a personal view and Dr Hirsch is a specialist in congenital heart disease, especially the specialty known as 'grown-ups with congenital heart disease' (GUCH), but if I were sick Dr Hirsch would be top of my list.

There's a stark equation in a heart transplant: someone dies so that someone else can live. Of course, there's little quality of life left for the donor, at least not in the way that most people would want to live, but nevertheless, for a family to offer a loved one's heart, there's an undeniable act of sacrifice at work.

The Al-Joulani family gather around Mazan's bedside to bid goodbye to a brother, a son, a husband and a father, but amidst the cruel horror of what has been taken from them, the shock, grief and anger there is something else, there is grace.

TWENTY-FIVE

No Plan at All

The night was punctuated by what sounded like the clatter of men running in groups up and down the staircase, moving from one room to another and kicking in doors. Half awake, I lie in bed knowing my own door could give under the fingertips of a shy child, and it seems only a matter of moments before I'll be kidnapped and chained to a radiator.

My self-important fear dissipates as the grey light of morning pours between the candy-coloured curtains and I drift back into a sort of sleep, just as the *muezzin's* morning prayer call drags me unwilling into wakefulness. My meeting with Abu Hotari is not until 'after the morning', which I take to mean before three but after twelve. So there's time to fulfil a little mission I have in mind.

In London I often pick up food at a takeaway restaurant run by a Palestinian named Mahomet. The food is good and reminds me of happy months spent in Cairo researching my first book. Although Mahomet is a serious, rather sad man, we often chat. Weeks earlier, when I'd told him I'd be going to the West Bank, he looked at me with what I now think might have been envy. I could go but he could not go, he'd said. It had been almost a decade since he'd seen his family. He missed them so much. He missed his country. I could see the grief in him and kicked myself for glibly saying I was going. His relations were becoming strangers, he told me. A parent had died and he couldn't go to the funeral. There were nieces and nephews growing up who wouldn't recognize him if they passed in the street. I asked if I could do anything for him, take anything to his family. He said no, but that I could simply visit and tell them he missed them. So this is what I'm doing.

I don't have an address, just the name of a hair salon in the centre of town. I ask around and am directed to a little street behind Al-Manara square where I find a barber's shop front decorated with green-and-white lettering. There's a great deal of activity inside, and I wonder if arriving and announcing *I'm a friend of Mahomet* might sound a little suspicious, particularly as I don't even know his surname. The first person I speak to is finishing a trim for a man who's pretty much bald. I wonder if the visit to the hairdresser is habit or denial. Neither the barber nor his client understands what I want, but in a typical Middle Eastern way the conversation is relayed to every other person in the room and someone even comes off the street to join in. The words *Mahomet* and *London* are parroted around in my accent, and soon another of the barbers comes in from another room and shakes my hand and asks if I could wait for a moment. I suggest that I come back later, but he won't hear of it. So I sit down and someone goes out of the shop and returns with a coffee and a glass of water for me. My time across the Middle East has taught me two things: patience, and that it's not doing nothing to sit and watch. So this is what I do. I watch as beards are lathered, nostril hairs snipped and gossip exchanged. The room bustles with activity: a couple of men are cutting hair, another is typing away at a laptop, one is setting up a new mobile phone and fielding instructions from others in the room. The man who'd brought me the coffee is looking out at traffic as if this were an occupation in itself. Everyone is very neat and smart in crisply ironed shirts, immaculate trousers and box-fresh shoes. My scruffy clothes and dusty boots look vagabondish at best, but I suspect no one judges me. I'm a visitor bringing news of a family member.

After an indeterminate stretch of watching and drinking coffee, two men come up and introduce themselves as Mahomet's cousins. I tell them my story and how I know Mahomet. They want to know how he is. I can't tell them that he's deliriously happy – I don't know him well but he's never seemed to be. Nevertheless, he seems physically well, and I tell them this, and also that he misses his home.

'We miss him,' the older cousin replies, which sums up the situation.

We talk a little, and people come and go from the shop. There's a great deal of warmth and affection between those who greet one another: hands are kissed before shaking, people look into each other's eyes when they say things. Backs are slapped, eyes widen with pleasure at exchanged information. Beneath one of the barber's mirrors is a framed photograph of a demonstration march. Crowds of people crush into the frame amidst a mass of yellow flags, and in the centre, a banner is emblazoned with an image of a young man who looks no more than fifteen. Elsewhere around the shop are pictures of what must be the boy's uncle or brother at about twenty-two, and then another of relatives in his thirties. I ask about the boy in the rally, and they explain that he's from their family; he is in fact the nephew of Mahomet.

'The boy's name is Mohammad. He's been in Israeli prison for a long time,' a man says sadly.

'And the other pictures, who are they? His uncles?' I ask.

'It is Mohammad. It is the same person,' someone says. 'Each time older.'

I look agog at this image of a life in jail. 'When is he coming out?' I ask. The younger cousin mumbles something ending in '*inshallah*' and the older one says quietly, but precisely, that Mohammad is not coming out.

I want to ask them about Hamas to get some on-the-ground perspective; in particular, whether it's safe for me – a person with no connections to the press or protection of any kind – to jump in a taxi to Qalqilya and go into the house of one of 'their' suicide bombers. It's the sort of plan that sounds as sensible as drinking a bottle of vodka and then trying to ride a motorcycle for the first time.

I don't ask because I've effectively appeared from nowhere, and despite their welcome, it doesn't seem that Mahomet mentioned I'd be passing through. And what with their nephew doing life without parole in an Israeli prison, I decide that mentioning Hamas and suicide bombers could seem a little suspicious. So instead I ask them about a taxi to Qalqilya, and they say something I don't understand. So I bid my good-byes and leave.

It's near midday. The sun is white and fierce, but in the shade it is desert cold. I check out of the hotel, am reunited with my passport, and find a taxi to take me to Qalqilya. As we drive along I watch the terraced hills of scrub and olive, the none-too-beautiful nor dramatic little slopes that have provided the scenery for the narratives of the Bible and so many conflicts ever since. The miles pass, mostly on good roads, occasionally with a diversion onto a track that's little more than a path. Signs in Arabic and English point to places I've heard of in news reports, always about something terrible: Nablus, Jenin. For long stretches the road is enclosed by tall wire fencing topped with barbed wire. Everywhere simple rustic villages are surrounded by razor wire and concrete towers.

Every movement here is watched, my driver tells me. At any moment – usually in the dead of night – a patrol of armoured vehicles can come to a halt in front of someone's house and a gang of paramilitaries in body armour can cart someone off, perhaps not to be seen again for months, years. Perhaps to be returned the next day, battered and shaken, but never again to be trusted. 'Because how', he says, 'do we know they haven't been blackmailed into working for the Shin Bet [Israel's internal security service]?'

I look through the questions I've scribbled down for Hotari. They seem irrelevant to what I'm doing, as if written by someone else. I realize I've produced a page of questions that are the sort of thing I imagine a proper journalist might ask. As we tear along a section of smooth traffic-less road, the vehicle's peculiar suspension swinging me this way and that, I think over what I really want from Abu Saïd. It's not so much facts, it's understanding. I want to see where Saïd came from, what sort of environment produced a young man who detonated a bomb packed with screws in a group of teenage girls.

Just after the bomb the MSN network offered their 'explanation': 'The bombers believe they are sent on their missions by God, and by the time they're ready to be strapped with explosives, say the sources, they have reached a hypnotic state. Their rationale: that by blowing themselves up in a crowd of Israelis, they are forging their own gateway to heaven.' The BBC similarly claimed the suicide bombers were 'motivated by religious fervour. They are likely to have shown particular dedication to the principles of Islam [...] and are taught the rewards that will await them if they sacrifice their lives.'

The received wisdom is that terrorists like Saïd are religious fanatics. Fatah had its roots in being an entirely secular group: theirs was originally a struggle of land and identity, not religion. Now religion – although not the end goal of the struggle – is fused with the concept of the nation. However, whether for God or land, I haven't, to this point, really questioned the idea that Saïd Hotari was a faith-blinded zealot blowing himself into heaven.

My entire mission suddenly feels wishy-washy, but this is the least of my problems. I don't know whether it's safe for me to go where I'm going, and I'm beginning to suspect that my taxi driver is anxious, too. As we come to the outskirts of Qalqilya, he is suddenly unwilling to go further. After a seemingly relaxed journey, he's now antsy, no longer satisfied with the scribbled notes on the paper I handed him when I'd got in the car.

It may be that his mother-in-law is making his favourite stew for lunch, or that he wants to get home to practise the guitar or buy some shoes or weed the garden. Or maybe, just maybe, he's nervous about bringing this clueless Westerner into a rather obvious kidnap scenario. What do I know? There haven't even been kidnappings in these parts since two Israeli reservists were beaten, strangled and burnt by a frenzied mob a few years before. A proper journalist wouldn't be thinking like I am; he would know what he's getting himself into. He would also have accreditation and the powerful force of the media behind him. But even with all that, he could still get nabbed and killed.

The streets are deserted around this part of Qalqilya. We stop by a black Toyota and my driver speaks to the man at the wheel. In the seat next to him sits a girl in a school uniform. She nibbles at a sandwich and looks at me, not sure which is more worthy of attention. The man seems to know who we're looking for and gives directions and a friendly nod before speeding off. The taxi driver noses around a corner where the houses open up from ramshackle stone and plaster to concrete low-rises. The roads are now more dust than tarmac. The driver is lost. 'Where?' he demands and throws up his hands.

'Where? I don't know,' I say. 'I've never been to Qalqilya.'

'Call,' he orders. I pass my phone to him and he calls. This is the third call. As he talks, he drives. Why doesn't he stop? How can he know we aren't going further away rather than closer? He tosses the phone back to me, and after five minutes, pulls over and turns to me. 'Where?'

'Why are you asking me where? What did the man on the phone say?'

Suddenly he doesn't understand me. What can they have been talking about? *Go around the block again until we finish sharpening our knives?* It suddenly seems more than reasonable to call the whole thing off. But something in me just can't stop.

'Go back that way,' I insist, pointing back to where the concrete low-rises had been. For once – and it is a rare phenomenon – I am correct. Two men are standing outside the apartment block we'd passed earlier. Perhaps they've been posted to look out for me. They're the only people on the street. They looked annoyed. The taxi drives up to them. 'Hasan Hotari?' I ask. He nods.

The driver nudges my shoulder. He wants to go. I'd rather he stay, but I hand him some money. He hardly counts it before speeding around the corner. All that's left of him is a waist-high cloud of dust.

TWENTY-SIX

Leave-Taking

The Sheba cardiac unit in the Tel HaShomer Hospital looks much like a modern hospital unit anywhere else in the developed world. The walls are dull shades of cream and taupe with a sort of plastic dado running along the entire length. Artworks of muted abstract shapes hang at regular intervals. A nurse walks by, a young man in a white coat with flared green scrubs beneath, and a porter pushes a trolley with electric pink rubbish bags stretched open. Signs in Hebrew mark the walls and are the only signifier that this isn't America or Europe. Donor plaques grace each new area: the Lilly and Edmund Safra this, the Ira and Jackie Rosenstein that. They signify wealth and philanthropy – *Jewish* wealth and philanthropy – and recall the half-century marriages of a bygone era.

It's surprisingly quiet in the hospital corridors. The grey-cream floor tiles gleam with cleanliness, reflecting the strips of fluorescent lighting above. Every few metres in the floor there's a pattern of tiles in mahogany brown, muddy golden yellow, and the grey of an overcast sky. Lavie's voice can be heard from his office. He's speaking with another surgeon, Dr Kassif. The dynamics of a heart transplant make for some of the most dramatic scenes in modern medicine. Two teams must assemble and work together, closely synchronized. Kassif will go to the Hadassah Hospital in Jerusalem with a perfusion nurse to extract the heart and Lavie will be waiting at the Sheba centre to carry out the transplant.

Even though Cohen is desperate for a new heart, another part of him, his immune system, will not easily accept it. Only powerful immunosuppressant drugs will allow the presence of another person's organ in his body. The first successful transplant, a kidney in 1954, used no immunosuppressant drugs (they hadn't been invented); however, the donor and the recipient were identical twins so the kidney was not perceived as alien. Every other attempt at transplant without immunosuppressant drugs has resulted in rejection and death. Surgical techniques have improved since the first cardiac transplant in Cape Town in 1967, but the operation is still basically the same. In terms of cardiac surgery, it's not an especially complex operation. What has improved is the quality of immunosuppressant drugs. Cohen's immune system's opposition to the new heart will be silenced with powerful drugs derived from horses and rabbits. His consent is confirmed with a signature on a legal document.

Cohen has not been permitted to eat or take fluids since he was given the news of the heart. He's been swabbed and his blood has been checked to ensure he has no infections. He's hugged his children. The pre-op sedative he's taken is still rippling through his system like a warm sea when he's anaesthetized. As Cohen drops into unconsciousness his last thoughts are, *I hope I wake up.*

The Al-Joulani family are told to make their farewells and spend their last moments with Mazan – a son, a brother, a husband. His heart beats, there's colour in his face, occasionally a finger may curl, a hand may twitch, but the family is assured, he is brain-dead. Some patients in his conditions exhibit what is called a Lazarus sign, which involves a sudden stretching of the arms and crossing them over the chest. Neurologists insist that this is a neuromuscular reflex coming from the spine and has nothing to do with signs of 'life'. But it makes consent for the removal of a heart that much harder for the family.

Dr Kassif and the perfusionist arrive at the Jerusalem hospital from the Sheba centre within an hour. They bring trunks of equipment, not because one hospital is better equipped than the other, but to ensure that the extraction team has exactly what it requires at hand. Transplantation is a very expensive treatment, and the smallest error or delay can disrupt the whole operation. Protocols for what to bring and do have evolved from an international collation of experiences. The team carries chests stuffed with bagged materials: scores of tubes of different diameters, plastic nozzles, needles all wrapped and re-wrapped in paper-backed plastic. There may be a careful order to the packing, but it looks as if a drawerful of bagged objects has been upended into the chest and the chest has been jammed closed. In other chests there are trays and liquids and three sealed cylindrical containers for the heart itself. There's only need for one of the containers, but should there be a problem – should the container become no longer sterile through an inadvertent touch – no one wants to hunt around the hospital for a sterile container for a human heart whilst ischemic time is ticking away. A germ-free, entirely sterile environment is nowhere more important than in an operating room, but with transplantation, it's even more critical because the patient's immune system is completely suppressed. A few bacteria from a cold or a cut finger could destroy a chance at life.

Dr Kassif will shortly remove and inspect the donor heart. The echocardiogram indicates that Al-Joulani's heart is in excellent condition, but until Kassif sets eye on the organ, neither team will proceed. Dr Kassif and his team unpack, and soon they're ready. They're keen to get started as soon as possible, but the Al-Joulani family is still saying goodbye to Mazan in the cramped intensive care ward. Heart donation can cruelly accelerate an experience of death. The Al-Joulani family are gently informed that the operation must soon begin. Intensive care wards are not designed with a family's emotional needs in mind. Space is minimal. Another family is a few feet away. There is no easy way to say goodbye forever.

A nurse wheels Al-Joulani into the operating room. The drapes covering his body are removed except for those around his groin. His chest is shaved and scrubbed with an iodine wash that stains his skin a brownish-yellow, and then he's re-draped so that his torso is framed and his head and neck are tented in such a way as to allow the anaesthetist an uninterrupted view. Nurses prepare trays of equipment for the teams that will extract the kidneys, liver and corneas, but preparation for the heart takes priority.

When all is ready Dr Kassif – who has washed and masked himself and is standing by in surgical scrubs – signals to a nurse to break the seals on the packets of surgical-grade aseptic gloves and surgical gowns and to wrap them on him. He stands in front of the draped patient. Only a nicotine-yellow stained rectangle of torso is exposed to him. Al-Joulani's head is hidden by the tented drapes behind which the anaesthetist regulates the ventilator and vital signs. Kassif takes a No. 10 scalpel and makes an incision down the middle of the chest, then changes to an electronic scalpel known as a Bovie. The Bovie's blade is an electric charge. An electrical element is placed under the patient, and when the tip of the Bovie touches the skin a current is formed, which creates an intensely concentrated heat that cuts through tissue. The advantage of the Bovie is that it cauterizes as it cuts, minimizing bleeding.

What blood there is a nurse dabs away with a cloth. Once the Bovie cuts down to the sternum, Kassif takes a sternal saw with a semicircular blade and saws through the thick bone. A surgical steel implement called a spreader is placed in the incision and ratcheted open as if to force apart a pair of sliding doors. A nurse cleans the opening and neatly edges it with a fold of surgical cloth so that the aperture in the chest becomes an ordered rectangular frame. Amidst the pink exposed flesh, the yellow streaks of fat, and the tributaries of bright red capillaries, the heart's motion is visible in thrusts and shudders.

Kassif cuts down towards the heart with the Bovie, tissue opening under its tip like a zip. Within a few minutes, the pericardium, the protective layer around the heart, is exposed. When this is opened, the pumping heart is visible in all its asymmetric vigour. There are shades of mauve and red, streaks of pearl white and knots of yellow. The colours glisten under the strong surgical light, but it's not the colour Kassif watches; it's the shape and movement of the organ, the rhythm and manner of contraction. He's satisfied and begins to clear the way around each of the veins and arteries known as the great vessels. With each contraction of the right ventricle, blood is pumped to the lungs to be oxygenated. With each contraction of the left ventricle, oxygen-rich blood is powered through the 60,000 miles of blood vessels in the body via the aorta. When the dissection to expose the great vessels is concluded, the moment has come to stop the heart. Cardioplegia (literally, heart-stopping) solution is perfused into the organ and the aorta is cross-clamped.

BEAT

After thirty-three years of ceaseless activity the heart of
Mazan Al-Joulani becomes still.

TWENTY-SEVEN

The Street of the Martyr

There's no one on the street but us. Just the road and a shuttered shop, its front painted purple, a wooden pallet supporting cases of fizzy drink wrapped in transparent plastic. It looks like a film set during lunch break.

'Hasan Hotari?' I ask. The man in the back, wiry and scarred with a broken front tooth, flicks his eyes from side to side. The other man, the broader of the two – keen eyes, white hair, thick moustache, strong forehead – nods. This is Hasan Hotari, father of Saïd Hotari, the boy who killed himself and twenty-one other young people with a bomb packed with screws. Saïd Hotari's prestige now means that his father is known as Abu Saïd, the father of Saïd.

Abu Saïd Hotari stands before me, solid, like a building with foundations three storeys down, a man who knows who he is. His large face seems kindly, avuncular, but the effect of the whole man – his physical size, his expression and the fact that he doesn't change it – speaks of the sort of strength that commanders have. He is frowning. '*Aina hir Tarjama?*'

I'd allowed myself to hope that Hotari would have a translator, to believe that the wiry man in the tracksuit with the scar across his face could, by the force of necessity, be that translator. It's a flimsy fantasy. The man doesn't look like such a person. He looks more like someone who hangs around the types of heroin dealers I'd pass by in Edinburgh housing estates when I was a student: suspicious, ready, eager even to commit any sort of rusty bladed injury on behalf of the big man. No, little chance this man can be a translator. I ask anyway.

'Is he a translator?' Hotari doesn't even bother to shake his head. 'I assumed it was all organized,' I lie.

I don't lie often. I'm not skilled enough, and I don't have the memory. It's something I try not to do. I do other things – probably just as stupid and just as unsuccessfully – but I avoid telling lies like people avoid walking under ladders. I can smell my own sweat. It's not just my lack of preparedness. There's something about Hotari that offers no room for the puerile game I'm playing. He exudes an adultness, an authority, and I feel like a schoolboy making excuses about his homework by pointing to a blank page and telling his teacher, 'But it was there, sir.'

Hotari speaks to me again in Arabic, none too friendly. I don't answer. We're silent as the dust from the taxi settles. I have my clothes and books and toothbrush in a rather too fancy moulded plastic carry-on case with smooth black wheels that glide friction-free along airport floors but screech and scrape here on the pebble-strewn cracked pavements of this part of Qalqilya. Resisting the silence and nervous to do something, I pull up the suitcase handle, which startles me with a loud click like an automatic weapon being cocked. No one reacts. Maybe it only sounds like an automatic weapon to me, because it's how automatic weapons sound in films. Real gunfire, I remember, doesn't sound anything like it does in the movies. When I heard the peculiar *puk puk* in real life for the first time I didn't know what I was hearing. But I think the men in front of me know the sound of the real thing too well to confuse the two.

The notion that somewhere I'm a professional seems increasingly ridiculous. I'm friends with proper foreign correspondents, journalists with their road-beaten canvas hold-alls, airline schedules and brass-bodied cameras. People with newspapers behind them and fixers in front, convincing adults with pertinent questions scrawled on spiral-bound notepads. They're realists to the man and the woman, spending nights in the Sheraton I'd passed in Ramallah, drinking one after another deliciously crisp vodka tonics at the bar. A bar like the ones in Belgrade or Beirut, in Addis or Athens. They bed down for a few hours in sheets that are changed every day and wake up to confront real problems and gather real facts. I feel like I've done everything wrong, like I'm swimming too far out to sea.

The wiry younger man next to Hotari is looking at me with something like disgust. The scar on his face isn't the sort of thing that happens walking into a door or tripping in the road. It stretches from ear to lip. There's a criminal deliberateness about this wound that does nothing for my self-confidence. Abu Saïd asks me again about a translator. I don't know what to do. Neither he nor his scary friend admit to speaking English, and my Arabic is useless beyond greeting people and trading insults. My only way of leaving is by taxi, and my taxi has left. The contacts I have in the West Bank are hard at work articulating puppets that say, 'Today the magic number is seven.'

I look up and down the street. There's not a sign of anyone. The pallet of drinks outside the shuttered shop looks as though it was delivered this morning, but it's untouched. The buildings are neat and freshly painted up to the height of a tall man's head, and then there's an exposed gap of muddy brick for a few feet. I notice for the first time that the roads look like they've been swept, rigorously so.

Hotari commands my attention and points up to his apartment. He and Scarface lead the way, not waiting for me to follow. I walk up the concrete stairs and step inside.

TWENTY-EIGHT

Stopping a Heart

Transplant staff describe cardioplegia solution as an agent for the preservation of the heart, but this is a euphemism. *Cardio* means 'heart' and *plegia* means 'paralysis'. The heart must be stopped in order for it to be removed. This paralysis once represented what was considered the moment of death until 'death' was medically redefined in 1967.

Potassium chloride, the active ingredient in cardioplegia solution, is the chemical agent of paralysis. It's the same compound that's used to carry out the death penalty by lethal injection in the United States. The uses are the same but the motivation is different: in a hospital, the aim is to save life, and in the death cells of a US penitentiary, it's to terminate it. When the cardioplegia solution is perfused into the heart of Mazan Al-Joulani, cardiac movement stops and the peaks and troughs on the monitor become a single flat line. As soon as circulation ceases, ischemic time begins, and from this point, every minute counts.

It is just before 2 am.

The great vessels (the tubes that bring the blood to and from the heart) cleanly exposed, Kassif now cuts through them using surgical scissors: first the superior vena cava, then the inferior vena cava, the aorta, the pulmonary artery and the pulmonary veins. Using both hands, he lifts the heart from the body cavity and turns to where three bowls of saline solution await. Dr Kassif washes the heart in one bowl after another: an action that curiously recalls the washing rituals in both Islam and Judaism. But in the operating theatre the purpose is not religious purification but physical purification – to clean the heart of blood. Once the heart is rinsed, Dr Kassif inspects it thoroughly. Satisfied, he then immerses it in a chemical solution, places it in a cold box, and covers it in ice. Mazan Al-Joulani is no more. An empty chest without a heart is a sight few people forget, a dramatic shift from person to cadaver. Dr Kassif steps out of the operating room and calls Dr Lavie.

Lavie is in the surgeons' waiting room. The news is on, filled with the horrific aftermath of the Dolphinarium bomb. Lavie picks up the call. Kassif tells him that the heart contracts well from both the left and right sides, there are no holes and it has a regular-sized aorta and chordae. It's a good healthy heart, vibrant and elastic. This is the green light Lavie has been waiting for.

Kassif and the heart are already in a car back to Tel Aviv when another team of surgeons begins to harvest the rest of Al-Joulani's usable organs – organs that will better the lives of three other people. Once the organs are taken, a junior surgeon neatly closes the chest, belly and eyes and cleans up the body for burial later that day.

Lavie makes his way through intensive care on his way to the operating room. The beds are still occupied by casualties from the bombing. Broken teenagers on life support. But Dr Lavie's attention is in front of him. He clears his mind and enters his theatre.

Yigal Cohen is there, unconscious and draped, his chest is exposed and stained with the sterilizing fluid. Lavie sets to opening Cohen's chest, exposing the sternum, sawing through and exposing his heart. Lavie's task, during the time the donor heart is racing from Jerusalem, is to attach the vessels of Cohen's diseased heart to a cardiopulmonary bypass machine. To do this he introduces a tube into each of the vessels of the heart and stitches them with 'purse string sutures', which are tightened to prevent leaks. The cardiopulmonary bypass machine, when switched on, will pump air into the lungs and oxygenated blood into the body, effectively replacing the work of Cohen's heart and lungs. Once Lavie has introduced tubes from the bypass machine into each of the great vessels and checked for leaks, he is in a position to cross-clamp Cohen's aorta, the final step before cutting out the failing heart.

And then he waits.

He knows that the donor heart is healthy and that it's speeding at 90 mph towards him accompanied by police outriders, but he also knows that the heart is not actually next to him. So he waits. Experience has proven that things that can happen, will, at some point, happen. If Lavie removes Cohen's heart and a crash or some bizarre incident prevents the donor organ's arrival, Lavie will have killed his patient with an unnecessary decision. So Lavie, like most cardiac surgeons, certainly those trained in the US (as he was), does not take the heart out until the donor heart is in the room.

Kassif calls Lavie again from the road and updates him on the characteristics of the heart, specifically its shape and size. Even in similarly sized people, hearts vary in mass and shape. Lavie makes preparations according to the description received, cleaning up the area around each vessel, cutting along tissue planes so that the arteries and veins are clearly visible and more easily accessed. When there's nothing else to do, he and the team wait.

Although the heart is coming from halfway across Israel, this is no more than sixty kilometres. In the US heart transplants are (generally) not accepted from more than five hours' flight away. There are no five-hour flights in Israel. People often think of Israel and the West Bank as much larger than they are. They assume a grand scale for the contested land, deserts and vast mountain ranges, but the area is tiny, smaller than Belgium and half the size of Switzerland. The delusion of scale perhaps comes from the sheer quantity and potency of narratives from the area. Judaism, Christianity, and Islam converge here, and then of course there's the modern history of conflict. Whatever the reasons, though the landmass seems epic, Jerusalem and Tel Aviv are only forty-four miles apart, Gaza even closer. There are private companies around the globe that own more land than the entirety of Israel. It's a tiny country with a very loud voice.

Lavie is informed when the new heart is ten miles away, five miles away, when it reaches the car park and when it's inside the hospital. As soon as the transplant box is placed outside the operating theatre a surgical assistant picks up the container with the heart inside and brings it in. Once it's next to him, Lavie looks at it, cross-clamps the aorta with locking forceps and then, with a few snips of his surgical scissors, cuts through the five vessels of Yigal Cohen's diseased heart. The bypass machine is activated, and it takes over the circulation and oxygenation of Cohen's body while a team of perfusionists and a surgeon maintain the flow, pressure and oxygenation. Lavie must now repair and prepare Cohen's blood vessels to be attached to the new organ. Just as an overstretched elastic is larger than a taut one, Cohen's diseased heart is considerably bigger than Al-Joulani's healthy organ, and Lavie must find a way to make the new heart fit. The ends of each of the great vessels must not only be the correct length, but also neat and symmetrical to allow an effective joining of tube to tube, known as anastomosis. Pressure inside an aorta is equivalent to the pressure inside a racing car's tyres – in other words, a secure anastomosis is vital. Lavie must ensure that, when the chest is closed, there won't be leaks; the tubes need to fuse together and then remain that way for decades to come.

The emblematic implement of surgery is a scalpel, but it could just as easily be a sewing needle. Surgery is as much about skilful tailoring as cutting. Seeing a great surgeon at work is a masterclass in sewing. Skilled surgeons make dozens of tiny identical stitches in near-inaccessible places and then tie knots at a rate of three per second using both hands. All this in conditions saturated with slippery blood and in areas often out of sight.

Whilst Lavie is making the final preparations he instructs someone on his team to remove the various bags and protective layers and to take Al-Joulani's heart out of its container. The heart is placed on a table, and Lavie moves to inspect it. He compares its shape and size with the vessels of Cohen's body. It too requires trimming and edging so the tubes can fit in their new homes. To make it fit, in the words of one surgeon, 'as if it were made by God'.

TWENTY-NINE

Tea and Time

The apartment door closes behind me. My eyes adjust to the light, and I see three more men sitting on sofas. I shake their hands, and Hotari motions for me to sit down.

My notebook is in my hand. It's one of those smart Moleskines with an elastic band and a useful envelope at the back. I normally use a much cheaper one, but I've brought the Moleskine in a pathetic attempt to give myself some gravitas. I pretend to make notes but all I come up with is an infantile illustration of the facial scar on the man in front of me and one sentence that reads: *I'm here in a group of men and there's no translator. What the fuck am I going to do?* I look up at the men and smile in what I hope to be a reporterly way. I flick though the pages of the Moleskine and see a number scribbled in a corner that someone had given me weeks before with the word *Abdel* written beside it. I vaguely remember that it's the name of a friend of a friend of someone, who's Palestinian and working for an NGO in the West Bank. 'Excuse me,' I say to the men.

I call the number and speak to a voice I've never heard before belonging to a man who doesn't even know I exist. His English is excellent, and he sounds clever and busy. I explain that I know this is a bizarre request, insane even, but there's nothing I can do but put it into words. I tell him that I'm a writer with an interview in Qalqilya, an important interview that I've waited years to do, and I have no translator, and I'm now sitting in front of four men and am unable to communicate. Might Abdel know of a translator?

'For when?' he wants to know.

'For now,' I tell him.

'Impossible,' he says. Can't he come? I beg, but he explains that he's more than an hour away, even by taxi, and anyway, he's in the middle of work.

I look around the room. There are sofas pushed against three walls. On one of the walls hangs a framed picture of young Saïd Hotari with his bomb strapped to his body, and behind him, Al-Aqsa mosque. Abdel says he will call back in ten minutes. After fifteen, I call, expecting the worst. He says, 'I will come, but it will be more than an hour.' It's fortunate for Abdel that he's an hour away, because if he'd been in the room, I would have kissed him on the forehead.

I communicate to Abu Hotari that a translator is on his way, and he alarms me by putting his hand into his jacket and slowly drawing out the thin barrel of what turns out to be pipe for smoking tobacco. One of the men responds to a voice from the kitchen and reappears with tea and chocolate biscuits. It's one of the many unifying factors of the Irish and the English: our morale improves with tea. As the small bare room fills with the sound of slurping from tea glasses and the reassuring smoke from Hotari's pipe, I lean back into the sofa and allow myself to observe.

In the way that some parents have framed pictures of their children's diplomas or other awards, Hotari has framed photo montages of Saïd with bombs, bandanas and mosques – including the famous image of himself with Saïd, arm in arm, Saïd gripping an automatic weapon. By the door is the light switch. Above this hangs a photograph of someone else crouching with a Kalashnikov with Al-Aqsa mosque superimposed above. It doesn't look like Saïd.

All these martyr pictures with banners and cloudy mosques are doing nothing to relieve the anxiety I'm trying to ignore. I can't imagine what we're going to do for an hour or more. We can't just sit here drinking tea and not talking. However, this is exactly what we do.

More tea is brought. I smoke a cigarette I was offered, and feel sick. I drink some fluorescent orange squash and then more tea. Hotari is very much the patriarch. All the men in the room look to him, none more often than the man with the scar. I worry suddenly that my iPad with its Find My iPad tracking function may be used by Shin Bet to launch a revenge drone strike against the family home of the suicide bomber and it will be my fault. I pull it out of my bag and turn the feature off.

The room warms. The afternoon sunlight streams though a window like a magnifying glass. Soon it's hot. Scarface shows no inclination to remove his long-sleeved tracksuit top, which remains zipped to the neck. When he stretches to retrieve his lighter, I notice he has thickly inked amateur tattoos under his cuffs. I'd feel better if the tattoos were more professional.

Every time someone enters or leaves the kitchen I see women within. At one point, the door cracks open and a toddler is pushed out. Hotari calls to the little boy, his voice suffused with joy. He gathers the child into his arms, playing with him, holding coins and making them disappear, watching with seemingly limitless tolerance as his wallet is removed and its contents thrown about the sofa.

The child sees me and waddles over. He tugs at a piece of clothing half out of my bag. Hotari remonstrates with him, but the boy is the only person in the room unimpressed by his authority. The boy continues pulling, and I unzip the bag for him, relieved to be able to demonstrate what a kindly and tolerant person I am. The child dives in, pulls out my clothes, and scatters the contents behind him. The pint-sized menace is not in the slightest influenced by Hotari's angry commands.

I sit by, embarrassed by the state of my clothes: unironed, unwashed, balled up. Then the boy grabs my iPad and holds it above his head, monkey style. I move over to him and pry it from the vice-like stickiness of his little hands, and Hotari scoops the child up from the mêlée. He screeches in indignation, furious that his game has been cut short. I find a sweet in my pocket and Hotari nods and looks as relieved as I feel when this quiets the child. As I stuff none-too-clean socks into my bag, I say a few platitudes about how lovely the boy is and ask his name.

'Osama,' comes the reply.

I explode into laughter, nervousness making it too loud.

'Osama. Good one. Ha ha ha … I like that.'

'No, his name … Osama.'

More tea arrives. I wish I hadn't turned off my iPad tracking function. I break my tea glass. The sun edges across the room.

THIRTY

Transplant

Dr Lavie's concentration is intense. Not only can a bad decision, a misplaced stitch or a rash incision cost Cohen his life, but every delay has tangible repercussions. To be precise, according to a recent study in Germany, each 5.78 minutes of ischemic time results in one more day in the intensive care unit. In monetary terms alone this can mean $10,000 every six minutes.

Whilst Lavie's hands snip and stitch, his brain begins patterning the heart of the Palestinian onto the body of the Israeli. He reviews actions he must take, calculates timings. His eyes are focused. He hears the tones of the machines around him. He absorbs words from the anaesthetist and replies to questions from the perfusion team. He moves quickly and precisely: cutting, sewing and knotting. He makes a final incision, the cut that will release the diseased heart. He lifts it out of Cohen's chest while he reaches to pick up the donor heart beside him – a heart that, a few hours ago, had been beating in the body of Mazan Al-Joulani.

But there's no time to dwell on this.

He re-engages with the operative reality and with a white surgical cloth places one heart in a container and the other into the chest of Yigal Cohen. He shifts the donor heart about in Cohen's chest cavity. He teases out the pulmonary artery. He turns the organ over in his hand and puts his finger in the opening of the inferior vena cava, double-checking which vessel is which before connection begins.

On a practical level, a heart without blood is a very different object to what one sees in a functioning chest. Unlike household electrical wires, the body's vessels are not colour-coded, and there's no time to make and unmake mistakes in connection. A meticulous knee or hip surgeon will visit a patient in person for a verbal confirmation of which limb requires attention, and to physically mark the correct limb with an indelible marker. It does no harm to be certain which leg to chop off – and no harm to be certain which vessel goes where.

As soon as the heart is out of the ice and within Cohen's body, it begins to warm up, and unless blood starts to circulate through it soon it will quickly spoil. Ischemic time accelerates massively within the body. In simple terms, imagine a meat product in a kitchen: it might last a number of days in a cold box, but it will spoil after a couple of hours at room temperature. The human body is at least a third hotter than the average room temperature, so the situation is acute. Swift action is required.

Lavie makes the first stitch, or suture, into the superior vena cava. This is the vessel that brings oxygen-exhausted blood from the upper body into the right side of the heart. Lavie judges exactly where to put the suture and where to align it on the prepared vessel in Cohen's body. After he makes the first two sutures, he pulls them together so that the heart draws in to meet the body in exactly the right place. From here on, a surgical assistant uses forceps to present the edge of each vessel to the tiny curve of Lavie's needle; and with quick neat stitches, he makes the joins.

Every movement is precisely judged. If the vessel is too long, it will bend and kink when the blood ebbs and pumps. If it's too short, it will stretch and leak. Stitches are made and then knotted off. The surgical knot is a reef knot with a double tie on one end. This looks straightforward and simple if you're using two pieces of rope, but within a living person's chest, in gloved hands slick with blood, it's more challenging. Surgeons train their fingers for hundreds of hours until these micro-movements are as natural to them as walking.

The stitching and knotting goes on without cease for ninety minutes. The thick white surgical cloth with which Lavie had picked up the heart is wedged between the heart and chest cavity. It's now sodden with blood, as if soaked in an entire bottle of red wine. Before long, Lavie is connecting the last of the great vessels, the aorta. It's the largest and thickest, not unlike calamari in look and texture. Nowhere is stitching more important than the aorta because of the quantity of blood that runs through it. In a single day, blood might travel 19,000 miles through the body, and the energetic impulse is nowhere more pressured than within the aorta. Stitches must be a certain depth and spacing. Here, imperfection isn't an aesthetic quality, it's a doorway to morbidity and death.

When the aortic anastomosis is concluded, Lavie releases the cross-clamp and blood floods into the heart. This is the critical point. This is the moment Lavie and his team will learn if the heart will beat again. As soon as Al-Joulani's heart is flushed with Cohen's warm blood, it comes to life. It contracts and expands independently, and without electric shocks or chemical stimulation, oxygenated blood courses through Cohen's body. This once-static organ, cut from Mazan Al-Joulani's body some three hours before, still as a rock or a lump of wood, has erupted into spontaneous vigorous movement. Its rhythm is confirmed by beeps and flashes of gradient on the heart monitor. One moment, it's a pound of flesh, and the next, a beating, living heart.

To Lavie, this is the 'magic moment'. Relief and joy is palpable throughout the operating room. The team watches the heart as it swells and tightens; even amongst professionals the sense of wonder remains. Despite spontaneous contraction, the beat is irregular. Lavie gives the heart an electrical shock with a pair of metal spatulas, and this resets it into a rhythmic pattern. When he establishes that the heart is beating well and that there aren't any leaks, he reduces the bypass machine flow until the heart of Mazan Al-Joulani takes on the full task of circulation for Yigal Cohen.

Lavie removes all the bypass tubes and closes each hole with a suture. He reverses out of the chest of Yigal Cohen until he reaches the sternum, which he closes with thick wire and surgical pliers. An assistant will finish the stitching. Before the operation, Cohen had been given a drug called Heparin – derived from, amongst other things, the intestinal mucous secretions of pigs – to prevent his blood from clotting. Now the team must nullify the effects of the Heparin so that Cohen's blood will clot when necessary, so that he won't die of blood loss at the smallest cut or accident. The team injects a drug to stimulate clotting called Protamine. This drug is made from a chemical found in the sperm of a certain sort of Arctic salmon.

Mission fulfilled, Lavie walks back through the post-operative recovery rooms still packed with the victims of the bombing. He's too exhausted to even look. When he arrives at the fire doors that lead to the family area he's confronted by a wall of TV cameras, microphones and a cacophony of shouting journalists. A reporter from CNN pushes a micro-phone in front of his face and barks a question: 'How did it feel to transplant the heart of a Palestinian into an Israeli Jew?'

Dr Yakov Lavie has worked for twenty-four hours and he says the first thing that comes into his head. It's an answer that will be replayed to the rest of the world over the next few days. And an answer that will dominate my life for the next decade: 'A short time ago I was holding the heart of an Arab Muslim in one hand and an Israeli Jew in the other, and do you know what? There's no difference.'

THIRTY-ONE

Translation

Abdel the translator, the angel, is outside the building. I stand up. I'd like to talk to him before we begin – mostly to greet him and thank him for saving me – but Hotari motions for me to sit down. Others go.

As soon as Abdel enters, I feel a great weight of anxiety lift. He's in his mid-fifties with greying hair, glasses and a waistcoat of the sort worn by photographer or fly fishermen, with lots of pockets and netting. He looks friendly and intelligent and exudes the kindly confidence of a well-liked university professor. Abdel shakes hands and exchanges detailed greetings with each man. As he comes to me, I look him in the eyes, and he nods briefly.

I begin my heartfelt thank you: 'There's not too much I can say right now that can convey my gratitude, but …'

He waves away my words and asks what I want from this meeting. I explain that I'm trying to get an idea about Abu

Hotari's son, about the family, and about how a young man becomes a bomb. He listens and nods. His English is flawless and displays a learnedness that befits his professorial appearance. He warns me that there are some areas that are sensitive, that even after a decade the issue is delicate. That some subjects should be avoided.

I've been sitting in this room for more than an hour and a half, and I'm anxious to begin. But on this side of the separation barrier, as in the rest of the Middle East, rushing headlong into business before gallons of tea and courtesy is unseemly. So I wait. Eventually, Abdel signals to me that this is a good moment to begin, so I start in on my questions, and he translates.

We begin in the past.

Hotari explains that he and his family fled their home in Qalqilya in 1967, when Israeli troops occupied the area following their victory in what they call the Six-Day War. They fled to a refugee camp in Kuwait and then to Jordan with whatever they could carry in their car. He says they tried to return home after the fighting, but they were not allowed. Life was difficult; they had nothing but they set up a small shop in the camp in Jordan and managed to survive.

They were allowed to return to the West Bank in 1999, but the children, who'd grown up hearing idyllic stories about their 'home', found themselves strangers in the place they were supposedly from. Their land was gone, and everyone they knew with it. This, he tells me, was part of a deliberate Israeli strategy to undermine social bonds by destroying communities and only allowing people to return from different areas.

Abu Hotari was fifty-nine and it was impossible for him to find a job, so he and his wife went back to Jordan to make a living. Saïd, however, had managed to enrol in a course to become an electrician, and his elder brother, Aleh, had stayed with him. The boys lived together and worked as much as they could, sending back funds for the rest of the family to help them survive. Abu Hotari felt terrible being separated from his boys. They had no one to cook for them or do any of the things that help and steady young men. They knew no one and so had no one to introduce them to job prospects or potential wives.

I steer the conversation to Saïd, trying to locate the source of his radicalism, but it becomes clear that his father has no more idea than I do – or he's not saying. Saïd took no part in the demonstrations against Israeli occupation, Hotari tells me. Even once the second intifada had begun. As a father, he'd been upset that his son seemed to have so little interest in the Palestinian struggle, or even in the idea of Palestine. 'But what about religion?' I want to know.

'He was a serious boy always, but had not been particularly religious until just before the attack.'

'Surely there were character traits ... Something out of the ordinary.'

Hotari says, 'No. Nothing.'

Saïd was ordinary and normal, gentle even. The only thing he was serious about was studying karate. Saïd was the last person he would have expected anything from. His brother Aleh was the trouble: he drank and took drugs and made problems that his younger brother Saïd had to sort out. It was Aleh, he thought, who would create a crisis, not Saïd.

I want to get an idea of what was happening in the days before the attack, how Saïd had been behaving, what precisely he'd said the last time his father or mother had seen him, but I discover that his father had not seen him for weeks, perhaps months before. His parents had been in Jordan; the two brothers were in Qalqilya, alone. He spoke with Saïd on the telephone but that was all. Only Aleh had been there.

'Wouldn't it have been possible,' I ask via Abdel, 'that you or your wife would have noticed something if you'd been there?'

As Abdel translates, I see the impact of the question before I realize exactly what I've implied. It hits Hotari like a blow to his belly. He makes a just audible grunt and the deep furrows of his frown deepen further. Abdel relays his response: 'Of course, had they not been separated from their sons, everything would have been different.'

I ask where Aleh is, and if I can speak with him about his last days with Saïd. As Abdel translates the question, the man with the scar jerks out of his blank reverie. He and Hotari exchange words. Hotari's tone is stern. Abdel informs me that the man with the scar is Aleh, the brother of Saïd Hotari. Abdel whispers that Hotari is insisting that Aleh keep his mouth shut, but Aleh is demanding that he be allowed to speak.

Abdel informs me that the situation is becoming delicate.

THIRTY-TWO

Same Heart New Body

The first awareness is voices, people talking near his bed. He wants to sink back into numb comfort, but there's too much noise. Nurses speak to each other, doctors on mobiles, machines bleeping and ringing, trolleys rattling.

He's in an opiate fog. Eventually, he scrambles through the agony and cracks open his eyes, an extraordinary pain hitting him in waves, an exploding counterpoint to the numbness. He feels encased in a ravaged body, sawn apart and held together with twisted wire. A woman comes over and drips sweet water into his parched mouth with a sponge. As the shards of sound, pain and sense assemble into recognizable consciousness, he comes to understand. He is in a hospital. He is Yigal Cohen, and he has another man's heart in his chest.

The impact of a heart transplant is something like that of a medically-controlled car accident. Not only is there the trauma of having your sternum cut open and wrenched apart and then wired back – not to mention the upset of having the most central part of you cut out and left in a bucket – but there's also the side effects of intensely potent immunosuppressant drugs pumping through the metabolism, of which nausea and diarrhoea are the most minor. There's also trembling, seizures, accelerated hair growth, diabetes and the possibility of a condition called Moon Face Syndrome, where the face swells into a circle. And of course, there is the threat of the most serious of all the side-effects, organ rejection, in which the patient will quickly die.

As if this isn't enough to contend with, Cohen quickly discovers that he, or rather his new heart, is the star of a global media story. Journalists are desperate to interview him and take his picture. This is not welcome news. Like most people after life-and-death surgery, Cohen would prefer to be left alone to recover in tranquil dignity. The last thing he wants is to be the centre of attention.

But Yigal Cohen is a man of strong qualities, and he's grateful for the heart. If his operation can do some good for others, so much the better. So as soon as Cohen is able, he forces a smile, gives the interviews, does what he can to help and generally goes along. Days pass, and when he's asked if he's willing to meet the father of the man whose heart beats in his chest, of course he agrees.

Mazan Al-Joulani's father Lotfi arrives at the hospital trailed by hordes of press. The hospital staff and the reporters are charmed by Lotfi's dignified grief and his manifest pleasure at meeting Cohen.

All he wants to do is listen to his son's heart beat in Cohen's chest.

He speaks with Cohen, poses for press photographs, and spends a few minutes with Dr Lavie. There are interviews, TV cameras and radio shows. Commentators on both sides of the conflict later complain that the story is becoming a distraction; a feel-good narrative that changes the focus from the horrific issues of the intifada even as the fighting rages on.

Lotfi is especially criticized within his own community. People claim that he's collaborating with the Israelis; rumours circulate that he was given money for his son's heart. False rumours. But a rumour doesn't have to be true, it just has to *be*. Lotfi Al-Joulani replies to criticism of himself and his family with simple, direct words: 'Even though our son was killed by a Jewish settler's bullet, [our aim was to] save the lives of others, no matter if they were Jews or Christians or Muslims.'

When I ask Dr Lavie if he remembers, he nods and says of course. When I ask him to describe Lotfi he says simply that he was 'a beautiful guy'. His consulting room was filled for a moment with the warmth of his smile.

Yigal Cohen was out of bed within the week and walking about.

It was a success, but, as with all heart transplants, one family was given the very thing taken away from another.

THIRTY-THREE

The Making of a Bomb

I want to hear from Aleh Hotari. He glances at his father, seeking approval but fearing rebuttal. He is Saïd's older brother, and he wants me to know … Saïd and Aleh shared everything. Their clothes, their meals, even their bed. They didn't know anyone else. Saïd had a job, but it was more difficult for Aleh. Life was hard. Saïd was a quiet boy, he says, and it's true he was not religious. In fact, the day of the bomb, Aleh had gone to Friday prayers but Saïd had stayed at home.

Aleh seems grateful for the stage, almost pathetically so. He grows more confident with each word as Hotari grows increasingly uncomfortable. I ask Aleh if he'd noticed anything strange about Saïd.

'Not really,' he says. 'Perhaps he became more quiet. He was hanging out with different people. I might not have noticed. I'd been going through … a difficult period.'

Not Saïd, though. Saïd was serious – never drank, never

smoked kif or even cigarettes. He practised karate but was gentle. Aleh didn't notice anything, except on the day of the martyrdom Saïd had asked if he could borrow Aleh's tracksuit jacket, and Aleh had reproached him, saying, 'Why do you ask? Take it, you are my brother.' Of course Saïd had known he would never bring it back.

I ask Aleh if he'd met any of Saïd's new friends – the 'different people' he'd been spending time with. He nods and is about to reply when his father interrupts. A disagreement ensues. Hotari barks a few words to Abdel the translator who tells me that the interview with Aleh is over. We must not continue speaking to Aleh, and if we are to remain in the apartment, we must respect his wishes.

Aleh deflates into silence. I feel for him. He seems to be the black sheep, the rebel, whether through drugs, alcohol or just attitude. He loved his brother, but perhaps he's always been judged against him. Perhaps never more than now. Perhaps he's wordlessly blamed for his death. Aleh had sat in the room while his father had referred to him in front of strangers as a problem. The scar across his face and the amateur tattoos imply a life on the darker side, and perhaps he's here in this house under strict and possibly necessary control.

I go to the bathroom to break the atmosphere and wash my face. When I return I ask if Hotari remembers 1948, the time Israelis call Independence and the Palestinians call *Nabka*, the catastrophe. He says he remembers it very well. He was a boy. They lost ten *dunams* (two and half acres) of land, but they remained where they were. In 1967, he said, the Israelis invaded and they fled and were not allowed to return for thirty-two years. Today access to their farm is blocked by the wall. They can see the land but not reach it, not plough, not sow, nor even harvest the olives. He has not seen the ocean for a decade, not once, no one in Qalqilya has. It's eleven kilometres away.

'Do you know,' he asks me, 'what it is like to be so close to the water and not even be able to see it, to touch it, to hear it?' He describes a catalogue of crimes committed by Israel in recent history and tells me that the disparity of military strength between Israel and Palestine makes martyrdom the honourable and inevitable course of action. But Hotari's bombastic talk of martyrdom does not hide the grief in this apartment. It's there like a pile of coal not quite covered by a snow fall of geopolitical justifications.

I feel for him, I do, but I've also pored over the pictures, spent hours with the fathers, brothers, sisters and friends of the young people killed by his son's bomb. I can't sit in this room and nod to moral justifications of asymmetric warfare and sacrifice and even heroism when a young man flicked a switch and ended twenty-one other lives and ruined so many more. I feel morally obliged to bring in the voices of these victims, in however small a way. It seems like a responsibility.

I whisper to Abdel: 'I've been spending a long time sitting with mothers and fathers just like him, mothers and fathers of young people – a brother, too – of the people who were killed that day by Saïd's bomb. These were immigrants from Russia. Most came for a chance at a better life – like him and his family in Jordan. Not because they wanted to hurt Palestinians. They're straightforward people who'd been told that the land was theirs. I want you to ask him, as someone who has lost a child, does he ever think of those mothers and fathers whose children are dead because of the actions of his son?'

Abdel looks at me in disbelief. He cannot ask this question, he says. It is unsafe. A bad question. For the first time, Abdel looks rattled. 'Just ask it,' I beg. 'Please just do it.' He raises an eyebrow and then turns and says a few words to Hotari in Arabic. The response is intense.

Hotari's voice gets louder as he is speaking like, a siren winding itself up. Abdel fixes his eyes on the room and translates the furious responses. I pretend to take notes. I've heard these things before, they have nothing to do with the question I asked.

Hotari is shouting of Zionism, oppression, people who would soon have been killing Palestinians, children slaughtered by snipers from concrete bunkers and armoured cars. How dare I ask him to identify with the victims; see them as people like him.

'But most were girls,' I plead. 'Teenage girls ...'

'Them too,' I hear. 'Soon they join the army and kill Palestinians, soon giving birth to more soldiers who would kill Palestinian children.'

Hotari eventually quietens. He no longer looks angry; he looks disgusted. I've achieved nothing. Picking at a wound till it bleeds. I've learned nothing and haven't even helped any of the bereaved.

Abdel whispers that it's time to leave. Perhaps because of the tea or my nerves, I need to go to the bathroom again. When I come out of the bathroom the situation has improved. Abdel has been working his magic. I want to offer my hand to Hotari, but it's dripping with water. Instead I look him in the eyes and say that I'm grateful for his hospitality and for allowing me into the home of himself and his family. I apologize if I've made him angry. He turns away and opens the door of the apartment and leaves. I look at Abdel and he mouths, 'Let's go.'

We follow Hotari out the door, but he goes up the stairs rather than down towards the street. I'm not nervous anymore, just relieved to be out of the tension. We walk to the roof. A shrieking metal door opens onto a flat rooftop. In the glare, Hotari's eyes are full of tears. I ask him again if there can be an end to it all. 'It can be solved in twenty-four hours if this is what was wanted,' he says.

He's looking at the solid mass of the separation barrier. It's close enough to hit with a rock, a mass of concrete 25 feet high, stretching to the left and right, almost encircling the town. It's like a maximum-security prison wall for the worst criminals imaginable.

I ask Abdel to ask Hotari what he wants.

'What I want,' he replies, 'is for each human to live his own freedom, with honour and respect. Why should it not be possible? The Israelis want control. They need control. They control the situation, and they don't really want peace. They want Palestinians to live in subjugation, and their plan is that they will die or go away and the children will give up and forget. But we will not go away. We will live in hell with dignity.'

He turns to me. 'I did not encourage Saïd to do what he did,' he says. 'If he had been happy it would not have happened.' He looks out over the walls enclosing us on three sides. I see Hotari for the first time. Not as the father of the *shaheed*, but as a parent who's lost a child in a suicide blast. I look past him to two other rooftops in front of us: black plastic water towers perched on spindly legs like primitive space satellites, solar panels and corrugated sheets of metal, potted plants dotted about. Beyond that, there are fields, bright green with the first growth of spring.

Hotari is at my shoulder. 'My land …' he whispers, pointing to the fields on the other side of the 25-foot wall.

PART III
Tribes

THIRTY-FOUR
The Politics of a Bomb

In his moving book *War*, Sebastian Junger describes how machine-gunners captured in combat in the World War One were shot on sight because it was felt that their weaponry was not in keeping with the unwritten rules of war. Artillery shells, mines, aerial bombs – they all make for even less discriminate killing than the machine gun, but until the advent of the suicide bomber, there was an illusion of space between the bomber and the bombed.

Military ordnance – i.e. anything commissioned and made by governments, is considerably more destructive than the improvised versions of bombs used by terrorists and insurgents. Each year many more non-combatant casualties are killed and maimed by military ordnance than all the improvised explosives put together. These explosive devices we have paid for with our taxes and supported with our votes. US arms contractors sold $209.7 billion in weaponry in 2015, representing more than half of the world's production. France ($15 billion) was a distant second in arms sales, with Putin's Russia ($11 billion) coming in at third place. *Forbes* magazine states that the US is 'still comfortably the world's superpower – or warmonger, depending on how you look at it'. In short *our* blast is much worse. Furthermore, whilst we're broadening the target area of responsibility to include ourselves, it's worth remembering that the actual explosive material used in IEDs and suicide attacks is itself mostly sourced from unexploded, stolen or re-purchased military ordnance.

A cursory look at some of the most widely used manufactured shells puts this in perspective. Take the CBU 87, a cluster bomb made by the US company Alliant Techsystems and designed to be released from an aircraft. More than 10,000 of these were dropped in the Iraq war. This exquisitely functional bomb ignites prior to impact spreading white-hot fragments at speeds in excess of 6000 ft per second and releasing hundreds of bomblets, which themselves are programmed to burst into thousands of body-piercing steel fragments. The most technologically advanced creator of IEDs can only dream of such a level of destructiveness. Other bombs in the CBU range have brightly coloured tennis-ball-sized bomblets that explode on delay fuses or remain unexploded for months, sometimes years, until moved, kicked, or picked up – many times by the curious hands of children – to devastating effect.

The facts of our own involvement in the genesis of today's blast-based weaponry do not detract from the horror of Saïd Hotari's bomb outside the Dolphinarium nightclub. His device, although advanced in relation to other improvised bombs in 2001, was primitive in comparison to even basic military ordnance; nevertheless, it caused massive damage to the people standing nearby because it had a uniquely sophisticated guidance system: a human body. Hotari's targets, other human bodies, were unprotected; they didn't have the heavy armour or body protection used by the military. His victims were a crowd of lightly clothed teenagers, mostly girls, waiting to get into a disco. His ten kilos of explosive, packed with screws, steel bearings and other jagged shrapnel, ripped through these young people, ending twenty-one lives and shattering hundreds of others.

I've discussed this bomb with many people in many Arab states. I've spoken to a broad range of Palestinians, particularly in Qalqilya, Ramallah and East Jerusalem. I've engaged with taxi drivers, mothers, doctors, teachers, filmmakers, farmers, builders, zookeepers and students – people from every range of political perspective, militants and their opposites. Most of these men and women seemed to have been fine upstanding people, and yet, even knowing the age, gender, civilian status and terrible injuries sustained by the young casualties outside the Dolphinarium, a great many of them spoke of the attack with nothing less than pride. They believed it to be a justified military response in the context of oppression and asymmetrical conflict.

The person who built the bomb, the people who planned the attack, the military branch of Hamas, and no doubt Hotari, too; they all knew what the bomb could do. Their ambition was maximum destruction and suffering. But just as gamblers rarely consider the reality that their wins are accrued from the losses of others, the proponents of violence do not see their victories as built on the very same suffering as they endure.

To put Hotari's ten kilos of explosive in perspective, let us look at Operation Cast Lead, the large-scale assault on Palestinian people by Israel in 2008–2009. During this operation, according to the IDF themselves, 100,000 kg of high explosive was dropped within nine hours on the tiny and densely populated town of Gaza. The stated aim was to stop Hamas missile attacks into Israel, attacks that Israel said threatened more than a million people but that had, in fact, killed no more than sixteen Israelis since 2004.[*] The Israeli military argued that Operation Cast Lead only selected military targets. They claimed that the civilian casualties were the direct result of Hamas using human shields around military targets.

At the final reckoning, Operation Cast Lead injured 5000 Palestinians and killed over 1400 people, 300 of whom were Palestinian children. The majority of the injured were unarmed civilians. Gaza is tiny and very densely populated. Indeed, according to the US census, Gaza is the world's sixth-most densely populated place.[†] Yes, the above numbers may include unintended casualties of war, but regardless, the men and women and 300 children who died were killed with explosives many more times effective than the one used by Saïd Hotari outside the Dolphinarium. And yet … many decent and upstanding Israelis with whom I've spoken, not to mention some non-Israeli Jews and non-Jewish Americans, believe the casualties and mortalities of Operation Cast Lead were justified within the context of the ongoing conflict.[‡]

Terrorists and those who make insurgent bombs are often portrayed in the Western media as reprobate criminals. A typical viewpoint is represented in this blog from the US: 'The bombs that terrorists use are among the most evil weapons ever invented. The explosives are bad enough, but Palestinians have chosen to add metal pieces to the bombs to increase their deadliness, and to deliberately wound as many Israelis as possible.'[§] In the case of the Dolphinarium attack, the bomb was

---

[*] http://mondoweiss.net/2012/11/dissecting-idf-propaganda-the
-numbers-behind-the-rocket-attacks.html.
[†] International database of the US Census Bureau Records.
[‡] Israel/Gaza: 'Operation Cast Lead: 22 days of death and destruction', Amnesty International, 2 July 2009.
[§] http://www.yourish.com/blog.

thought to have been made by Tarek Akesh,[*] a bomb-maker trained in Syria who gained legendary status for his bomb-making skills and ability to avoid capture. It was rumoured that he'd made bombs packed with copper screws so that the metal couldn't be removed with surgical magnets; there were also stories that Akesh put rat poison in his bombs. In the 2014 conflict, Amnesty International criticized Palestinian armed groups for 'a flagrant disregard for the lives of civilians by repeatedly launching indiscriminate rockets and mortars towards civilian areas in Israel'.[†]

Daniel Tregerman, a four-year-old child, was killed in front of his sister by a Hamas rocket; 453 Palestinian children were killed; 1500 Palestinian civilians, seven Israelis ...

Weapons designers working for the military and the corporations that make ordnance for state use are seen as upstanding members of society. Yet they're constantly honing the technology of blast, and, in particular, shrapnel. There are flechettes – little darts designed to enter the body and cause maximum damage, which are sometimes cast in plastic to avoid X-ray detection. White phosphorus – put in artillery shells, which burns through flesh until it reaches bone. Bomblets – fabricated in bright colours that attract children and are designed not to explode until touched. Anti-personnel mines that maim, not kill, as a victim of a double amputation is a more effective drain on resources and morale than a corpse.

We have weapons and strategies in place with the aim of destroying the will of an enemy by poisoning and maiming civilian populations, and yet as the historian Eric Prokosch points out, the weapons designer is not portrayed as an evil killer: 'He's a statistician, a metallurgist, an engineer with terms like kill probabilities, lethal area estimates, effective

---

* Middle Eastern Intelligence Bulletin (MEIB), October–December 2010.
† Amnesty International, 26 March 2015, Index number: MDE 21/1178/2015.

casualty radius."* Nor are the manufacturers or the people who press the buttons condemned. Nor are we, who tacitly support the development and sale of these weapons with our votes and taxes. We avert our attention from any implication of responsibility for our weapons and foreign policy whilst comfortably agreeing on the moral reprehensibility of suicide bombs like that of Saïd Hotari.

I've heard that Ahmed Jabari, the assassinated military leader of Hamas, was no more of a child-hating psychopath than Ariel Sharon. Tarek Akesh, loved by his friends and family, is a hero to tens of thousands of people. George Bush is known to be warm and decent. Hitler painted watercolours and loved his dog.

---

* Eric Prokosch, *The Technology of Killing* (1995).

THIRTY-FIVE

The Missing Heart

There's one last piece to the story.

When I get back from Ramallah, I go to see Dr Yakov Lavie. He's a man of integrity and decency, talent and intelligence – qualities I had the privilege of experiencing from my parents. On top of this, no one could be more generous with his time, or more helpful. Lavie's as busy as a head of state and yet he never fails to go out of his way to do his best for me. Nevertheless, when I ask him to help me get in touch with Yigal Cohen for an interview, he tells me straight: 'It's not going to happen. He doesn't want to speak to anyone. Forget about him.'

The bomb outside the Dolphinarium seized my attention but it had been Yigal Cohen's Palestinian heart that refused to let me go, summoning me like a drum. Calling me for a decade. And yet I haven't been able to get to him. I've found witnesses, relations and victims, and even Hotari's family. I've met and talked to so many people over the years, but I can't get to Yigal Cohen.

I'm not sure what I want to ask him, but as time passes he becomes the most important interview I don't have. Each time I try to find a way to him, the message comes back that it is not possible. I'm told that he has other health complications, that he's gone through so much with the media and that he lives far away from Tel Aviv and Jerusalem with his wife and wants to 'get on with his life in peace'. I empathize with his point of view, but I can't stop feeling that I can't properly address the story without him.

I try to forget, as Lavie advises. I examine what might be miles of microfilm in the news archives of the Tel Aviv libraries: interviews, pictures, editorials. However, it doesn't matter what I tell myself; everything falls apart without Cohen.

I get in a taxi, head to the hospital.

———

I grew up amidst human hearts and their diseases.

That little boy in the prologue? That was me. Those hearts in the fridge? Those were real. My parents weren't serial killers; they were pioneering cardiologists. Terms like *pulmonary artery*, *mitral valve* and *aortic stenosis* were as common in my childhood as words like *dog*, *ball* and *ice-cream* were to other children. My parents were obsessed with hearts.

While physicists of the sixties and seventies were trying to find a way to build a bigger atom bomb or beat each other to the moon, cardiologists like my parents were trying to save people from the number one killer in the Western world. Their colleagues included the greatest surgeons of the day: Donald Ross, Marc de Leval and Magdi Yacoub. Long before the internet made the spaces between doctors less significant, these people were part of an international group of cardiologists, physicians, researchers and surgeons: John Kirklin, Denton Cooley and Dwight McGoon in the US; George Trusler in Canada; Billy Kreutzer and Luis Becu in Argentina; Aldo Castañeda in Guatemala; Christiaan Barnard in South Africa; Åke Senning in Sweden; Gerard Brom in Holland ...

These are some of the people who roamed the world and often ended up in our house, people who improved the treatment of heart disease so radically that most heart conditions today are treatable. These doctors were not only supremely talented, but many – certainly the ones I knew – were outsiders. My father was an Irishman; Ross a South African; de Leval a Belgian; and Yacoub an Egyptian. And my mother, perhaps most threatening of all, was a woman.

My father was part of the first cardiac catheterization team in the UK and arguably the leading cardiologist of his day. He was president of the British Cardiac Society and editor of the *British Heart Journal*. But my mother was the one to push the boundaries of patient-centred advancement. She took the well-being of her patients personally, perhaps because so many of them were children. If one died, she had to know why.

In those days, a lot of cardiac patients died. But when a heart failed in a way my mother didn't understand, she wouldn't simply accept it and move on; she'd go to the morgue and get the heart. She'd keep it, discuss it with my father, and look at it until it revealed its malfunctions. She'd convene with colleagues from every corner of the globe in our kitchen, eating, drinking, smoking cigarettes (it was a long time ago) and discussing cardiology until late into the night. Sometimes, if my mother couldn't resolve a particular heart's defect between our home and the hospital, she'd take the heart, or a piece of it, across the world, often to Buenos Aires, where one of the great cardiac pathologists of the day lived. But aside from frequent international flights, my mother was obliged to look after four lively children. So she kept her beloved children and her beloved hearts all together in the same place: our home.

Which is why there were always hearts in the family refrigerator. Frozen organs in shopping bags in the freezer compartment; ventricles on the top shelf; muscle tissue and valves below. All human. Beneath them, the usual things of course: chocolate mousse, roast chicken, salad. Perhaps it sounds macabre, even gruesome. Today it would generate the kind of headlines that are the lifeblood of tabloid newspapers. But to my siblings and me, the presence of hearts in the fridge was an unremarkable part of daily life. It was normal.

Perhaps this is why, when I heard about the heart transplant between a Palestinian and an Israeli, somewhere in me, I thought it would heal the world.

THIRTY-SIX

The Politics of Small Talk

I walk into Dr Lavie's office and I play my ace and beg him to call Yigal Cohen. He starts to shake his head but I interrupt: 'He can't refuse you, Yakov. You put his heart into his body. You saved his life.'

He disagrees, giving credit to the Al-Joulani family, to the transplant team, to Cohen. He insists that he's no more than a player in a larger team. I keep at him, and eventually Lavie sighs and agrees to make the call. No promises he tells me, but he'll try. Twenty-four hours later I receive the message. Cohen has agreed to an interview.

Cohen lives in the north of Israel, and I head to a train sub-station near where I'm staying. I'm searched at the gate by a strictly Orthodox man with a shaved head and side-locks that graze his shoulders. He carries a machine-pistol that looks like something a James Bond villain would use. I'm staring at the weapon when he finds a penknife in my bag that I use for fruit.

He confiscates it. I plead for its return as it is a much-loved object and he asks: 'What, you are allowed to carry knives in your country?'

At that moment four or five people walk past us with automatic weapons slung over their shoulders. Our eyes meet. 'The situation is a little different there,' I say.

He passes me my knife back and says he hopes I'm not a terrorist and like the shadow on a speeding train, the briefest of smiles flashes across his face.

The train is soon before me, compact and ugly in a snub-nosed sort of way, but clean and quick. Inside, children shout, a few young people wear battle fatigues, and lots of weapons are piled against the moulded plastic and strips of hard-wearing, unremarkable textile of the train seats. We hum efficiently past miles of pebbly beaches and white-capped, jade-blue sea. At some point the train halts, and we're ordered out of the carriage while it's rigorously searched for bombs. Then we're back on and zipping along the coast.

I sit gazing out the window and thinking about Yigal Cohen and his Palestinian heart. I wonder if the heart has brought anything with it, changed him in any way. Years before, the chat show host Jay Leno had quipped: 'An Israeli man's life was saved when he was given a Palestinian man's heart in a heart transplant operation. The guy is doing fine, but the bad news is, he can't stop throwing rocks at himself.' Funny of course, but symptomatic of some Americans' emotional distance from a conflict in which their country plays such a significant part.

Politics aside, there are many people who claim it's possible for a heart to carry memory – that a new heart not only brings improved circulation, but also the donor's character traits and lived experiences. Most doctors dismiss any kind of cellular memory as fantasist, but I've read dozens of cases in which people have reported taking on characteristics peculiar to their donors, characteristics that they could have known nothing of until later confirmed. An enthusiastic meat eater became a vegetarian; an academic had vivid dreams of the violent death of his donor; a tough 57-year-old foundry worker in the US became obsessed with classical music after receiving a heart from a young African American killed in a gangland shooting – there was no way he could have known the boy was a classical violinist who had been caught in the gunfire.

I asked Sir Magdi Yacoub about organ memory and he said it was absolute rubbish; but another important heart surgeon, Susan Vosloo in South Africa, said she wasn't so sure. She told me the story of a shy young girl she'd known for years who, post-transplant, inherited (she suspected) the characteristics of the fashion model whose heart she'd been given. Susan's husband, an anaesthetist, overhearing her acknowledgment of the possibility of heart memory, commentated: 'But Susan, you read the horoscopes.'

The scientific explanation of the many, often astonishing, character changes recorded by some recipients of transplanted hearts is that they're the psychotropic side effects of potent immunosuppressant drugs. A more numinous point of view was summed up by the late psychologist Professor Paul Pearsall who wrote in *The Heart's Code*:

> As one who has become emotionally close to hundreds of transplant patients and their donors' families, who has held a beating heart in his hand and felt its amazing spiritual essence, and who has not only read about but observed and taken part in experiments on invisible subtle energy, I have little doubt that the heart is the major energy centre of my body and a conveyor of a code that represents my soul.*

Anyone who starts talking about souls tends to get nudged off the serious contender list when it comes to science but

---

* Paul Pearsall, *The Heart's Code* (1998).

accepting organ memory does not require full immersion into a world of faith. In the nineteenth century the German neurologist Leopold Auerbach discovered that a complex network of brain-like nerve cells exists in various parts of the body, giving rise to the possibility that there could be a brain-like functioning in other areas of the body. More recently, Richard Davidson, a neuroscientist from the University of Wisconsin researching the recordable effects of compassion meditation, attached sensors to the head of the senior lama of a Tibetan monastery. The other monks burst into laughter and Davidson presumed that this was because the venerable lama looked funny with the electrodes attached to his head. But it turned out that the monks were laughing because Davidson was trying to study the effects of meditation by attaching the electrodes to the lama's brain rather than his heart.

More recently, Davidson has discovered that the monks may have been closer to the truth than he supposed: studies have shown that the heart rates of experienced meditators change more markedly than those of novices. In an entirely separate study, psychologist Barbara Fredrickson at the University of North Carolina discovered that the vagus nerve, which extends from deep within the brain stem down to the heart and regulates emotions and bodily systems, is more evidently stimulated by those experienced at meditation than novices. I don't know whether organ memory exists, but as I head up the coast of Israel in a train, I hope that Cohen has been touched by the Palestinian heart beating in his chest.

A short time later my finger is on the buzzer of the Cohen family's home. A lively woman with bountiful black curling hair, a thin smile and wide-apart eyes shows me in. Yigal is seated on a low sofa, and he rises with effort. He's still recognizable from the decade-old pictures in the newspaper: a big man with a strong jaw, large in frame, but the power and bulk have fallen away. His brown, almost amber eyes are widely spaced, like his wife's, but sunk deep into his head. He wears jeans and a crew-necked sweater, clothes that may once have been the right size but now are baggy. He smiles in welcome, but it's clear he's not well: there's a greyness to him, a suffering inscribed in the lines on his face.

A hospitable array of snacks is put before Yigal and me. Olives and hummus and crunchy things that make too much noise as I eat them. We settle down and talk about his life and the years leading up to the transplant. I suspect that the only reason he's doing this interview is because Lavie asked him to, but he's still helpful. Dry, precise, and uncompromising. A real *sabra*.

I listen to his story, his early life, his parents, the progress of his disease. He tells me about the media circus after the transplant: newspapers, TV broadcasters and radio journalists jostling for interviews. He confirms what Lavie had said about the transplant, sentences that affected me so much: *deep inside we are the same.* He speaks about gratitude and the moment the donor Al-Joulani's father, Lotfi, put his ear to Cohen's chest so he could hear his son's heart. I ask him if he feels any different now, having a Palestinian heart – if there have been any unexpected changes of character. He looks at me as if I've just asked him if he believes in leprechauns and shakes his head. I tell him about some of the instances of organ memory I've encountered, and he says that anyone who believes that emotions or experiences are contained in a heart needs their brain transplanted.

I stay a couple of hours, longer than I should, having seen Cohen clench his fists now and then as if squeezing away waves of pain. When it feels like the interview is over, he sits back and asks me which paper I'm writing for. I reiterate that I'm not a journalist and I'm hoping to write a book. He understands this but someone must be paying for it?

'Not yet,' I tell him.

'So it's like a hobby,' he suggests.

I feel uncomfortable with this, perhaps because it's too close to the reality. I shake my head and say hopefully someone will publish it.

'When?'

'In a few years …?'

'Who is actually paying you, and the expenses?'

'No one … me.'

Now I feel like a fool. Okay, maybe it is a little like a hobby.

He relaxes into his chair, as if realizing that all the careful efforts he's learned to make when speaking with a proper writer are unnecessary.

I start to get up when his voice stops me. He tells me that Israeli Jews have an obligation to get along with the Arabs, those who remained in the country after 1948, but that all the others in the West Bank and Gaza, 'They just want to kill us.'

I'm astounded. I wonder if I've heard correctly.

'You don't believe that, do you?' I ask. 'I mean, if they all wanted to kill you, why did a Palestinian family give you a heart?'

'Maybe they wouldn't have known it was going to a Jew.'

I tell him it is not what I had heard, and he shrugs.

'And all those interviews you gave?' I ask. 'The photos with the father?'

Sure, he was grateful, he tells me, sincerely grateful, and he did his best to play along with the media circus, to do what he could to help, but it doesn't change anything. He sees my expression and tries to explain further.

'It doesn't mean anything. It's a pump,' he tells me. 'Not even a month later, one of the donor's cousins, another Al-Joulani, he was shooting at Jews.'

I wander out of Cohen's house, dazed, and I get back on the train. It was all going so well: the gratitude, the grace, the peace, the heart ... And then just as I was leaving, this one shining beacon of hope was stamped on, like a walker jumping off a path to crush a butterfly. If I'd left a few minutes earlier, things would have been different. But now it feels like everything is fragmenting.

THIRTY-SEVEN

Nothing Comes from Nothing

It crosses my mind to omit the last few minutes I'd spent with Yigal Cohen, editing them out as if they didn't happen. The thought obsesses me, after my return to Tel Aviv, after my return to London, after my return to everyday life. When Cohen told me, *they just want to kill us*, I realized that the symbolism his heart transplant carried for me meant nothing to him.

I look into what Cohen told me about Mazan Al-Joulani's cousin killing Israelis a month after his transplant, and it turns out to be true. Ali Al-Joulani had been a house painter and a distant cousin of Mazan Al-Joulani. He worked for Israelis all his professional life, and one morning, out of the blue, he drove to a military centre in Tel Aviv and shot at soldiers with an automatic weapon. Ali had no military training and didn't know how to use the weapon, so fortunately, he didn't kill or seriously injure anyone. Unfortunately, he was soon shot in the head by an Israeli with professionally lethal training.

Ali Al-Joulani it seems, acted independently, with no connection to Hamas, Fatah, or any other armed organization. His family were dumbfounded. Most Palestinians have surprisingly little social contact with Israelis – or none at all – but Ali was a man with close daily interaction, and indeed very good relations with the Jewish people he knew. His Israeli boss had even wanted to come and console the family as soon as he had heard about the shooting. The violence felt like it had come out of nowhere.

But of course, when King Lear tells his daughter 'nothing will come of nothing', he couldn't have been more wrong – his daughter's silence was not nothing and his reaction unleashed bloody chaos in his lands. Nor did Ali Al-Joulani's bloody madness come from nothing. The Israelis had built a massive checkpoint right where Ali had been brought up, and every day crowds of Palestinians on foot and a three-hour tail of cars waited to pass through the checkpoint, to be interrogated by young conscripts with mirrored sunglasses and automatic weapons. Perhaps it was this that drove Ali to violent despair? Perhaps not. Nevertheless, like Saïd Hotari, Ali's transformation into terrorist or *shaheed* was a shock to his family. As his brother put it: 'If I had seen him with a gun I wouldn't have believed it.'

Yigal Cohen wasn't in any way malicious when he said he believed that Palestinians wanted to kill the Jews; nor is he alone. It's a widely held sentiment in Israel, especially after the Dolphinarium bomb, and not unsupported in Hamas's original mission statement. But I'd hoped for something else. I expected some kind of confirmation that the heart transplant signified a hidden grace, some potential, something greater. I wanted reality to hum with the power of the symbol I saw. I thought it would heal everything but what is left … the truth is simple, it has symbolic meaning for me but for Cohen it is just pumping oxygenated blood though his body.

THIRTY-EIGHT

Heart Failure

I'm sitting at my mother's kitchen table. The fridge is different and the only heart in sight is a cut-out paper one stuck on the door by one of her seven grandchildren. Otherwise everything is the same.

The core of my entire story has turned out to be little more than a projection of my imagination, no more permanent than a picture drawn with a Shabbos pen in disappearing ink. The transplanted heart had given life to my mission, but it feels like the heart has failed. I'm left without grace, or much hope. If I can't find salvation through Mazan, or Cohen, or Dr Lavie, or through the gift of a beating heart, where can I look?

My mother suggests I get in contact with my cousin Judy. She has become the family expert on genealogy and sends me records and photographs and documents from a synagogue with the information that my mother's estranged father, my grandfather, was, without question, Jewish. His parents were born in England and he was born in South Africa. A South African Jew.

This 'new' part of my ancestry makes me smile. On a word-less level, it makes sense to me. It is a connection with a people I have always been drawn to, a people, in fact, I love. But really, how Jewish am I? A bit, not at all? At what point do I – does anyone – become really Jewish? For thousands of years the answer was, *when they have a Jewish mother.* Other than genes and a half-hearted attempt to make contact with her on her twenty-first birthday, my mother's father had very little to do with her. She knew nothing of that side of her family. During World War Two my mother was sent away from London to a boys' boarding school whilst so many of her unknown relatives might have been sent to the camps.*

If there is a Jewish genome then it would be in me. If this is true, I have Jewish blood. If Jewish tradition is fact, then neither myself nor my mother is Jewish. But then, in 1970, the Israeli government officially amended Jewishness to include anyone with a Jewish spouse, Jewish father, or any Jewish grandparent. There is a terrible resonance in this, because by so doing they followed the blueprint for racial identity used by the Nazis. During the Third Reich, they changed the defi-nition of who was Jewish to account for anyone with traceable Jewish ancestry to three or in some circumstances two of their grandparents; and after the Holocaust, many such Germans and Poles, stripped of their national citizenship, defaulted to this identity that in some cases had been forced upon them, and fled to Israel. The majority of the teenagers waiting outside

---

* My father, being an Irishman, was not obliged to enlist – nevertheless, he volunteered and fought for the US Air Force (despite having no connections with the USA) and was awarded the Legion of Merit. I remember asking him as the first Gulf War broke out why he signed up. 'It is not like this now,' he told me. 'It was right against wrong.'

the Dolphinarium that terrible evening in 2001 were just such immigrants. They arrived following the break-up of the Soviet Union, on the back of an Israeli government drive to encourage immigration, which involved free air tickets and in some cases, a cash incentive. Some of the parents of those individuals waiting outside the nightclub passed their entire lives not knowing they were Jewish, or – like me now – could be defined as Jewish enough to immigrate to the State of Israel.

I tell my mother everything – about the sons and daughters, the bombs and memorials, the hats and cups of coffee, the guns and checkpoints, the parades and marketplaces. The prejudice, the hospitals and the hearts. When I pause for a breath, she steps away from the table, and when she comes back, she's holding an old newspaper. There's a photograph of a young and attractive woman on the steps outside a hospital in London. The woman holds a child of about eighteen months. The date is 3 May 1968 and the article is titled 'Britain's First Heart Transplant'.

'What's wrong with the baby?' I ask, pointing to the plump and far-from-bonny boy.

'Nothing much. He's greedy and doesn't know how to say no to food.'

'Why is he in hospital, then?' I ask.

'He's not in hospital,' she says. 'He's mine.'

I look closer.

'He's you,' she says.

The caption describes the woman in the picture as Dr Jane Somerville, the cardiologist responsible for the transplant. My mother tells me about the operation and the circumstances around it. It was a failure, the patient died, but then, heart transplantation was wildly new. She explains that it was five months to the day since the first successful heart transplant in the world had been performed.

THIRTY-NINE

The Politics of a Heart

Maybe I need to go back there, another five months and several thousand miles south to the place where a part of my own history began. There I will find an intelligent, handsome young man with piercing blue eyes and an unusually acute brain. A man with an ambition to make his name on the world stage. He was a maverick who grew up so poor he had to walk barefoot to school across the semi-desert of his homeland. He was born into a religious tradition that saw itself as a Chosen People on a land given to them by God. It's likely that his name is known to you, because in 1967, his achievement of a heart transplant changed the definition of life and death, as well as the very idea of what science could do for humanity. This man was Christiaan Barnard, and the place South Africa.

From one side of the earth to the other, cardiologists like my parents were looking for ways to curtail the ravages of heart disease, and a select few believed the way forward for the most hopeless cases lay in transplantation. Leading the race to carry out the first successful heart transplant were Norman Shumway at Stanford, Richard Lower in Richmond, Virginia, and Adrian Kantrowitz in New York.* The US was the clear front runner, but Vladimir Demikhov in Moscow had written the first monograph on transplantation and had successfully transplanted dog hearts before anyone else. By 1967, any of these surgeons were capable of carrying out a human heart transplant. Certainly, the least likely of all to win the race was the young Afrikaans surgeon Barnard, who was working in a hospital at the tip of the continent in a country more famous for its institutionalized racism than any medical or scientific advances. The son of an impoverished white preacher, Barnard and his brother Marius grew up as social outcasts because of their connections to the 'coloured' community of the Karoo.

Barnard himself had to contend with a degree of prejudice: his rakish good looks, self-confidence and brash Afrikaans accent didn't make him popular with his peers when he was visiting and training in the US. In 1962 Barnard was offered a prestigious appointment in America, but he gave it up, and with it, ceded his position in the race for the first heart transplant to Shumway and Lower. But when visiting the US later in the sixties, Barnard happened to pass by the laboratory where Richard Lower was about to transplant a dog's heart. Lower invited him to watch the operation and Barnard was amazed by the elegant simplicity of the technique. He was transfixed by the possibilities the operation opened up and determined to replicate it himself. He found out all he could about Lower's method as well as Shumway's latest research, and returned to Cape Town with a renewed sense of mission.

---

* I have spent considerable time in South Africa interviewing and researching the first heart transplant but some of the information is gleaned from Don McRae's excellent book *Every Second Counts*.

Soon, with the assistance of a team of doctors and his gifted lab assistant Hamilton Naki, he replicated and then mastered Lower's operation.

In contrast to the secrecy and intrigue behind the Cold War battles to dominate sport and space travel, the main figures of cardiac transplantation shared their research and techniques with selfless generosity. Shumway and Lower not only allowed Barnard to know all the details of their techniques and discoveries, but they donated an expensive heart bypass machine to his hospital to help him advance. And Demikov in Moscow was such a guiding force that Barnard called him 'my teacher'. When Barnard reviewed the information he'd received from the Americans, he couldn't believe that Norman Shumway and Richard Lower had made as much progress as they had but hadn't already tried the transplant on a human patient.

The reason was fundamental: both Lower and Shumway were cautious and careful scientists. It was one thing to risk the lives of dogs but they weren't going to let the desire for victory compromise the quality of their work or the life of a patient. There was another factor as well. It related to the definition of death. Life had up to this moment been defined by the beating of the heart. Yet, a heart transplant required a donor with a *still-beating heart*. Thus, if anyone were to remove a still-beating heart for the purposes of a transplant, he would, by definition, be committing murder.

But Barnard had no such qualms. Yes, throughout most of the world, death was defined by the cessation of a heartbeat. And yes, certain ambitious district attorneys in the US had made it known to the surgeons that they'd raise the issue of unlawful death if a heart transplant went ahead, but in South Africa, the legal definition of death was entirely in the hands of the physician who signed the death certificate. And the issue of public opinion wasn't a factor since the rulers of the country weren't remotely interested in any of the opinions of the majority of their public. Barnard had legal leeway, a viable technique and the confidence that he could succeed: all he needed was a potential recipient who was going to die without a transplant and a donor who was, in every practical if not broadly accepted sense, dead. Barnard lacked only a patient and a heart.

Around the world, cardiologists were in a dead heat. Shumway, however, wasn't simply concerned with the ethical and legal technicalities; he was concerned about the psychological impact of a heart transplant on the public. The heart was so closely identified with the self, he realized, that people needed to be prepared for the process of putting one person's heart in the body of another. Accordingly, in November 1967 he issued a press release to the *Journal of the American Medical Association* and told an auditorium full of cardiologists that he was ready to transplant a human heart. Adrian Kantrowitz in New York was right behind him. He gained consent from the parents of an infant with fatal congenital heart disease to proceed with an experimental transplant, and all he needed was a suitable donor.

A few days after the press release, Barnard, too, found himself a patient: 53-year-old Louis Washkansky, a wrestling coach with a failing heart. Washkansky, a Jewish-Lithuanian immigrant, was a courageous and resolute man who'd agreed to the transplant whatever the risks. He was someone with just the sort of toughness that might pull a patient through such a procedure.

And then Barnard got a call from a doctor friend who'd admitted a young man with a severe and lethal head injury. The dying patient not only had a healthy heart and no other signs of disease, but he was the same blood group as Washkansky. It was *manna uit die hemel*, as they say in Afrikaans, a gift from heaven, and Barnard seized his opportunity. The young man's family was persuaded to allow the heart donation, and Washkansky was scrubbed, sedated and prepped for the operation. News came in from the US that Adrian Kantrowitz had already attempted and failed to transplant the heart of an encephalitic baby (born without a brain) into an infant patient. Barnard was determined not to fail.

It was 22 November 1967. Everything was set for this little-known heart surgeon thousands of miles away in South Africa to perform the world's first heart transplant. But before he could continue, he had to get permission from the hospital authorities, and there he hit a wall. Not because of the definition of death, or the experimental nature of the operation, or the high risks involved, or even the question of obtaining consent from the prospective donor. The obstruction was unique to this apartheid regime. Washkansky was 'white', and the prospective donor, the young man with the traumatic brain injury, was defined as 'coloured'.

Barnard had written to Val Schrire, the highly respected head of cardiology at the Groote Schuur Hospital, explaining that he intended to 'take a Bantu [a word the apartheid whites used for black Africans] with heart disease, because it's a disease common to them with no known cure'. Barnard's language *take a Bantu* and *it's a disease common to them*, and the implication of experimentation, is shocking today. But the fact is, Barnard didn't care what colour or race the person he operated on might be; he simply wanted to carry out the operation. But Val Schrire did care, and he'd refused permission. The idea of using 'a Bantu' – one step up from the dogs they'd been practising on in the laboratory – did not sit well with him. Also, he feared it would look to the rest of the world as if they were harvesting not only labour and riches from the Bantus, but organs too.* Dr Schrire said he'd give permission for the

* This is my inference rather than Val Schrire's stated view at the time.

operation on the condition that the transplant was white to white; and Barnard had no choice but to accept.

Washkansky had been shaved, scrubbed and prepped for the operation. Barnard had the perfect donor, brain-dead but with a healthy, beating heart. He'd hoped that, given the unique circumstances, permission from the hospital would be a formality but the operation was cancelled. If a heart transplant were to happen in apartheid South Africa, it would have to be 'white to white'.

By 1967 apartheid was being imposed on the population of South Africa with all its ideological seriousness.* Racial segregation was written into the law so non-white races were zoned into specific living areas and couldn't use the same public transport, beaches, libraries or education facilities as the ruling elite. They couldn't sit on the same park benches. Marriage and sexual relations between any race and whites had been made illegal, and even blood transfusions were not permitted between the darker races and their pale rulers. The law of apartheid was not so much a new ideology as a codification of the segregation that had already existed for decades within South African society. The laws were set up to ensure that those defined as 'white' or 'European' (less than 20 per cent of the population) would have total political and economic control over the non-white majorities.

Of course, to enshrine racism into law requires an objectively provable difference between these races. The operation that Barnard wished to do, would, if successful, undermine the

---

* I am very grateful to Andre du Toit, Professor of Political Science at Cape Town University for his wisdom and the time he gave in educating me about the apartheid government. Although he is not responsible for any errors I may make, if any of the points about this period are particularly erudite one can assume they come from him and other academics listed in the acknowledgments.

basis of racial difference on which apartheid was built. If an organ was shown to be interchangeable between a black and a white person, the notion of an essential difference between the two would be corroded, especially if the organ was a heart; not only biologically central to life, but symbolically at the centre of human identity.

Barnard himself didn't believe in God nor any biological difference between races, and he didn't care what colour or race the person he operated on might be. He simply wanted to advance medicine and himself. He was frustrated by the permission being denied for his transplant. One of the theatre nurses, Dede Freedman, told me that, half a century later, she still remembered him sitting on the floor of the changing rooms in his underpants that night, his head in his hands, despairing at the lost opportunity. Washkansky was sent back to his ward, and after a few words of encouragement from Dede, Barnard went home. The next day, he resumed the search for a donor.

The problem for Barnard was that as each day passed, Washkansky became weaker. Cardiologists at the hospital were amazed that he was alive at all; but he was a stocky man with a strong desire to live and an indomitable sense of humour.

Opportunity came with misfortune. A week after the aborted inter-racial transplant, Denise Darvall, a 25-year-old bank clerk on her way home from work, decided to pull over and buy a caramel cake for tea from the Wrensch Town Bakery in Salt River, just outside Cape Town. It was a sudden impulse, and one that was to end her life. As she crossed the main road with her mother, they were struck by a car driven by a drunken off-duty policeman. Denise's mother was killed outright, and Denise was rushed by ambulance to the hospital with a badly fractured skull.

That evening, in a room in the Groote Schuur hospital, a floor away from where Washkansky lay fighting for each breath,

Ed Darvall was given the news that he'd lost not only his wife but any hope for his daughter's survival. A member of Barnard's transplant team arrived shortly afterwards and told him about the groundbreaking operation they were longing to try. The doctor explained that a brain injury like the one Denise had received was not only a form of death, but was rare – rarer still, Denise was the same blood group as a man named Washkansky who would be dead within a matter of days unless they attempted this radical new operation. Would Darvall consider authorizing the donation of his daughter's heart? Ed Darvall's salient memory of his daughter was of a beautiful, loving girl whose first impulse was to help others. So he, a man who'd lost his wife and daughter in one terrible afternoon, agreed to the donation with the words: 'You must try to save this man.'

Christiaan Barnard now had a white heart for his white patient. In the early hours of 3 December 1967, Barnard opened the chest of Leo Washkansky while Barnard's brother Marius switched off the respirator that was keeping Denise Darvall breathing. Up to this point in history, the continuation of life had been defined by the beating of the heart; without oxygen, Denise's heart would eventually stop beating. But it was Marius who likely made the courageous, if contentious, decision to stop her heart himself and end her life. He, it is claimed, administered an injection of potassium chloride – an act that was kept secret for four decades. By stopping her heart, Marius allowed Christiaan to remove the organ from Denise's body and rush it into another operating room. Thirty steps later, Barnard sutured Denise's heart into the body of Leo Washkansky.

At 6:13 am on a warm Sunday morning in December in Cape Town, the heart of Denise Darvall began beating in the body of Leo Washkansky. Christiaan Barnard had performed the world's first successful heart transplant in Cape Town, South Africa.

The operation affected the society of 1967 in a way that couldn't have been predicted. The media response was unprecedented: within days, the hospital was mobbed by the world's press. Barnard was flown to America to appear on a special edition of a TV show with an audience of twenty million viewers. He lunched with President Johnson in Washington and appeared on the covers of *Time*, *Newsweek*, and *Life* magazines. His heart transplant became the lead story throughout the world and arguably the single biggest story in medical history. He was fêted and photographed, interviewed and adulated, and with his chiselled good looks and unshakable self-confidence, he became, for a moment, the most famous man in the world.

Half a century later most people know that Christiaan Barnard was the man who performed the world's first heart transplant. His operation gave people a sense that modern medicine could accomplish anything. It also altered the way people thought about their lives, affecting their imaginations and aspirations. Just as the first pictures of Earth from the *Lunar Orbit I* space vessel made people reconsider their very identity, the exchangeability of a human heart changed what people thought of when they thought of 'I'.

Barnard seized an opportunity to propel himself and South Africa into scientific history, but in doing so, he provided the 'feel good' news story that the apartheid government desperately needed. Soon after hearing news of the transplant, South African Prime Minister John Vorster issued a memo, saying: 'We must take every opportunity for the international prestige this breakthrough gives us [...] We can link a moment of medical history to a positive image of the country after all the propaganda directed against us around the world.'*

---

* Donald McRae, *Every Second Counts: The Race to Transplant the First Human Heart* (2006), p. 199.

Barnard himself did nothing to counteract the positive press his oppressive government was receiving, nor did he ever use his fame to combat racial injustice. He even told a group of international reporters that the apartheid rulers were not the villains they were made out to be, pointing out his own hospital's equitable treatment of black and coloured patients. This was true. Barnard had insisted that his intensive care unit be unsegregated. However, segregation was a fact in the rest of the hospital and indeed the country. Non-whites had lower status, lower pay and fewer rights.

The ruling elite made as much as they could out of the fact that this scientific breakthrough came from within their country, their ideology. The reality was, though, that this medical breakthrough was less about ideology and more about an ambitious and talented individual making use of decades of work from doctors and surgeons in different corners of the world. Barnard was remiss in failing to acknowledge the fact that so much of the work that made his transplant possible had been done by others – in particular Richard Lower and Norman Shumway, who had been so generous with him and his laboratory assistant Hamilton Naki. Today it's known that heart transplants are best done male-to-male or female-to-female. That the heart in South Africa was moved from a woman to a man, and from a Christian to a Jew, raised some eyebrows, but crossing the frontiers of gender and religion was not a transgression in the way that crossing a racial frontier would have been. That's not to say that gender and religion weren't important social markers in apartheid society, but transgressing them wasn't a threat to the economic and political status quo.

Amidst the storm of adulation and publicity still raging a month later, an opportunity arrived for Barnard to perform a second transplant. The new patient was a dentist called Phil

Bleiberg. The putative donor was a garment worker named Clive Haupt who'd collapsed and suffered a lethal stroke whilst playing touch rugby. He had been a young, fit, otherwise healthy man with an excellent heart and the same blood group as Bleiberg. The problem was again one of racial difference, Haupt was *coloured* and Bleiberg was *white*.

This time Barnard didn't bother to ask permission from the authorities. When a government minister ordered him not to proceed, Barnard silenced him.

'*Moenie met my twis nie,*' he said. Don't argue with me.

Barnard was no longer a cog in the machine of an important national hospital; he was a global celebrity. Only a few days before, the Pope himself had met Barnard and said: 'I bless your achievement and I invite you to proceed along the same road, doing good as you have up to now.' Barnard gambled that his celebrity would protect him from apartheid authorities, and he was right. The second transplant was televised, seized by the world's press, and another great success.

Barnard and his team had learned a great deal from Washkansky's case. Haupt's heart was a better fit in every way, and Bleiberg recovered well and was photographed on the beach within a few days. In truth, it was a deceptive photo call as he was carried there on a litter, and then carried back to bed where he remained for weeks after. But Bleiberg did return home eventually, announcing to the world's press that he'd made love to his wife for the first time in many years.

After the triumph of Barnard's second transplant, the implications of a *coloured* person's heart being interchangeable with a *white*'s was, at the very least, an embarrassment to the apartheid government. Ray Hoffenberg, the neurologist who'd helped Barnard by pronouncing Clive Haupt 'dead', was a courageous opponent of apartheid government. He was 'banned' the following morning under the Suppression of Communism Act. Banning prevented him from practising medicine and was like an extreme house arrest. His banning was in reality more to do with his active political opposition to apartheid than the interracial transplant, but the timing was pointed. Barnard, a close colleague, did nothing to help him.*

But the cat was out of the bag, and there was no way to coax it back in. Barnard's first transplant, between a slight young Anglican white woman and a thickly built middle-aged Lithuanian Jewish man, didn't challenge the racial constructs on which apartheid was built. But when retired dentist Phil Bleiberg was walking around with a *coloured* heart, it was absolute proof that whatever surface differences there were between races, on a physical and biological level, there was an exchangeability of organs, a physiological parity of the most symbolically potent object in the body. This was the very opposite of apartheid's *apartness*. Indeed, as one scholar put it, transplanting the heart involves 'the highest level of interpersonal intercorporeal transfer that it is possible in the physical dimension'.[†]

The Guardian in the UK asked: 'If a white man can use a coloured man's heart after death, can he sit on the same park bench as him when both are living?'[‡] A South African diplomat in London went as far as issuing a statement that the transplant did not alter Bleiberg's status as a white man under South African law. And the American magazine *Ebony* summed it up, saying:

> For the first time, Clive Haupt's heart will ride in the uncrowded train carriages marked For Whites Only... It will enter fine

---

* Sir Raymond Hoffenberg became head of the Royal College of Physicians in London.
† William R. LaFleur, 'From Agape to Organs: Religious Difference between Japan and America in Judging the Ethics of the Transplant', *Journal of Religion and Science*, vol. 37, September 2002.
‡ *The Guardian*, 2 January 1986.

restaurants, attend theatres and concerts and live in a decent home ... Haupt's heart will literally go to hundreds of places where Haupt himself could not go because his skin was a little darker than that of Bleiberg.

Not quite thirty-five years later in Tel Aviv, Yakov Lavie would put the heart of a Palestinian Muslim into the body of an Israeli Jew.

FORTY

Apart Hate

The key distinction between the South African heart donor and recipient was not race, it was the policy of apartheid. To pronounce the word properly it must be divided into two words: *apart* and *hate*. The word is from the Afrikaans meaning 'separateness' or 'apartness'. It describes a policy of racial segregation involving political and economic discrimination against 'non-white' communities in South Africa. The practical aim of the policy was to ensure that control and wealth would remain in the hands of 'Europeans' who had emigrated to South Africa over the centuries and developed society for their own benefit – as well as for any other 'whites' who arrived in the decades since.

Prime Minister D.F. Malan announced the creation of the apartheid state of South Africa on 28 May 1948 – two weeks to the day after the state of Israel was declared. Both new states were recent manifestations of much older ideologies: both were built on lofty principles; both aimed to protect the interests of a 'race' of people. As Malan put it upon assuming office for the new apartheid state: 'Today South Africa belongs to us once more. South Africa is our own for the first time [...] and may God grant that it will always remain our own.'

This ruling Afrikaans class descended from Dutch immigrants of the sixteenth century. They had their own branch of Calvinist Christianity, the Dutch Reformed Church, and they produced a revised version of the Bible, which supported an idea that the Afrikaans were a people who made God's wishes manifest. As part of a nationalist movement in the nineteenth century some Afrikaners retold their history as a domination over other races in fulfilment of biblical prophesy. Their land became a divinely promised land. Scriptures were interpreted to make their way of life not just a political reality but a divinely inspired order. It didn't matter that Afrikaans people had no historical connection with the Middle East of the Bible; they appropriated the stories of exile and God's chosen people for their own nationalizing purposes.

It should be noted that by no means all Afrikaners believed that the land was given to them by God. Indeed, a contemporary joke went along the lines of, 'If they think they are God's chosen people, fine. Let's see them parting the Vaal river.' Nevertheless, the Bible was used by some as a sacred justification whilst others sought refuge in the logic of modern 'science' to support their dominion over other races. Writers like Gustav Preller, an Afrikaner historian, wrote that the sovereignty of their race was not merely God's plan but also manifest in scientific reality:

> The Boers [Afrikaners] have always been unique among the European peoples that have come into contact with the natives in different parts of Africa. Today science brings us proofs that the cerebral capacities of what we conveniently call the 'native',

are, when he has reached the age of puberty, distinctly inferior in comparison with those of the white children of a civilization of 5000 years.

Apartheid rule was subject to constant revolt from those not included in the ruling elite – protests, strikes, acts of sabotage, violence – and it is worth looking squarely at the fact that all of these acts of resistance were dubbed 'terrorism' by the South African government. The US and many European governments also agreed that the ANC, including its leader Nelson Mandela, were 'terrorists'. We'd much rather remember the international censure eventually focused on apartheid that came from the left wing of the global political ambits – but this came only after decades of international support for the regime.*

The apartheid response to international criticism when it came was bullish: they refused to be the whipping boys for the world's problems. They complained that their critics didn't understand the African culture and didn't understand that *they* had been the ones to create a paradise out of the primitive desert they'd found on arrival. They argued that their black populations were much better off than the native populations in other African countries ruled by black Africans, and over the decades (up to its eventual collapse) they spent a fortune on public relations and marketing strategies to explain to the world that the regime was in fact decent, upstanding and guardians of the very values their critics held so dear.

---

* There was also an important and courageous force of resistance from within the white South African community.

FORTY-ONE

A Way Forward

I heard terrible things about 'the Jews' from some Palestinians in the West Bank and appalling things about 'the Arabs' from some Israelis. Apparently, 'the Jews' want everything for themselves and don't care about anyone who isn't Jewish. As for 'the Arabs', they don't even know what they want – other than to hurt Jews.

In apartheid South Africa blacks and whites to an extent knew each other. They worked together. Children (sometimes) played together, certainly many white children had black nannies who grew up with Zulu and Xhosa lullabies. It is a fact that the apartheid government had to pass laws to keep white and black races apart, to stop them loving and making love with each other. It is not the same in Israel and Palestine. The Pulitzer-winning journalist Richard Ben Cramer[*] recounts meeting a Palestinian man who told him that he grew up

---

[*] Richard Ben Cramer, *How Israel Lost: The Four Questions* (2004).

convinced 'the Jews' had horns and a tail. The man recounted how, when the Israeli occupying army arrived in his village in 1967, he knew they couldn't be Jewish because they had no tails.

The message of Israeli Prime Minister Benjamin Netanyahu towards the Palestinians is one rooted in fear: 'If the Arabs put down their weapons today, there would be no more violence. If the Jews put down their weapons today, there would be no more Israel." Fear engenders defence, and in the case of Israel, a powerful military. As Richard Ben Cramer puts it, for any military man, 'The cardinal ethic is fight to win – and never give up ground. For twenty years at least they have faced fear and inspired fear – it's what they know. Force has been their calling card.' Netanyahu is the only Israeli Prime Minister out of the previous six who has not been a general – he was a colonel. If Israel today is a democracy, it is a military one. It has become a military democracy for the Jewish people.

The Dolphinarium bomb in 2001 played right into the hands of the militaristic right wing of Israel. Not only did it silence the once-powerful voices of the liberals, but it converted a number of former peace advocates into right-wing militants. It also cleared the way for the Separation Wall that cages the residents of the West Bank – and those in favour of it argue, brought to an end the devastating series of suicide bombings that preceded its construction.[††]. In many ways the bomb was a

---

* Speech at the Knesset at the end of 2006.

† *How Israel Lost.*

‡ It is argued that the wall brought to an end the devastating series of suicide bombings that preceded its construction – I would dispute this. In January 2006, Shin Bet's annual statistics showed a considerable drop in 'terror attacks' from 2005. The main reason for the sharp decline, Shin Bet said, was 'the [Hamas-called] truce in the [occupied] territories'. *Haaretz* (2/1/06) commented that 'the security fence is no longer mentioned as the major factor in preventing suicide bombings, mainly because the terrorists have found ways to bypass it'. The 'main

resonant validation for Netanyahu, who was then an aspiring politician. It seemed to validate his doomsday warnings against relaxing occupation or seeking any equitable solution for Palestinians.

I would go as far as saying that the Dolphinarium bomb marked the beginning of the end of liberal democracy in Israel. Of course there are notable exceptions. In 2003 a group of Israeli pilots signed a letter criticizing the occupation and refusing to fly missions that targeted Palestinian towns and cities. A decade later a former head of the Shin Bet made a comparison between the occupation in the West Bank and Nazi treatment of Poles in World War Two. Another former chief of Shin Bet, Cami Gila, put it plainly and bravely: 'We are making the lives of millions unbearable." A courageous and effective organization called Breaking the Silence gives Israeli soldiers an anonymous platform to report human rights abuses. Nevertheless, Netanyahu's government shifts further and further to the right with attacks on Israeli human rights organizations and their supporters including brutal arrests and beatings by soldiers and police. This is a world Palestinians have known for decades but such violations are now routinely carried out on Israelis opposing the Status Quo.[†]

Before I left the West Bank for the last time I spoke to a Palestinian called Bashir. He told me how he had spent seven years in an Israeli jail for (unsuccessfully) throwing a grenade at a jeep full of Israeli soldiers. He was incarcerated through his teenage years into his early twenties. During his last years in

---

reason for the reduction in terrorist acts', the report emphasized, was the Hamas truce, and the organization's 'focus on the political arena'.

* These interviews were in Dror Moreh's 2012 Oscar-nominated documentary *The Gatekeepers* – an extraordinary, brave and powerful film.

† 'Disturbing the Peace: The Use of Criminal Law to Limit the Actions of Human Rights Defenders in Israel and the Occupied Territories', Hrdata.org.il, 2016.

prison, an Israeli guard his own age offered him a sip of Coke and from this seed of kindness a profound friendship grew between the two young men. Bashir had never properly met an Israeli before this. He had never before considered the possibility of humanity amongst his oppressors. Meeting this individual, he told me, meant he could no longer deny this shared humanity.

When released, Bashir was given a hero's welcome is his home town, but there was disappointment when he announced that he no longer believed in fighting. Armed struggle is justified, he told me, but in this context, it is more an expression of rage than strategic gain. 'How is it possible to live in a land that you have died for?' he asked. Violence in this struggle would end in death 'and gain not one dirham of land'. He became committed and active in non-violent methods of advocacy. A year later after his release he had a daughter whom he loved more than anything. When she was nine, she was shot dead by the IDF. People flocked to his house to support him, sing *shaheed* songs and vent hatred against the Israelis. Those who mourned the loss of their fighting hero were certain that the death of his daughter would make him turn again to armed struggle. But he refused. He drove the people away from his house. This is my tragedy, he screamed at them.

I asked Bashir if it were possible see a way forward after this.

'Of course there is a way,' and what he said then awes me still today: 'We must understand their pain. The conflict will not end until we understand their pain, until we Palestinians go to Yad Vashem and know the reality of their history and the fear that drives them. And they too must understand what they have done to us and what they are doing today. And they must understand that we will never give up. Never.'

FORTY-TWO

The Quality of Mercy

I've known about Christiaan Barnard my entire life. He was my parents' colleague and a part of their professional and social circle. But I'm only beginning to understand the implications of his first heart transplants in apartheid South Africa half a century later.

The heart is a muscle. It is roughly the size of a fist. It weighs about a pound. But it is more than that. The transplant between Washkansky and Haupt is more than the story of scientific breakthrough. The transplant between Al-Joulani and Cohen is more than the story of surgical success. Something more remains, I tell myself. It is the symbol. As Jung put it, symbols are 'expressions of the intuitive perception which can as yet be neither apprehended nor expressed differently'.*

The heart is both the physical pump Cohen described and

---

* C.G. Jung, *Contributions to Analytical Psychology*, trans. H.G. & Cary F. Baynes (London 1928; reprinted 1942).

the symbol 'that says something about a person's innermost centre, depth and ultimate unity," as theologian Karl Rahner puts it. When people point at one another, they point at the chest with its heart, not to the head with its brain. The concept of *life* is not just physically but culturally connected to the organ of the heart. The heart has been and will always be a synecdoche of life.

Your heart is you.

Concepts like *identity* and *feeling* are no more than symbols themselves: no cardiac surgeon has ever observed love, no brain surgeon has seen thought. Heartbreak is a feeling most of us have had, Takotsubo cardiomyopathy is a rare cardiac condition where the heart actually breaks down from grief. The role of the cardiac muscle in your chest, which has beaten perhaps half a million times while your eyes have been on this book, is more than one thing simultaneously: both a life-sustaining pump *and* a symbol of feeling, of love, of inner identity, of divine life, and of life itself.

This is a just a story. A way to understand a complicated moral problem. It is symbolic, and also, it is real. It did really happen. But it is only one individual's glimpse into the lives and tragedies of others. I've always sought to describe what I've seen and heard but perhaps this book is no more than an articulation of my own need to find justice and seek something worth living for amidst all the suffering. To find that precious quality Thomas Aquinas called 'mercy'.

---

* 'The Sacred Heart' (2009): I am grateful to for the work of Liliana Leopardi, Professor of Art History, Chapman University, Orange, California for this scholarship.

Epilogue

As will be clear by now, I'm not a scientist, historian, sociol-
ogist or psychologist; I'm not an academic; I'm not even a
journalist. I'm no more than a person writing what he's seen,
heard, read and thinks.

I am hopeful that the inclusion of the apartheid narrative
will be fruitful rather than divisive but I know I'm dreaming.
It's too difficult. Many of my friends in Israel are horrified
by any juxtaposition of Israel and apartheid South Africa. So
offended, in fact, that I've too often veered away from such
comparisons because of the fury and pain they elicit. I could
say Israel today is not the same as apartheid South Africa in
the sixties, and I believe it, but I also believe that history rarely
provides exact analogues.

People can look at the same object and see something
different, or they see nothing at all. Simply put, I can point at
a plant and see a weed, another person will see a flower, and a
goat will see lunch.

Israel and the so-called Israeli lobby spends a considerable amount of money on political lobbying and the influencing of international public opinion. A policy commonly known as *hasbara** funds pressure groups and channels money to thousands of people who are – amongst other more positive attempts at explaining the Israeli government's point of view – paid to attack journalists and infiltrate social media discussions between groups of individuals.[†] Indeed, Tel Aviv and Haifa universities now offer programmes in *hasbara* supported by the Department of Propaganda (Hasbara) and the Foreign Ministry. They include tuition on debating, PR and editing Wikipedia.

One US ambassador, Chas Freeman, put it like this: 'The tactics of the Israeli lobby plumb the depths of dishonour and indecency and include character assassination, selective misquotation, the wilful distortion of the record, the fabrication of falsehoods and an utter disregard for the truth.'[‡] *Hasbara* is not restricted to politics; ask any professional journalist in Europe who writes about the Middle East and they will tell you that if they write an article critical of Israel's policy or actions, they are often systematically attacked by groups and individuals, some of whom are paid to do so.

The reasons I see parallels between Israel and apartheid South Africa are straightforward and personal: over my trips to Israel and the West Bank, I saw queues of Palestinians showing their differently coloured ID papers at the fixed checkpoints and I found it impossible *not* to think about the apartheid – in this case the pass laws used to control the populations of

---

* 'Explaining' in Hebrew.

† A fuller explanation of *hasbara* can be found in the excellent Israeli publication 972 http://972mag.com/against-hasbara-explaining-ourselves -to-death/107603/.

‡ Ambassador Charles W. Freeman Jr (USFS, retired): speech at Watson Institute for International and Public Affairs, Brown University, 4 February 2016, Providence, Rhode Island. Courtesy of John V. Whitbeck.

non-whites. Travelling between Israel and the West Bank, I couldn't help but think of the *Bantustans* created for the black South Africans – self-governing zones with drastically lower standards of health, education and employment than the 'white' territories, theoretically independent of the white government but always at the mercy of its security forces. This may not be merely a personal view. Massimo D'Alema, former prime minister of Italy, revealed at a dinner in Jerusalem that Ariel Sharon had told him that the *Bantustan* model was the most appropriate solution to the conflict with the Palestinians. A guest present suggested that he must be paraphrasing Sharon. 'No, sir,' D'Alema had said, 'That is not interpretation. That is a precise quotation of your prime minister.'*

During the apartheid era the US and British governments cosied up to the apartheid rulers, but they were not alone. Israel and South Africa were, to quote my esteemed friend Rian Malan, 'as thick as thieves'. In the 1970s Prime Minister Yitzhak Rabin of Israel welcomed South African leader John Vorster and praised 'the ideals shared by Israel and South Africa'. Alon Liel, the head of the Israeli foreign ministry's South Africa desk, put it more clearly in 2006: 'After 1976, there was a love affair between the security establishments of the two countries and their armies.'†

It has become taboo today to even draw parallels between Israel's treatment of the Palestinians and the apartheid treatment of their non-white populations – but perhaps it is in turning away from seeing any similarities that Israel has missed vital lessons from the demise of apartheid. Judging from the way Netanyahu's government continues to ramp up pressure

---

* The remarks of the former Italian PM were reported in *Haaretz*. This and the 'live' quotation came to me came to me via the excellent series of articles by Chris McGreal for *The Guardian*.
†Chris McGreal in *The Guardian*, 7 February 2016.

on the Palestinian people it would seem they believe there's no need to compromise so long as they have the unconditional support of the USA. The leaders of apartheid thought so too, at least whilst enjoying the cool breeze of the Cold War. Perhaps this is why they were (at least initially) quite nonchalant about efforts to enforce boycotts and disinvestment. Israel could not be said to be nonchalant about the threat of boycott and sanctions. They are hysterical. It has become illegal to support it. Imagine, a country, which has justly prided itself on exceptional levels of free speech, now making it illegal to speak out in favour of boycott. The loudest shouts of protest against the new laws came from within Israel itself. Outside of the borders the Israeli propaganda machine has worked hard to equate any support for sanctions against the country with outright anti-Semitism. What a shock for all those lefties, those campaigners against the original apartheid (some of whom are today behind the Israel boycott movements), what a shame for all those committed anti-racists (many of them Jewish) who are now being told that if they support economic and cultural sanctions against Israel they are ipso facto anti-Semitic.

History relates that it was not so much the ANC that forced the apartheid government to its knees as sanctions, divestment and the cultural isolation of global moral opprobrium. However, when the apartheid government glimpsed the world from this newly vulnerable knee-height perspective they at least realized the wisdom of making peace from whatever power they still clung onto. There is a lesson there. Crucially, the apartheid rulers understood that peace would be impossible unless they took the enormous risk of trusting their enemies. There is a lesson there, too. For both Palestinians and Israelis.*

In 1967 the transplant of a human heart across racial frontiers in apartheid South Africa underlined the falsehood of

---

* My thanks to Rian Malan for this, amongst many insights.

an ideology that claimed a biological division between two people. The transplant of Mazan Al-Joulani's heart into the body of Yitzak Cohen, a transplant between races, between enemies, to me at least, echoes this – and beats out the absurdity of any ideology that puts one people over or against another because of race or creed. Unless you believe the land is given to you by God, these supposed absolutes are proven to be constructed, decided and assumed, the definitions cultural rather than genetic – in other words, myth.

As for myths, they are not nothing. On such foundations all nations are built: amalgams of partly fabricated, mostly fabricated, or loosely based on other partly fabricated stories and texts. The celebration of Thanksgiving in the United States didn't happen the way it's told;* nevertheless the story is a rallying point for cooperation, giving thanks and the ideal of friendship across cultural lines. The chieftain Vercingetorix of Gaul was not in truth the originator of modern France, but he was used by leaders from Napoleon III to President Mitterrand to forge an idea of French identity.† King Canute and the waves, Robert the Bruce and his spider, St Patrick and the snakes ... As professor of religion Roald Kristiansen puts it, '[myths] create unity and a national identity ... a desire to create a future by looking back on past ideals'.‡

---

* The first Thanksgiving Day, as most Native Americans know so well, actually happened in 1637 to celebrate the safe return of a band of heavily armed volunteers who had returned from Mystic, Connecticut, where they slaughtered 700 Pequot Indians: men, women and children. The story was put together from different contemporary sources at the end of the nineteenth century.

† 'Our Ancestors the Gauls': Archaeology, Ethnic Nationalism, and the Manipulation of Celtic Identity in Modern Europe, Michael Dietler, *American Anthropologist*, New Series, vol. 96, no. 3 (September 1994), pp. 584–605.

‡ Roald E. Kristiansen, associate professor at the Department of History and Religious Studies at the University of Tromsø.

Going back to the comparison between Israel today and apartheid: my view is that it is valid to discuss it, but is it useful? The danger of making such comparison – and it is a toxic and terrible danger – is that it becomes a vehicle for easy moral outrage. It can encourage the idea that all the positive things Israel has constructed and achieved (and there are so many) require dismantling, and worst of all, it can lead one to the false belief that this struggle is one of good versus evil. It is not. It is a conflict between communities, who, as Rabbi Yeshayahu Leibowitz put it so nicely, 'in consequence of centuries of history […] feel passionately that this is their land'.* This is a conflict that outside powers exploit for their own interests; a conflict that will inevitably destroy both cultures unless people on both sides can see the reality of one another's suffering and right to live in peace.

Perhaps you feel reading this book and in particular because I raise the comparison with apartheid, that I am partisan. All I can say is, as Dante pointed out in his *Divina Commedia*, there's a special place just inside the gates of hell for those who *'non furon ribelli né fur fedeli'*, those who neither rebel nor are faithful, neither resist nor support. The issues between Israel and Palestine are not right versus wrong as each side would have us believe – but to say nothing? I'm guided by the words of that great Brazilian educator Paulo Freire, who told us so memorably that 'washing one's hands of the conflict between the powerful and the powerless means to side with the powerful, not to be neutral.'†

The fact is, if the State of Israel decides to define somebody as Jewish enough to 'make Aliyah', to immigrate to Israel, they can assume rights superior to any Palestinian

---

* Rabbi Yeshayahu Leibowitz, *Judaism, Human Values, and the Jewish State* (1995), p. 241.
†Paulo Freire, *The Politics of Education* (1985).

– even those Palestinians who were permitted to remain in the country since 1948. Thus someone from Vladivostok, Vienna, or Virginia Beach with a single Jewish grandparent, someone who might never before have had the slightest connection with Israel – someone like myself – has the legal right to turn up and assume benefits that Palestinians, even those with hundreds of years of history in the country, are denied. In my case, when I found out about my Jewish grandfather, I applied for citizenship – and guess what – all I have to do is present the relevant birth certificates and I'm in. All the rights can be mine … better rights than a Palestinian who's lived for generations in Jerusalem, much better than a Palestinian in the West Bank and immeasurably better than a Palestinian in a refugee camp – even if they still wear the key to their grandmother's house hanging around their neck.

Some people view any laws or actions that strengthen Israel as a place only for a Jewish majority as just – and they have reasons, amongst them: that God actually gave the land to the Jews, or that the British (who once held the mandate) gave Palestine to the Jewish people. Or there's the argument that the land was nothing, pretty much empty, until developed by the Jewish immigrants. The first two points are hard to deny: the British, because of the Balfour Declaration, and God, because no one has been able to reliably check with Him. On top of this, as Rabbi Leibowitz explains with his characteristic way of cutting to the quick: 'The idea that a specific country or location has an intrinsic "holiness" is an indubitably idolatrous idea.'* Not to mention the fact that despite the fact that Israeli identity cards define all Israeli Jews as followers of Judaism, about half are avowedly secular and don't believe for a moment that they're legitimized by any god. The third argument, that the land was empty and undeveloped, reminds

---

* *Judaism*, pp. 226–27.

me of the joke I heard about the Victorian explorer David Livingstone 'discovering' the Victoria Falls in 1855, and the thousands of Africans living next to the mile-wide waterfall being astonished because they just hadn't noticed it before.*

So many times when in Israel I asked people about the origin of an old home, gallery, or business, I was told that the 'Arab' owners had 'left'. As if they got swamped by a sort of nomadic ennui and no longer had interest or use for the property or land. Once, in an achingly beautiful house in Jaffa overlooking the Mediterranean, I was told smilingly of how the house had been found with toys left in a child's room, cupboards full of a family's possessions, even bread in the kitchen. The subtext is that the previous occupants left willingly – so what better to do than occupy the empty space. Questioning whether Palestinian families left their homes 'willingly' or were forced out misses the point. What everyone agrees on is that in 1948 they fled. Whether Plan Dalet (the Israeli military strategy for taking over the land then known as Palestine) was a tactic of deliberate ethnic cleansing, or the panicked evacuation by Palestinian families was an accidental by-product of violence, is still being debated by Israeli historians. What no one denies is that the Palestinians fled because they feared that they would be killed, injured or dishonoured. Surely it is obvious that the cupboards were full because they intended to return?

In the dark days of 1991 when Tel Aviv was in range of Saddam Hussein's Scud missiles, a great proportion of residents fled the city. Weren't they right to do this? A missile – perhaps with chemical agents – falling on your child's playground school, or on your house ... But imagine the outrage if on their return the Tel Avivites had found their homes occupied by Palestinian families enjoying the delicious, still-warm

* I first heard this (much better told) from British comedian Mark Lamarr in The Assembly Rooms in Edinburgh, in 1987.

pita bread left on their tables, and then, to rub salt into the wound, a law was passed changing the ownership of their homes to the new occupiers.

The land now known as Israel was far from empty when the first waves of Jewish immigrants arrived following the pogroms in the nineteenth century. This fact is accepted by anyone not ideologically conditioned to reject anything that doesn't accord with their views. This is not to take away from the achievements of this new nation; the unparalleled industrialization and technologically sophisticated transformation of olive groves, orchards and scrub to high-intensity farming. This is not to take away from the extraordinary – and once so hopeful and idealistic – act of building a society, a functioning nation out of an idea. These Jewish immigrants were motivated by the same thing that's driven people for millennia: a desire to live their lives safely, protect and feed their families, educate their children and, initially at least, build a society according to the values of their culture while protecting themselves from people who would kill them because of who they are. But none of these motivations, these ambitions and achievements preclude the reality that people had been living on the land and calling it home before this nation was created.

Nevertheless, the narrative persists that if you go far back enough, *originally* this was the land of the Jews, that they were here first, that they were exiled long ago and now, after millennia, they can return. That is, a family in New Jersey whose roots trace back to Lithuania for instance, might say, within this narrative, that if you look back far enough you will find their great-great-etcetera-grandparents actually left Jerusalem at the order of the Romans. Considerable research has been carried out trying to find a Jewish gene rooted in the Middle East, a gene that would link Jewish people and link European and Russian Jews to this Middle Eastern territory. Proof would strengthen the idea of return being historically valid. However, despite some fallacious claims (the most widely held being the idea that those with the name Cohen are proven to be genetically descended from the original priests of the temple in Jerusalem, the *Kohanim*) there is no valid scientific evidence that most Jews originated from Israel/Palestine. As geneticist Eran Elhaik of Johns Hopkins put it to me: 'All the papers about the Cohen modal haplotypes are nonsense and have been disproved by multiple authors, even though they are still shown on Wikipedia.' In an interview with the Israeli newspaper *Haaretz* he said this:

> From the scientific point of view, the notion that all such Jewish people are returning to their homeland becomes, quite simply, a myth.* […] The various groups of Jews in the world today do not share a common genetic origin. We are talking here about groups that are very heterogeneous and which are connected solely by religion.†

At the beginning of this book I suggested that as religion loses its rational credibility, science, for some, becomes the omnipotent force. One thing science does is undermine attempts to claim racial absolutes. Discoveries in modern genetics repudiate the idea that humanity is divided into discrete races with clear and marked differences. Geneticists today don't talk of races, they talk of clusters. As the Swedish geneticist Svante Pääbo puts it: 'If we start walking east from Europe, when do we start saying people are Asian? Or if we walk up the Nile Valley, when do we say people are African? There are no sharp distinctions.' It may be easier for enemies to believe that there's an absolute distinction that unifies one people, or that there's a discoverable difference separating

---

* This idea was first brought to my attention in Professor Schlomo Sand's extraordinary book, *The Invention of the Jewish People* (2008).
† *Haaretz*, 28 December 2012.

them from other people; that there's a divide between 'white' and 'black' or Ashkenazi and Sephardi, Jewish and Muslim. But these lines don't exist; there's no single genetic marker, no white gene, no Jewish gene, no gene for Palestinian, Christian, or Muslim. Perhaps that is why people need to wear a certain sort of hat, or eat only certain foods.

I am certainly not implying that legitimacy for Israel rests on genetic testing. If this were so, why not try to determine if Palestinians are genetically different from all other Arab peoples in the region? No. What kind of hypocrisy would it be to decry the racial politics of apartheid and then jump on the idea that if 'the Jewish people' could genetically prove their racial connection to the Middle East, Israel would be legitimate. Who am I to posit legitimacy anyway? That is for the United Nations, the General Assembly, the Security Council, and all the other round tables, and anyway, they have defined it. Do not think for a moment that I doubt Israel's right to exist. Israel is legitimate. I have seen it with my own eyes and not in a UN resolution, not even in Yad Vashem, the Holocaust museum. I've seen her legitimacy amongst Israelis. I've seen it amongst the group of children, the four- or five-year-olds holding hands in their high-vis waistcoats as they got off a bus near the Dolphinarium. There is legitimacy. At least for me.

The situation as I write is as volatile as it has ever been between Israel and Palestine. The occupation of the West Bank continues, illegal settlements increase, Palestinian homes are bulldozed, olive trees are destroyed, innocent Israelis are attacked with knives in the street, lies are told on both sides. Today in Israel support of the occupation and indeed of illegal settlements has become equated with patriotism – opposition to these is somehow equated with anti-Semitism – which recalls George Orwell's observation that language in politics is given a semantic nudge in order to distort reality.* Nevertheless, I believe that peace is achievable. I listen to those ex-heads of the Shin Bet saying peace is the only viable strategy for Israel. I listen to Bashir telling us to understand our enemy's pain. I think of one heart beating in the body of another.

My father died before there was peace in Ireland. He wanted it, oh so badly, but he thought it impossible.

But then it happened.

Do I sound confused? Very well. I am confused. I contain, as Walt Whitman wrote, 'multitudes'.† The closer I get to the situation, the messier it becomes. Neat guidelines vanish, clear-cut conclusions become false, the dualisms of positive and negative dissolve.

When a heart emerged from the carnage of the Dolphinarium bomb I was one of those for whom it was like a spark of light on a dark night of the soul. Whatever it did or did not mean in a wider context, it felt to me like a moment of grace, and I am not alone. Dr Lavie, who held the hearts, said: 'We are in a political and emotional tornado and things are blurred but there is a ray of light and these are the things that give you the strength to continue.'

And for me the transplant was something that:

> ... falls as they say love should,
> Like an enormous yes.‡

On a physical level, the truth of Cohen's heart is that it pumps oxygenated blood throughout his body. On a symbolic level ... well, I found any search for a single truth perplexing. But, as anyone who dips into semiotics soon discovers, symbols resist complete understanding. All I can hold onto as truth is

---

*George Orwell, *Politics and the English Language* (1946).
†Walt Whitman, *Leaves of Grass* (1855).
‡Philip Larkin, 'For Sidney Bechet' from *The Whitsun Weddings* (1954).

that even at the edges, people are people. Fundamentally decent, crucially flawed, all of us wanting happiness for our loved ones, our people, ourselves, all of us wishing to avoid suffering, all of us loving our children.

All of our hearts beating.

Acknowledgments

I am not sure if any books are easy to write, but no book of mine has been as hard as this. These pages represent a fraction of what has been written and researched over the past decade. During this time I have been helped by a great many souls; whether you are here or not please know that I thank you.

To those brave people who were at the Dolphinarium, their relatives and friends, who had the courage to revisit this trauma and share it with me – thank you.

Towering intellects across many disciplines in the world of research and academia have been generous with their time and expertise: André du Toit, Irena Slavutskay-Tsukerman, Schlomo Sand, Eran Elhaik.

Thank you William Sieghart for many hours of advice and support, Angelique Chrisafis and Fiachra Gibbons for their support and friendship; Fiachra's wise words and unrelenting enthusiasm were gifts I still treasure. Francesca Marciano for sage counsel, Jenny Dyson for being an all-round star, Eric Ransdell for friendship and picking up that unbelievably expensive hotel bill in Tokyo as well as fifteen pages of killer notes, Julian Ozanne for unparalleled friendship and support so far beyond any call of duty. David Kuhn and Becky Sweren. Much more work than reward – so far ... your excellence shines forth.

The staff of The London Library for every book they found for me and every late return they have endured – and in particular the Carlyle Membership, which has allowed me to continue being a member.

I am so grateful to Anna Lena Vaney: time and time again you gave given my little Camille and I a home in your home.

Dr Dror Sofer, trauma director of the Tel Aviv Sourasky Medical Center, Dr Susan Vosloo, cardiac surgeon at the Christiaan Barnard

Acknowledgments

Memorial Hospital, Professor Olivier Raisky and Sébastien Gerelli of the Necker Hospital in Paris (you know what you did) and my magnificent mother, Professor Jane Somerville. Special thanks to Dr Yakov Lavie of the Chaim Sheba Medical Center in Israel – this could not have happened without you.

All my friends in Israel especially the Hirsch family, Raphael, Shira, Eran and Roni: such kindness, hospitality, intelligence and so many different opinions. The Rosenbergs for inviting a stranger to Aruchat Shabbat not to mention stopping your dog from eating me. My dear friend Efrat Gosh. Tal Engel. Thank you to the brilliant and incomparable Dahlia Scheindlin and my respect and gratitude to the staff of the excellent +972 *Magazine*.

To my friends in the State of Palestine, I think of you every day and long for the day when there will be sanity and justice and equality. Thank you to all those who spoke to me, helped me and housed me, in particular Reem Shilleh, Mohamad Yaqubi and the legendary Hamoudi.

Thank you to those who read the manuscript and especially to those who gave me notes: William Goodlad, Crispin Somerville, Jane Somerville, Stuart MacFarlane, Kate McCreery, Eric Ransdell. Thank you Colm Farren, a very, very good editor – the best I've known. Copy editors lie awake at night hoping to avid the manuscript of a dyslexic – thank you Djinn von Noorden for elegantly wrestling this unruly beast.

Those beloved people who time and time again have picked up the bill when they didn't need to. I hope you know how much I appreciate it. I suspect you wouldn't want to be identified so let's just say: J.O., E.R., C.A., H.S., J.K., A.L.V. and L.R.S.

My heartfelt thanks to Saul Rosenberg, a man with an extraordinary facility of language and a mind that is actually beautiful in its intelligence and clarity. We disagree strongly on the politics of Palestine/Israel. We have discussed and disputed many things over many years – sometimes lapsing into months of silence as one or the other of us can no longer bear what seems like the myopia or intransigence of the other. But Saul, you kept helping me, in generous and time-consuming ways. Saul, you helped make a book better knowing it contained much with which you disagreed. Thank you my friend.

Finally, thank you Antony Farrell, Kathy Gilfillan and Vivienne Guinness of the Lilliput Press in Ireland. In all the world, you were the ones with the courage to commit. Lilliput is the smallest publisher I have had and honestly the best and the bravest.